Alberto Minujin, Mónica González Contró, Raúl Mercer (Eds.)

Tackling Child Poverty in Latin America

Rights and Social Protection in Unequal Societies

CROP International Poverty Studies

Edited by Thomas Pogge

1   *Maria Petmesidou, Enrique Delamónica, Christos Papatheodorou, and Aldrie Henry-Lee (Eds.)*
    Child Poverty, Youth (Un)Employment, and Social Inclusion
    ISBN 978-3-8382-0912-8

2   *Alberto Minujin, Mónica González Contró, Raúl Mercer (Eds.)*
    Tackling Child Poverty in Latin America
    Rights and Social Protection in Unequal Societies
    ISBN 978-3-8382-0917-3

Alberto Minujin, Mónica González Contró,
Raúl Mercer (Eds.)

TACKLING CHILD POVERTY IN LATIN AMERICA
Rights and Social Protection in Unequal Societies

ibidem-Verlag
Stuttgart

Bibliografische Information der Deutschen Nationalbibliothek
Die Deutsche Nationalbibliothek verzeichnet diese Publikation in der Deutschen Nationalbibliografie; detaillierte bibliografische Daten sind im Internet über http://dnb.d-nb.de abrufbar.

Bibliographic information published by the Deutsche Nationalbibliothek
Die Deutsche Nationalbibliothek lists this publication in the Deutsche Nationalbibliografie; detailed bibliographic data are available in the Internet at http://dnb.d-nb.de.

Cover photo: *Little expressions.* © copyright 2001 by Xavier Kriscautzky
Translated by Alan Molina Zúñiga

Gedruckt auf alterungsbeständigem, säurefreien Papier
Printed on acid-free paper

ISBN-13: 978-3-8382-0917-3

© *ibidem*-Verlag

Stuttgart 2017

Alle Rechte vorbehalten

Das Werk einschließlich aller seiner Teile ist urheberrechtlich geschützt. Jede Verwertung außerhalb der engen Grenzen des Urheberrechtsgesetzes ist ohne Zustimmung des Verlages unzulässig und strafbar. Dies gilt insbesondere für Vervielfältigungen, Übersetzungen, Mikroverfilmungen und elektronische Speicherformen sowie die Einspeicherung und Verarbeitung in elektronischen Systemen.

All rights reserved. No part of this publication may be reproduced, stored in or introduced into a retrieval system, or transmitted, in any form, or by any means (electronic, mechanical, photocopying, recording or otherwise) without the prior written permission of the publisher. Any person who does any unauthorized act in relation to this publication may be liable to criminal prosecution and civil claims for damages.

Printed in the EU

We wish to thank in a very special way Verónica Bagnoli, who has provided an active and ongoing collaboration in the preparation and execution of this book. Her help, without a doubt, has been priceless. We also want to thank Alberto Cimadamore and Luis Daniel Vázquez Valencia for their personal and institutional support. We also extend our thanks to Mark Robinson supervised by Jace Shinderman.

The editors

Table of contents

Alberto Minujin, Mónica González Contró, and Raúl Mercer
INTRODUCTION 9

PART I
THE CONTEXTS OF CHILD POVERTY 31

Ana María Osorio and Luis Fernando Aguado
STARTING AT THE BEGINNING A SOCIAL EXCLUSION INDICATOR CENTERED
ON THE MOTHER-CHILD DYAD FOR COLOMBIA 33

Héctor Nájera Catalán
CHILD POVERTY AND INEQUALITIES AT THE GEOGRAPHIC LEVEL:
A SPATIAL ANALYSIS. MEXICO 2010 55

Robin Cavagnoud
FAMILY POVERTY, TEENAGE WORK, AND SCHOOL DESERTION. AN OVERVIEW
OF A COMPLEX RELATIONSHIP BASED ON THE CASE OF LIMA (PERU) 87

Jorge Paz
PRODUCTION AND REPRODUCTION OF CHILD POVERTY IN LATIN AMERICA.
AN ANALYSIS CENTERED ON THE EDUCATIONAL DIMENSION 105

PART II
SOCIAL POLICY AND CHILD PROTECTION 137

Camilo Pérez Bustillo
HUMAN RIGHTS, HEGEMONY, AND UTOPIA IN LATIN AMERICA:
INTERCULTURAL DIMENSIONS OF POVERTY AND INDIGENOUS
MIGRATION IN MEXICO AS CASE STUDIES 139

Yedith Guillén Fernández
CHILDREN RIGHTS: A FRAMEWORK FOR THE CONSTRUCTION OF
SOCIAL POLICY AND FOR THE ERADICATION OF POVERTY IN LATIN AMERICA
AND THE CARIBBEAN 161

Jorge I. Vásquez
POVERTY AND CHILD POVERTY: ELEMENTS FOR THE DEBATE IN THE
PREPARATION OF A SOCIAL PROTECTION POLICY IN HAITI 187

Ianina Tuñón and Agustín Salvia
VULNERABLE CHILDHOODS AND SOCIAL PROTECTION SYSTEMS:
CHILD ALLOWANCE IN ARGENTINA 207

Cristian Herrera, Alejandra Vives, Camila Carvallo, and Helia Molina
INTEGRAL PROTECTION OF CHILDHOOD THROUGH THE "CHILE GROWS
WITH YOU" (CHILE CRECE CONTIGO, CHCC) SUBSYSTEM: ANALYSIS
OF A POLICY TO BREAK THE INTERGENERATIONAL CYCLE OF POVERTY
AND INEQUALITY 227

PART III
INEQUALITIES AND CARE POLICIES 255

Charles-Édouard de Suremain
THE "WOMAN/MOTHER" AS THE ONLY RESPONSIBLE PARTY FOR CHILD
POVERTY? CRITICAL ETHNOGRAPHY OF SOME HEALTH PROGRAMS
AGAINST CHILD MALNOURISHMENT (LATIN AMERICAN EXAMPLES) 257

Juan Antonio Vega Báez
COMPARATIVE STUDY OF THE DAYCARE PROGRAMS IN MEXICO (2007–12)... 267

Ma. Cristina Torrado, Ernesto Durán, and Tatiana Casanova
DO EARLY CHILDHOOD POLICIES PERPETUATE THE HISTORICAL
INEQUALITIES BETWEEN COLOMBIAN GIRLS AND BOYS? 285

Nelson Antequera
REFLECTIONS ON CHILD POVERTY, QUALITY OF LIFE, AND
LOCAL PUBLIC POLICY 307

INTRODUCTION[1]

Alberto Minujin[2]
Mónica González Contró[3]
Raúl Mercer[4]

> Recreating childhood means generating a space in culture where that reality can be thought of as a new intergenerational link, and as an emancipatory category, and not merely as a period of pure submission to adults.... Child autonomy is a core concept, given that the goal is to provide fundaments to nothing less than freedom. As it is known, without freedom, the person is not possible.
>
> Eduardo BUSTELO, *The recreation of childhood*

The core purpose of this book is to show that the debate on poverty in Latin America, specifically childhood and teenage poverty, must be part of a larger discussion involving justice, freedom, citizenship, identity, participation, and

---

[1] This introduction has been prepared by members of the Working Group for the Investigation of Child Poverty in Latin America (GT) and is based on a work by Alejandro Acosta (doctor in Education, Director of the International Center for Education and Human Development [CINDE], *aacosta@cinde.org.co*) and María Cristina Torrado (PH.D. in Psychology, Coordinator of the Observatory of Children Universidad Nacional de Colombia, *mcristina.torrado@gmail.com*). The authors like to thank Alejandro Acosta and Maria Cristina Torrado for their contribution.
This document is the exclusive responsibility of the authors and it does not necessarily reflect the opinions and orientation of the institutions they belong to.
GT is a body of a consortium formed by researchers and comprising Alberto Minujin, Valeria LLobet, Raúl Mercer (Argentina), Ernesto Durán, María Cristina Torrado, Alejandro Acosta (Colombia), Helia Molina, Cristian A. Herrera and Alejandra Vives (Chile), Alberto Cimadamore (Norway) Verónica Bagnoli, Mónica González Contró (Mexico). Institutional Affiliates: Equity for Children (USA/Argentina), Flacso (Argentina), Universidad Nacional (Colombia), CINDE (Colombia), Universidad Católica (Chile), CROP (ISSC/UiB).

[2] Alberto Minujin, Mathematician and Statistician. Specialist in demography and social policy. Director of Equity for Children/Equidad para la Infancia/Equidade para a Infância, *minujina@newschool.org*.

[3] Mónica González Contró, PH.D. in Fundamental Rights. Researcher with the Instituto de Investigaciones Jurídicas of UNAM, *monica_contro@yahoo.es*.

[4] Raúl Mercer, Pediatrician and public health specialist. Coordinator of the Social Science and Health Program of the Facultad Latinoamericana de Ciencias Sociales, Argentina, *raulmercer@gmail.com*.

peace on a global level. It attempts to promote efforts in our region to generate our own line of thinking about social policy. Our focus is on lasting alternatives that are unconstrained by traditional views about social policy's formulation and implementation.

The current context shows us that the world may be experiencing its most severe crisis since the 1920s. Although income-related poverty has decreased in Latin America, particularly in comparison to other regions, this trend is both non-sustainable and less than expected considering the investments made.[5] As a measurement of inequality in income distribution, the Gini index shows that inequality continues to prevail in the region. For children, poverty persists because of their lack of rights and the intergenerational transmission of poverty.

Human beings must be the protagonists of the decisions that affect them. Therefore, it is necessary to provide new definitions and context to citizenship. That is why it is so important for girls and boys to be recognized as full-fledged citizens. In doing so, it is vital to analyze public policies as part of a larger research and social mobilization effort that seeks to address the issue of inequality and improve children's standard of living.

In this context, the nature of child poverty and inequality in Latin America must be conceived of in a way that deepens the debates on the social determinants of exclusion and marginality, incorporating reflections on how new and old inequalities articulate in the restriction of the rights and in the exercise of citizenship by boys, girls, and teenagers (NNyA, as per the acronym in Spanish).

In that sense, this material may serve as a catalyst for debate and analysis that advances the study of child poverty and inequality and identifies potential ways to address the problem in the region.

The works included in this publication were selected by an academic committee in response to an international call under the International Seminar "Childhood Poverty, Public Policy and Democracy," organized by Equity for Children (*http://www.equityforchildren.org/*) and Comparative Research Programme on Poverty, CROP (*http://www.crop.org/*), with the support of Flacso and UNAM, held in Mexico D.F., in February 2014.

---

2 While it is true that in the last decade both poverty and extreme poverty have been reduced, as of 2011, 40.5% of children were poor, 16.3% lived in extreme conditions, and inequality remained the highest in the world.

I. Background

This publication is the result of research and collaboration initiated by the Working Group for Investigation-Action on Child Poverty and Inequalities and by the Project for Connectivity in Graduate Studies on Children Rights and Policy (GT) commissioned by Equity for Children with the support of the regional offices of the United Nations Development Programme (UNDP) and the United Nations International Children's Emergency Fund (UNICEF) in 2010. It aims to boost academic training for the application and democratization of knowledge required to strengthen childhood policy in Latin America.

Since 2011, a group of academicians was convened by Equity for Children to develop an information and analysis tool that contributes to the debate about the conditions of inequality faced by children and teenagers in Latin America. They also explored policies aimed at overcoming the factors generating these conditions of inequity and exclusion. They approached the concept of child poverty from a critical and scientific perspective, in the broad context of social exclusion and inequalities related to, among other areas, gender, ethnic origin, and social class.

The GT coordinating team included researchers from Equity for Children Latin America, Comparative Research On Poverty-ISSC/University of Bergen, Flacso-Argentina, the Observatory of Children of the Universidad Nacional de Colombia, Chile's Universidad Católica, and CINDE-Colombia.

The first concern in the child poverty analysis was recognizing its increasing complexity inside the home, including aspects of social relationships such as gender, age, and ethnic relations that often give rise to many forms of inequality and that cannot be considered in isolation. The second concern was the interrelationship between the home and its relationship with stakeholders from the state and civil society, the latter of whom build barriers or bridges to the exercise of rights to the following: a quality environment, adequate public areas and services, violence rates that do not restrict the mobility of women and children, dignified public transport, and decent jobs. Third, the team considered the intergenerational transmission of poverty and the effects of poverty both at different stages of life and over the long term.

II. Reference framework

Below are a series of conclusions from the review process at the international seminar "Childhood Poverty, Public Policy, and Democracy":

1. Childhood teenage and social justice

The inclusion of the rights of children and teenagers as guiding principles in the formulation of public was achieved through the social, academic, and political mobilization of the past 20 years. However, identifying the issue and defining it in technocratic terms does not necessarily lead to a political solution.

Views on social justice have been guided by the debate between transcendentalist justice theories and the comparative approaches. The former seeks to analyze whether institutions can be made fair, as posited by transcendental institutionalism based on the theory of justice in Rawls. The latter is about comparisons based on realizations that allow eliminating evident injustices. These debates have extended the issue of social justice as a matter of redistribution and equity by positing the subjects of *identity* and *difference* (Fascioli, 2011: 53).

In this way, social justice is related to issues of distribution (*economic*), recognition (*cultural*), and representation (*political*) as manifested in the nation-state, a frame of reference rendered obsolete by globalization. Fraser indicates that failing to account for globalization results in the injustice of *mis-framing*. This injustice relates to the *what*, the *who*, and the *how* of justice and further elucidates the debate on the right approach to theorize about justice (Fraser, 2008). In adopting the perspective of the participant, Fraser states the following:

> I have proposed to conceive present-day arguments about distribution, recognition and representation as a species of "abnormal justice," in which the taken-for-granted parameters of "normal justice, such as a shared sense of "who counts," are up for grabs. At the same time, however, I am also trying to clarify the aspirations of those social movements that seem to me to carry our best hopes for emancipatory change. (Fraser, 2008: 253)

Child poverty is relevant to each of these areas. Economic injustice is present in the material deprivation endured by poor children. Discrimination and horizontal inequalities are related with the lack of recognition of the identity and injustice in the acceptance of the differences. Lastly, problems such as child trafficking, child pornography, and the movement of "unaccompanied" minors must be considered in a global rather than national context.

From another perspective, postcolonial authors proposed that there are more radical forms of exclusion, that is, *a priori*, structural exclusion that hinders them from being understood; because they do not have access to any possibility in the sphere of representation, they are "subalterns." Therefore, they establish that "the continent of exploration of the postcolonial thought is constituted by the processes that subjectively construct differences under conditions of extreme inequality" (Boutang and Vidal, 2007: 13).

Faced with this situation, the authors propose generating in Latin America a geopolitically endemic thought that is merged for the south and in opposition to Eurocentrism. In this way, the dominated are not favorably inclined to repeat the practices of the colonizers (Boutang and Vidal, 2007: 12).

Although Sen's (2010) last book on justice acknowledges Rawls, he posits that beyond formulating a theory of justice, it is necessary to base concrete actions by citizens on their moral feeling toward situations of injustice to further advancement in the development of justice.

Even if guided by different motivations and strategies, human beings must be protagonists of their decisions, giving new definition to the idea of citizenship.

2. Social citizenship and childhood

Social justice and equality among citizens is a political ideal of democratic societies that cannot be reduced to formal language as it appears in constitutions, legal regulations, and social policy documents; on the contrary, it must become apparent in the welfare and exercise of fundamental freedoms by the people.

As Cortina (1998) declares, the idea of citizenship, inherent to the emergence of the modern ruleoflaw, has traversed a long historical process to reach the meaning we give to it today. On the one hand, the status of citizens has ceased to be an elite privilege and has become a condition to which every member of society aspires. On the other hand, the idea of citizenship has expanded to incorporate political participation, cultural identity, and welfare as individual rights recognized by the state.

In a democratic culture, citizenship is related to the awareness of human rights, trust in social institutions, social bonds and cohesion, and participation and autonomy.

The subject of children's citizenship has gained prominence in recent discussions.

> The notion of childhood citizenship has become a way to re-think the position of children as members of the community and as holders of rights.... This "turn toward citizenship" in the field of childhood studies received the approbation of the Convention on the Rights of the Child and is a significant regulatory milestone for children. (Llobet, 2012: 19)

Quoting Roche, Llobet (2012: 20) states: "The rights of children and teenagers encompass both inclusions and exclusions, and citizenship is restricted or partial. In this way, the forms of social inclusion of children and teenagers, from a regulatory standpoint, are problematic, to say the least.". From the perspective of feminist theory, citizenship is not a homogeneous phenomenon.

Based on this idea of citizenship and in reference to the issues of social justice and the capacity for action of the governments and the role of public policy, it is important to recognize that, as Llobet states,"the issue of child citizenship, and of the social construction of childhood, is unclear in social policy, despite the 'the issue of childhood' being at the epicenter of social protection" (Llobet, 2012: 11). They have been justified with revisions to human capital theory, specifically the idea that state spending on children mitigates greater expenditures in the future. Social protection policy anticipates returns in the adult life of children because of those early-year interventions, the benefits of which have been proven by neuroscience. However, those policy interventions fail to take into account the necessary and sufficient actions that boost the subjectivity and intersubjectivity, exploration, creation, and leisure implications of growth in children.

A broad concept of citizenship allows for the inclusion and recognition of new social stakeholders. In other words, this notion of citizenship reveals the ways in which state and society develop and exercise their rights.

The recognition of new expressions of citizenship is justified in the literature on politics and social development, supporting the formation of a fair society in which everyone is able to fully enjoy fundamental rights and a shared sense of identity and belonging. This seems to overcome the elitist character that the exercise of citizenship, and the concept itself, had in other historical moments.

On the other hand, in recent years social movements have brought new dimensions to the concept of citizenship. The institutional and/or legal view of citizenship has been informed by feminist thought, multiculturalist or environmentalist theses, and various social movements that are constantly reinventing social interaction and the sense of welfare and social justice. This is why citizenship appears as a dynamic, ever-changing concept, situated in specific political contexts and historical moments.

The granting of certain rights to children and teenagers leads to the idea of *childhood citizenship*, in which childhood is divested of its "underage" connotation and is recognized in full ownership (Brailovsky, s.f.).

In this concept, and in relation to the recognition of children and teenagers as holder of rights, there have recently been discussions of *child citizenship*. Even though several arguments exist around the subject, the idea clearly expresses the intention of transcending the representation of childhood as an underage, giving them agency as full citizen in the ampleness of their rights (Brailovsky, s.f.).

Recognizing children and teenagers as citizens breaks the traditional paradigm restricting their participation in the political and social sphere, a rupture which is only possible if we recognize them as individuals at every stage of their life.

How can we understand childhood and teenage citizenship? Although it is essential to recognize them as social stakeholders and grant their participation in the social, political, and cultural life of their community, we can consider welfare and inclusion as equally important dimensions of child citizenship. It is in daily life, the context in which children live, that they must be treated as citizens, because it is there where their relationship with the state and society takes shape.

The concept of intersectionality involves the interrelationship of various categories of difference: gender, ethnic origin, age, and social class, among others. That is to say, the experience, determinants, and cycles of "poverty" will not be the same for girls and boys, for Mapuche girls and white girls, for 5-year-olds and 12-year-olds. According to intersectionality, child citizenship must be considered within the framework of interrelationship. Not only are the rights of individual children interrelated but so are children themselves. Social exclusion studies have pointed to the confluence of intersectionality and time-related dynamics, using the concept of "concentrated disadvantages" (Saravi, 2006), that must be confronted to achieve full access to social, political, and economic rights that are intrinsic to citizenship (conceived in opposition to social exclusion).

In other words, for children to fully exercise their rights as citizens, they must participate in the public arena and benefit from the welfare they deserve, including the socialization processes guided by the democratic ideals of equality and respect.

3. Child poverty and inequality

The issues of poverty and inequality are inextricably tied to the ideas of social justice and citizenship. These discussions have allowed a more rigorous analysis of the issues of poverty and childhood (Alberto Minujin and Shailen Nandy). The authors indicate that "the measurement and analysis of child poverty requires the consideration of a wide range of measurements and non-monetary factors that have a widely documented impact on child survival, development and welfare." Based on sound methodological approaches to measuring child poverty, the publication "calls politicians, researchers and activists to immediate action to make the reduction of child poverty and inequality a central issue in their agendas and to use their influence to ensure that children are granted the priority they deserve in international, regional and national policies" (Minujin and Nandy, 2012: 3 and 572).

Viewing the issue of poverty by incorporating the rights approach, while not neglecting the risks of depoliticizing said approach, must confront social inequalities beyond considerations of wealth and treat children as individuals connected to networks of social relationships.

With respect to childhood, considering problems derived from a lack of material access to life options that guarantee development above the minimum survival level, there is a tendency to obfuscate the frontier between biological immaturity and its materiality, and the social processing of the same, with its results in terms of psychosocial normality patterns. In that sense, it is a challenge to sustain this tension without naturalizing inequality as "particularism," or without naturalizing "normality" as an individual result of an adequate/expected development.

On the other hand, the issue of poverty, and how to measure it, presents a series of challenges. Although the measurement of poverty must entail a multidimensional approach, this approach may become detached from the conceptual and political debates surrounding "poverty." Likewise, the local political visibility adopted by the measurement strategy and its results in various countries risks limiting the debate surrounding the nature of societies notable for their levels of poverty and inequality. Lastly, the international context that points to the validation of scales between countries obstructs how poverty is affected by political action on the local, regional, and global levels. This has not helped in evaluating the impact of public policy on people's living conditions.

4. Social policy

As previously mentioned, we must recognize that there has been major progress in legislation and policies aimed at guaranteeing the rights of children and teenagers in the region; however, child inequality and poverty still inhibit the exercise of fundamental rights by younger citizens.

Children from the most excluded sectors grow up as "second class citizens," lacking rights and with asubordinate role in society.

Likewise, the territorialization of inequality must be considered in terms of relational and structural processes that are resistant to change; in turn, the institutional modalities of organization of childhood welfare and exercise of rights may obfuscate institutional exclusion processes.

These reflections lead us to the following questions:

- How can we guarantee the welfare of younger citizens in highly unequal societies that are socially segregated?
- How can we bridge the gap between children and teenagers of different social classes, regions, and ethnic groups, and even among those who live in urban centers?
- How can we formulate childhood and teenage policies that are not based on failed views and practices in favor of policies that invite new perspectives and approaches to management and evaluation, breaking new ground for social policy in Latin America?

Highlighting the limitations of studies on social policy in relation to childhood problems (and, conversely, of childhood studies that have social policy as a setting) is an emergent budding matter. In effect, those studies mostly tend to focus on socioeconomic inequalities and not on the categories related to gender, ethnicity, and interage relations (Tilly, 2005).

Policies that will guarantee the enjoyment of rights by the child population and seek to break the intergenerational transmission of poverty and inequality are required. It is also necessary to consider the true effects of the conditional subsidy programs and those aimed at the poorest persons. Do these policies actually reduce inequality?

According to Sanhueza and Atria (2013), when social investment is focused on the poorest and the most vulnerable, while leaving to the market the regulation of services for the richest, it is unavoidable that services for the poor will be worse than the services for the rich. As for education, this means that the poor will all attend low quality establishments, while the rich will all attend quality establishments. Instead of reducing inequality, this trend will deepen it in the long term.

By maintaining segmented services of varying quality, social inequality between groups of children is strengthened and naturalized. The construction of an inferior citizenship for poor children is widely reinforced early in life.

Clearly, interactionist, ecological, and constructivist perspectives toward childhood, centered on intersubjectivity, involve enormous challenges in relation to the traditional ways of developing, executing, and evaluating policies and programs. It is clear that global conventions and declarations, such as the International Convention on the Rights of the Child, the Jomtien and Dakkar Declarations on Education for All, and the United Nations Head of State Summits on Childhood, have supported action from civil society, international cooperation, academia, and government sectors to include childhood and teenage issues in the public agenda of our countries. However, they have proven to be insufficient.

In this context, it is necessary to reinforce any gains realized, preventing them from being co-opted by approaches and practices that debase them while maintaining the declaratory aspects. Progress made on legislative issues is important, given the responsibility of the state as the main guarantor of rights, in conjunction with the family and civil society. There are possibilities to incorporate policies and/or programs with other social and economic policies and programs that may generate major synergies.

For that purpose, it is important to look at issues such as the relationship between quality and coverage. Increasing coverage at the expense of quality negatively affects both of these objectives. Therefore, it is essential to consider quality in terms of integrality and complementarity, with the related challenges for institutional practices and realities that, due to their origin and approach, are necessarily classifying, fragmented, and disjointed.

Given the enormous diversity both among and within our countries—as well as the growing decentralization in many counties—it is also necessary to take into account the differential perspective in the design and operation of policies and programs that fail to distinguish between deconcentration, delegation, and actual decentralization and that one would expect to reduce regional inequalities for the benefit of the most excluded areas.

5. The Latin American context

It is important to note that Latin America has recently experienced a democratic resurgence, including the creation of new legal frameworks and the implementation of policies and programs aimed at reducing poverty. In this context, the issue of child and teenage poverty has received more public attention; however, social injustice and inequality have not improved as much as expected.

In effect, and despite the disparities, Latin American countries share historical and socioeconomic processes that affect their domestic social dynamics, characterized by persistent inequalities and a unique position in the global arena. In addition to poverty, there are major differences in living conditions and in development opportunities among the population. We may say that a significant number of the people suffer from "citizenship poverty."

> the poor are not only the victims, in one way or another, of an inadequate distribution of income and wealth, but also lack the material and immaterial resources to meet the social demands and habits required of them as citizens. Therefore, poverty is, above all, poverty of citizenship. (Bustelo, 1999: 40 and 41)

Today, millions of Latin Americans lack the tangible and intangible goods considered as necessary to guarantee their welfare. Therefore, they lack conditions to participate in social life and also opportunities to enjoy a satisfactory life. It is well known that Latin America is the most unequal region in the world, because of the enormous gaps in the quality of life between different demographic groups.

The 2013 CEPAL Report on the Social Panorama of Latin America shows that between 2000 and 2011 childhood poverty was reduced by 14 percentage points, and extreme poverty was reduced by 10.5 percentage points. Likewise, the numbers show that the intensity of poverty also dropped and, in every country analyzed, there were reductions in both poverty and extreme poverty. However, despite the improvements, in 2011, 40.5% of children, or 70.5 million children, were poor, and 16.3% were in extreme poverty (CEPAL, 2013: 16).

In 2010, 10 out of the 15 most unequal countries in the world were in Latin America, which, as we have pointed out, contradicts the idea that economic growth would guarantee a substantial reduction of poverty and inequality.

As some analysts point out, this situation shows the failure of the development model, under which economic growth would directly lead to an increase in the welfare of the people. Also, Sen recognized that the freedoms enjoyed by the people depend on other determinant factors, such as social and economic institutions (e.g., education and healthcare facilities), as well as political and civil rights (e.g., the freedom to participate in public discussion and scrutiny) (Sen, 1999).

Social exclusion has been one of the important subjects in social science because, as Llobet indicates, and based on Weber's concept of "social closure," it was among the concerns of Durkheim, Merton, and Simmel, and most recently

> as Norbert Elías indicated, in his *Essay on the Established and the Outsiders*, interdependence between different groups does not emerge from social prejudice. Rather, the socio-dynamics of the relationship between established groups and outsiders is determined by the nature of their bond, not from any of their individual characteristics. (Llobet, 2013: 6)

Regarding childhood and teenage poverty, Llobet continues: "In principle we may note that the 'exclusion' of children and teenagers relates to a particular relationship between the State and them, and not to a social process directly or indirectly linked to poverty" (Llobet, 2013: 3).

In this way, the dynamics of inclusion and exclusion are strategies of the state which, as pointed out by Fraser, go beyond the process of redistribution during the twentieth century, since today they compete with claims for recognition. For that reason, they have to be analyzed in the context of the "mis-framing" caused by globalization (Fraser, 2008: 16).

For Lahire (2008: 46–47), there are many differences between people and groups of people other than their relative equality in a certain historical moment. According to the author, "The issue of inequality is clearly indivisible from the belief in the legitimacy of a good, knowledge or practice, that is to say, indivisible from what we may call the *degree of collective desirability* maintained for the latter."

In that same sense, Jackson (2011) posits the need for revising the notion of prosperity to prevent it from being reduced to the idea of "having more" or "consuming more." According to him, individual and collective prosperity is not limited to material safety, as it also involves social and psychological dimensions such as emotional stability or the feeling of belonging to a community.

It is worth remembering that if social protection is understood as a citizen guarantee, it must essentially focus on the realization of economic, social, and cultural rights (Cecchini and Martínez, 2011).

It is necessary to review the legal framework, because while the enforceability and judiciability of those who deal with childhood is complex, they have serious difficulties and contradictions in terms of its application. Diligence is required to ensure that the financing of policies and programs does not become pro-cyclical and detrimental to the poor. This is also the case for the fiscal structure and oversight of public spending.

Likewise, it is essential to have feasible and reliable information systems that are used by various stakeholders that can be used for research and for management, monitoring, and evaluation purposes. Universities, research centers, and national science and technology organizations must be able to systematize their work on childhood and teenage poverty.

In addition, it is also necessary to continually train and develop the human talent working with children, families, and institutions, from the many sectors, at different stages of the life cycle, in the state and in civil society.

III. Structure and content of the book

This material is the result of a synthesis process that started, as described at the beginning of this article, with a call to participate in an international seminar held in Mexico D.F. in 2014. After the selection process, each work was submitted orally and analyzed in depth by a professional in charge of reviewing it. Each submission was discussed among the participants, and the discussions were recorded for systematization.

After that, there was a screening process to select the works that would be included in this publication, taking into consideration their academic quality, their original contribution to the subject matter, and the feasibility of their completion within the established schedule.

Then, the editorial team was responsible for establishing an interactive dialogue with the different authors to make relevant adjustments to the content. Lastly, all the works underwent a final review and editing.

The book includes three parts:
- Part I: The contexts of child poverty.
- Part II: Social policy and child protection.
- Part III: Inequalities and care policies.

Each part comprises a group of lectures aligned with the posited axes. In any case, the epistemic limits of the works are unclear, and as such, they have ramifications that relate to each other as communicating vessels between the different perspectives proposed by the authors.

It is important to note the diversity in terms of thematic axes, in the territorial origins of the works, and in the multiplicity of methodological perspectives that nurture and diversify the analytical frameworks. Despite this diversity, there were common perspectives and fields of investigation throughout the material that had a transversal nature. These included childhood, poverty, rights, and the Latin American context. In this way, this book provides a holistic and critical view of the multiplicity of children and teenagers, their problems, and the social policies that prevail in the region.

Due to the universal dimensions of childhood and rights, contributions and experiences started coming together to collectively build a scaffolding of knowledge that translated into this work with an integrating spirit. Positioning childhood centrally in these investigations helped provide an enhanced entity to this social collective of childhood, often invisibilized and denied of their rights.

PART I: The contexts of child poverty

"Starting at the beginning: A social exclusion indicator centered on the mother-child dyad for Colombia," by Ana María Osorio and Luis Fernando Aguado.

In this paper, the authors construct a composite indicator that reflects the use of and access to key social goods and services during early childhood in the Colombian context. This paper accords with the basic rights outlined in the Convention on the Rights of the Child, which is essential in the accumulation of human capital to decrease the likelihood of falling into poverty during adult age; it incorporates aspects related to education and the independence of the mother that affect quality of life, and the partial indicators used may be construed as intermediaries in the framework of the Commission on Social Determinants of Health. This can potentially make an impact through public policy.

"Child Poverty and Inequalities at the Geographic Level: A Spatial Analysis. Mexico 2010" by Héctor Nájera Catalán.

The understanding of the geographic concentration of inequality is important from the standpoint of poverty and social justice. The core questions of the article are as follows: What is the geographical distribution of child poverty at the municipal level? What is the spatial pattern of deprivation/contextual poverty? Is there a nonseasonal geographical link between childhood poverty and contextual deprivation? Where is this relationship stronger? A measurement of childhood material deprivation and contextual deprivation is developed from municipal data from the Sample of the Population and Housing Census (2010).

"Family poverty, teenage work, and school desertion. An overview of a complex relationship based on the case of Lima (Peru)" by Robin Cavagnoud.

The work of children in the framework of family strategies is an unavoidable phenomenon in contemporary Peruvian society, which has three fundamental social spaces: family, work, and school. In the metropolis of Lima/Callao, the relationship of working children and teenagers between these socialization spaces brings up many questions, such as their schooling paths. This article analyzes the school abandonment process that affects working teenagers in Lima as a factor in the reproduction of childhood poverty in Latin America.

"Production and reproduction of child poverty in Latin America. An analysis centered on the educational dimension" by Jorge Paz.

This work aims to explore the potential for equalization of opportunities to impact the gap of the educational results between poor and nonpoor children. If this impact is verified, the challenge would then be to calibrate the current conditional transfer programs and to expect that, within one or two generations, the said interventions start to yield results. Education, as can be seen, is one of the focuses of Conditional Transfer Programs (PTC), and schooling is one of its main goals. That is also what the Millennium Development Goals proposes, and also what is sought by everyone involved in one way or another on the conceptual framework of the equalization of opportunities.

PART II: Social policy and child protection

"Human rights, hegemony, and utopia in Latin America: Intercultural dimensions of poverty and indigenous migration in Mexico as case studies" by Camilo Pérez Bustillo.

This paper seeks to analyze the main outlines of a conceptual framework to approach the migration of indigenous children—of Mexican, Central American, and Andean origin in transit to the United States via the territory of Mexico—as a case study of the complex and multidimensional relationship between poverty, indigenous people, and migration in these contexts. The emphasis here is on poverty and inequality as structural factors that trigger the decision to migrate, commonly assumed in liberal mythology as a "rational," individual, and "voluntary" choice but understood here more as forced migration" process.

"Children rights: A framework for the construction of social policy and for the eradication of poverty in Latin America and the Caribbean" by Yedith Guillén Fernández.

This study posits the need for developing an integral social policy, based on childhood rights, to eliminate child poverty in Latin America and the Caribbean. It also argues that the right of children to have access to social benefits provided by the state has been framed as part of their family unit, or home, but that children are citizens in their own right, who have specific needs and the right to have access to public services, as well as the right to participate in the benefits provided by their societies.

"Poverty and child poverty: Elements for the debate in the preparation of a social protection policy in Haiti" by Jorge I. Vásquez.

The text presents a conceptual framework that explores the importance of considering, for the contemporary debate on poverty and its corresponding expression in Latin America, the analysis of three logical aspects that define and reformulate the development of both public policy and private initiatives for the reduction of poverty. These aspects refer to the ongoing reformulation of the issue of poverty, the determination of who the poor are, and therefore, assuming that certain levels of consensus on the subject have been reached, the consideration of why the conditions that perpetuate impoverishment continue to be reproduced. It highlights aspects of governance and strengthening of the state as a key element in developing any public policy that involves long-term planning, articulating multisector demands with a rights-oriented approach, and considering the importance of the development of an active citizenship. This analysis is made based on the case of Haiti.

"Vulnerable childhoods and social protection systems: Child allowance in Argentina" by Ianina Tuñón and Agustín Salvia.

Considering the case of Argentina, a society where major social inequalities persist in the exercise of basic childhood rights (food, health, and education), the authors ask: To what extent does this fragmented system of economic aid aimed at children as the subject of public protection reach the poorest sectors and improve their economic, social, and educational opportunities? More accurately, does a conditional income transfer program explicitly targeting excluded children, such as the Universal Allowance per Child (AUH), have a positive impact on food safety, school exclusion, and child work? Answering these questions allows us to reflect on the challenges faced by income transfer programs and their effects on childhood rights.

"Integral protection of childhood through the 'Chile Grows with You' (Chile Crece Contigo, ChCC) subsystem: Analysis of a policy to break the intergenerational cycle of poverty and inequality" by Cristian Herrera, Alejandra Vives, Camila Carvallo, and Helia Molina.

This work focuses on analyzing the policies of the ChCC program, exploring its development process and the factors that influence its evolution, final content, and current results. Among the main findings, it highlights that the main actor in the political endorsement of ChCC was the president of the Republic, who made it a priority during her campaign and at the start of her mandate. The design of this policy had a technical component in the Presidential Advisory Council and a political component in the Committee of Ministers for Childhood, where the political ministers of the relevant sectors of the government discussed the final characteristics and components of the program and promoted its execution. Currently, the policy faces challenges in readapting itself, acquiring new momentum to reach teams and families, and performing a systematic evaluation to improve results.

PART III: Inequalities and care policies

"The 'woman/mother' as the only responsible party for child poverty? Critical ethnography of some health programs against child malnourishment (Latin American examples)," by Charles-Édouard de Suremain.

Although both women and gender relations have attracted considerable attention from mass media and scientific literature, research on the representations of the "wife/mother" continues to be scant. This is particularly true with respect to their social role and relationship to efforts aimed at fighting poverty, and, more specifically, childhood malnourishment. Based on the analysis of the discourses and the institutions of the implied and explicit stakeholders engaged in health and nutrition issues in Latin America (Bolivia and Peru), the paper explores the ideological and anthropological challenges related to the notion of the wife/mother as a "responsible party" with respect to child malnourishment in addition to child poverty, childhood inequality, and health care.

"Comparative study of the day-care programs in Mexico (2007–12)" by Juan Antonio Vega Báez.

This work seeks to answer the following questions: How has the issue of child poverty developed over the last decade in Mexico? How did the social policy of child care change from a solidarity-benefactor model to a mixed social/private and social/residual model that has had the effect of reproducing discrimination and child poverty? Why is there not a Universalist conception in childcare policy, particularly with respect to the indigenous population, which is the most impoverished and most discriminated against? It is possible to have a global post-2015 social agenda that includes the issue of care, and not only child survival? For that purpose, the paper considers the social determinants of health and childhood policies in analyzing the level of discrimination in access to childcare services in Mexico, particularly in the case of the *Estancias Infantiles* Day Care Programs initiated in 2007. One of the premises of the study is that the crisis in care and the exploitation of the reproductive work of women have an impact on the generational transmission of child poverty in Latin America.

"Do early childhood policies perpetuate the historical inequalities between Colombian girls and boys?" by Ma. Cristina Torrado, Ernesto Durán, and Tatiana Casanova.

Based on secondary sources, this article analyzes the issue of early childhood poverty and inequality in Colombia.It recognizes monetary or multidimensional measurements that take the household as the analytical unit, as well as the more recent ones that take children as unit of analysis. The analysis allows the conclusion of the enormous inequality between regions of the country and between demographic groups, with indigenous and Afro-descendent communities showing the highest poverty rates, and, simultaneously, a high percentage of children under five. In recognizing other intervening dynamics with respect to inequality, it shows the relationship between armed conflict and rates of early childhood poverty.

"Reflections on child poverty, quality of life, and local public policy" by Nelson Antequera.

The article posits the relationship between child poverty and local public policy as it relates to the concept of development and poverty behind state intervention through programs, projects, and budgets. It also refers to concrete situations of poverty that transcend these areas and therefore challenge the policies and practices of the state. Based on qualitative data on child poverty in the municipality of La Paz (Bolivia), it shows that in daily life, child poverty is suffered not only as a deprivation or lack of access to resources and services but also as an expression of abandonment and violence. It thus highlights that the concept of development and poverty, which has been promoted as state policy to overcome of child poverty, is insufficient to meet these challenges. Based on the concept of "the quality of life of a community" as an alternative proposal to the understanding of development and poverty, it proposes a few guidelines for a local public policy that could engage with the problem of child poverty with the community as the protagonist.

Bibliography

Acosta, Alejandro, 2009, "Protección de la primera infancia: abuso, violencia, abandono, niños de la calle, explotación laboral," in Palacios, Jesús and Castañeda, Elsa (coord.), *La primera infancia (0-6 años) y su futuro, volumen Infancia de OEI. Metas Educativas 2021. La educación que queremos para la generación de los bicentenarios*, Spain, Fundación Santallina.

Andrenacci, Luciano and Repetto, Fabián, s.f., *Universalismo, ciudadanía y Estado en la política social latinoamericana*.

Banerjee, Abhijit and Duflo, Esther, 2012, *Repensar la pobreza. Un giro radical en la lucha global contra la desigualdad global*, Bogotá, Taurus (1st ed. in English, 2011).

Boutang, Yann Moulier and Vidal, Jerome, April 2007, "De la colonialidad del poder al Imperio y Viceversa," *Nómadas*, Bogotá, no. 26.

Brailovsky, Daniel, s.f., "Sujeto político y sujeto de derecho. Algunos apuntes acerca de la literatura académica sobre niñez y ciudadanía." In *Coordenadas en investigación educativa*, in ww.educared.org.ar.

Bustelo, Eduardo, 1999, "Pobreza moral: reflexiones sobre la política social amoral y la utopía posible," in Bhattacharjea (comp.), *Infancia y política social*, Mexico, UNICEF.

Bustelo, Eduardo, 2007, *El recreo de la infancia*, Buenos Aires, Siglo XXI.

Calvo de Saavedra, Angela, 2012, "Guía para el Seminario de Campo: Martha Nussbaum. La textura emocional de la democracia," *Childhood and Teenage, Agreement between Universidad de Manizales and CINDE*, PHD in Social Science.

Cecchini, Simone and Martínez, Rodrigo, 2011, *Protección social inclusiva en América Latina: Una mirada integral, un enfoque de derechos*, Santiago de Chile, CEPAL.

CEPAL, 2013, "Panorama Social de América Latina. Documento informativo," http://www.ce pal.org/publicaciones/xml/9/51769/PanoramaSocial2013DocInf.pdf, (retrieved on January 11, 2014).

Cohen Tirado, Sofia, 2011, *Segregación residencial, marginalidad y estigmatización territorial en la construcción de identidad social urbana infantil*. Pontificia Universidad Católica de Chile, Master's Thesis.

Collier, Paul, 2007, *The Bottom Billion. Why the Poorest Countries Are Failing and What Can Be Done*, Oxford University Press.

Comisión Gubelkian, 1995, *Abrir las ciencias sociales. Informe de la Comisión Gubelkián para la reestructuración de las ciencias sociales*. Coordinated by Inmanuel Wallerstein, Centro de Investigaciones Interdisciplinarias en Ciencias y Humanidades-Siglo XXI (eds.), Universidad Autónoma de México.

Cortina, Adela, 1998, "Ciudadanía social," Madrid, El País.

Doctorado en Ciencias Sociales, Niñez y Juventud, 2012, *La Justicia. Seminario de Campo*, Agreement between Universidad de Manizales and CINDE.

Easterly, William, 2006, *The White Man's Burden. Why the West's Efforts to Aid the Rest Have Done So Much Ill and So Little Good*, USA, Penguin Books.

Fascioli, Ana, 2011, "Justicia social en clave de capacidades y reconocimiento," *Areté. Revista de Filosofía*, vol. XXIII, No. 1, http://www.scielo.org.pe/pdf/arete/v23n1/a03v23n1.pdf (retrieved on January 17, 2014).

Fitoussi, Jean-Paul and Rosanvallon, Pierre, 1997, *La nueva era de las desigualdades*, Buenos Aires, Manantial.

Fleury, Sonia, 2004, "Ciudadanías, exclusión y democracia," *Nueva Sociedad*, No. 193.

Fraser, Nancy, 1997, *Iustitia Interrupta. Reflexiones críticas desde la posición "postsocialista,"* Bogota, Siglo del Hombre.

Fraser, Nancy, 2008, *Escalas de justicia*, Barcelona, Herder.

Galofré, Fernando (comp.), 1981, *Pobreza crítica en la niñez, América Latina y el Caribe*, Chile, CEPAL-UNICEF.

Herrera, Cristián et al., 2014, "Protección integral de la infancia a través del programa 'Chile Crece Contigo': análisis de una política para romper el ciclo intergeneracional de la pobreza y la inequidad," *Lecture: "Child Poverty, Public Policy and Democracy" International Seminar*, Mexico.

Honneth, Axel and Margalit, Avishai, 2001, *Recognition. Source: Proceedings of the Aristotelian Society*, Supplementary Volumes, vol. 75, http://www.jstor.org/stable/4107035.

Honneth, Axel, 2009, *Crítica del agravio moral. Patologías de la sociedad contemporánea*, Argentina, Fondo de Cultura Económica-Universidad Autónoma Metropolitana.

Jackson, 2011, *Prosperidad sin crecimiento*, Barcelona, Icaria-Intermón Oxfam.

Kliksberg, Bernardo (comp.), 1993, *Pobreza. Un tema impostergable. Nuevas respuestas a nivel mundial*, Caracas, CLAD-PNUD-Fondo de Cultura Económica.

Lahire, Bernard, 2008, "Cultura escolar, desigualdades culturales y reproducción social," in Tenti, Emilio (comp.), *Nuevos temas en la agenda de política educativa*, Buenos Aires, SigloXXI-UNESCO.

Llobet, Valeria, 2012, "Políticas sociales y ciudanía. Diálogos entre la teoría feminista y el campo de estudios de infancia," *Frontera Norte*, vol. 24, No. July–December (48).

Llobet, Valeria, 2013, "Estado, categorización social y exclusión de niños/as y jóvenes. Aportes a los debates sobre la exclusión social a los estudios de infancia y juventud," in Llobet, Valeria (coord.), *Sentidos de la exclusión social. Beneficiarios, necesidades y prácticas en políticas sociales para la inclusión de niños y jóvenes*, Buenos Aires, Biblos.

Llobet, Valeria et al., 2014, "Infancia, pobreza y desigualdades en Argentina: tensiones y transformaciones en los últimos dos decenios," *Lecture: "Child Poverty, Public Policy and Democracy" International Seminar*, Mexico, 2014.

Pilotti, Francisco (coord.), 1994, *Infancia en riesgo social y políticas sociales en Chile. Desarrollo y perspectivas del Servicio Nacional de Menores y su relación con las políticas sociales, la sociedad civil y el marco jurídico.*

Minujin, Alberto and Nandy, Sheilen (ed.), 2012, *Global Child Poverty and Well-being. Measurement, Concepts, Policy and Action*, The Policy Press, University of Bristol.

Rabbani, Martha J., 2009, *Ciudadanía, justicia social y lucha por el reconocimiento*, *www.derecho.unal.co/unijus/pj26/3Ciudadania.pdf* (retrieved on January 12, 2014).

Sanhueza and Atria, 2013, *Focalización: un atentado contra la igualdad*, *http://voces.later cera.com/2013/08/27/claudia-sanhueza/*.

Sachs, Jeffrey, 2007, *El fin de la pobreza. Cómo conseguirlo en nuestro tiempo*, Bogotá, Debolsillo (1st ed. in English, 2005).

Saraví, Gonzalo, 2006, "Biografías de exclusión: desventajas y juventud en Argentina,"*Revista Perfiles Latinoamericanos*, No. 28.

Sen, Amartya, 1999, "Romper el ciclo de la pobreza: invertir en la infancia,"*Lecture at the World Meeting of the Inter-American Development Bank*, IDB, Paris.

Sen, Amartya, 2002, "¿Qué impacto puede tener la ética?," in Kliksberg, Bernardo (comp.), *Ética y desarrollo, la relación marginada*, Buenos Aires, El Ateneo-Banco Interamericano de Desarrollo.

Sen, Amartya, 2010, *La idea de justicia*, Colombia, Taurus (1st ed. in English, 2009).

Siteal, 2013, "01 Resumen estadístico comentado. Desarrollo en América Latina. 2000–10,"*http.siteal.org/sites/default/files/rec_siteal_1_2013_08-06.pdf* (retrieved on January 15, 2014).

Tilly, Charles, 2005, "Historical Perspectives on Inequality," in Margolis (ed.), *The Blackwell Companion to Social Inequalities*, Oxford, Blackwell.

Torrado, Ma. Cristina *et al.*, 2014, "¿Perpetúan las políticas de primera infancia las desigualdades históricas en las oportunidades de los niños colombianos?,"*Lecture: "Child Poverty, Public Policy and Democracy" International Seminar*, Mexico.

UNESCO, 2011, *Informe sobre las ciencias sociales en el mundo. Las brechas de conocimiento*, México, UNESCO-Foro Consultivo (1st ed. in English, 2010).

Wintersberger, 2006, "Infancia y ciudadanía: el orden generacional del Estado de bienestar," *Política y Sociedad*, vol. 43, No. 1.

Part I
The Contexts of Child Poverty

STARTING AT THE BEGINNING
A SOCIAL EXCLUSION INDICATOR CENTERED ON THE MOTHER–CHILD DYAD FOR COLOMBIA[1]

Ana María Osorio Mejía[2]
Luis Fernando Aguado Quintero[3]

> I. Introduction. II. Why a social exclusion indicator centered on the mother–child dyad? III. Structure of the indicator. IV. Data and methodology for the development of the indicator. V. Results. VI. Selection of the components and the variables represented by each component. VII. Sorting the departments with the indicator. VIII. Limitations. IX. Conclusions. X. Bibliography.

I. Introduction

In recent years, there has been a growing interest in measuring the quality of life for children (Ben-Arieh, 2008; Brooks and Hanafin, 2005; CEPAL and UNICEF TACRO, 2010; Minujin, 2013; UNICEF, 2014) and in figuring out its main determinants (Kilburn and Karoly, 2008). Since the enactment of the Convention on the Rights of the Child in 1989, an extensive regulatory framework has been developed. The International Society for Child Indicators in 2007, in addition to a specialized magazine, *Child Indicators Research*, has emerged out of the academic sector. However, despite the aggregated research, preventable inequalities remain: "Quality of life for children is dependent on a multitude of factors, including their sex, the relative affluence of their households, neighborhoods, and countries, and

---

[1] This document is part of a research project called "Childhood and Social Exclusion in Colombia," financed by the Technological Research and Development Office of Pontificia Universidad Javeriana, Cali campus, Colombia. We appreciate the data-processing assistance of Beatriz Elena Jaramillo, student of the Statistics Program of Universidad del Valle, Colombia.
[2] Assistant Professor, Department of Economy, Regional Development Research Group, GIDR, Pontificia Universidad Javeriana, Cali Campus, Colombia. e-mail: anao@javerianacali.edu.co.
[3] Associate Professor, Department of Economy, Regional Development Research Group, GIDR, Pontificia Universidad Javeriana, Cali Campus, Colombia. e-mail: lfaguado@javerianacali.edu.co.

whether or not they are growing up in a rural or urban environment" (UNICEF, 2014: 4).

This paper seeks to develop a composite indicator centered on the mother–child dyad, based on the use of and access to key social goods and services during early childhood in the case of a developing country: Colombia. These goods and services include the mother's reading capacity and decision-making autonomy, prenatal care, legal visibility before the state, child care, early stimulation, access to books, breastfeeding, and vaccination schedule. The existing research on these indicators' inequalities is marked by attributes such as level of income, level of education, racial identity, and geographical region. These findings indicate that indicator inequality may be prevented through satisfactory public policy aimed at childhood development—first centered on the mother during pregnancy and then continuing after the child is born.

This indicator represents progress in the empirical investigation on the quality of life for children, which can be replicated in other countries. It is useful in its quantitative assessment considering the mother–child dyad and including variables seldom used in the empirical literature for developing countries. These refer to minimum elements that may be altered by public policy in the short term and that would improve quality of life in the contexts where the social exclusion chain starts—during pregnancy, birth, and the first five years of life.

Composite indicators constitute a useful tool to simplify multidimensional and complex phenomena, such as quality of life in childhood. They also facilitate the measurement, evaluation, monitoring, and comparison of trends in different indicators and the scope of public policies—both temporally and geographically. Likewise, they enable comparisons between groups classified on the basis of demographic variables—for example, sex, race, and age (Moore et al., 2008; OECD, 2008; Saltelli, 2007). A 20-year overview of the debate on the indicators of child welfare, including their related domains and causes, can be found in O'Hare and Gutiérrez (2012).

The pertinent data come from the 2010 National Demography and Health Poll (hereinafter, ENDS)[4], Principal component analysis (hereinafter, PCA) is applied to determine the weight of the partial indicators, using

---

4   The 2010 ENDS was financed by the Asociación Probienestar de la Familia Colombiana (Profamilia), the Social Protection Ministry (MPS) and the government of the United States, through USAID. The micro-data are available at *http://www.dhsprogram.com/data/dataset/Colombia_Standard-DHS_2010.cfm?flag=0*.

polychoric correlations, due to the discrete nature of the variables. The main results show that the best performance in the aggregated index corresponds to the capital of the republic: Bogota. And the lowest performance corresponds to departments located in the periphery—specifically Vaupes, Chocó, La Guajira, Guainía, and Vichada. These results underscore the urgent need to incorporate vertical equity elements from a territorial perspective in public policy for childhood in Colombia.

The document is organized in six sections. The first section is this introduction. The second and third sections present the conceptual nature and the characteristics of the indicator, respectively. The fourth presents in detail the data and methodology used in the development of the indicator. The fifth and sixth sections present the results and conclusions, respectively. The document concludes with a bibliography.

II. Why a social exclusion indicator centered on the mother-child dyad?

Social exclusion during childhood can be understood as a complex process that we can call child poverty. In effect, according to Minujin (2013: 12), the analysis of child poverty involves three domains:

Deprivation: "The lack of material conditions and services that are essential for development."

Exclusion: "The result of misalignment processes, through which the dignity, voice and rights of children are denied, or their existence is threatened."

Vulnerability: "The inability of societies in controlling threats against children that exist in their environments."

The exclusion in the use of and access to key social goods and services during early childhood denies children their right to welfare, and therefore, undermines their quality of life in two time frames: in the present, as subjects of rights as defined by the Convention on the Rights of the Child, and in the future, through the accumulation of human capital and skills required to become integrated into the social, economic, cultural, and political life as adults. Child welfare incorporates a broad spectrum of quality-of-life dimensions and local and universal values (Ben-Arieh and Frønes, 2007: 249-250): economic conditions, peer relations, political rights, and opportunities for development.

Given that social exclusion is multidimensional, an indicator that seeks to reflect it must include multiple and differentiated dimensions. The indicator developed in this paper centers on social exclusion of children in early childhood arising from two reasons. First, in terms of regulation, it constitutes the priority target population for any public policy. Second, early childhood is the optimal context to maximize the performance of programs that aim at improving the accumulation of human capital (Kilburn and Karoly, 2008; Walker *et al.*, 2011).

Focusing on the mother–child dyad is essential to breaking the intergenerational transfer of poverty (Valenzuela and Benguigui, 1999: 40-46). An individual's well-being—both in the present and in the future—is largely dependent on the quality of childcare services provided to the pregnant mother and the newborn (UNICEF, 2007; World Vision, 2011). Children's well-being in the initial stages of life is a direct outgrowth of their living conditions before they were born (Logan *et al.*, 2007). In principle, access to basic social services for the pregnant mother is paramount. These forms of intervention include prenatal care, attending to birth, and registration of the birth in the civil registry. During the first five years of life, the access, availability, and use of services and resources by the mother and the child (i.e., the mother's reading capacity and decision-making autonomy, child care, early stimulation, access to books, breastfeeding, and vaccination schedule) define a "trauma-less" transition from childhood to adulthood that reduces the chances of falling into poverty, and therefore, facilitate an adequate integration into the social and economic sphere (Aguado and García, 2008; Aguado *et al.*, 2008).

III. Structure of the indicator

The indicator has the following characteristics:
- Complies with the basic rights contained in the Convention on the Rights of the Child [rights-based approach, welfare as a present-day right (Ben-Arieh, 2007: 3-4)].
- Accumulates key inputs of human capital that reduce the likelihood that an adult will fall into poverty [welfare-based approach, skills for the future (OECD, 2009: 24-26)].
- Incorporates aspects related to the education and decision-making autonomy of the mother as they relate to the child's quality of life [a mother's autonomy improves both her health and that of her children (Bloom et al., 2001); similarly, a mother's level of education is directly correlated with a child's early development (see Walker *et al.*, 2011: 8)].

- The partial indicators used may be construed as intermediaries in the framework of the Commission on Social Determinants of Health (Solar and Irwin, 2010); therefore, they positively impact children through public policy in the short term.
- In addition, these findings can be applied transnationally; the indicator may be replicated in other developing countries for comparative purposes that measure children's living conditions and promote social policy alternatives that positively impact children.

The indicator suggests a temporal perspective that incorporates the life cycle and the development of the children, emphasizing the use of and access to key social goods and services and the availability of resources at the appropriate time, and on a preventive basis, as elements of public policy that benefits children (see figure 1).

Figure 1. Access, use, and key social resources during early childhood.

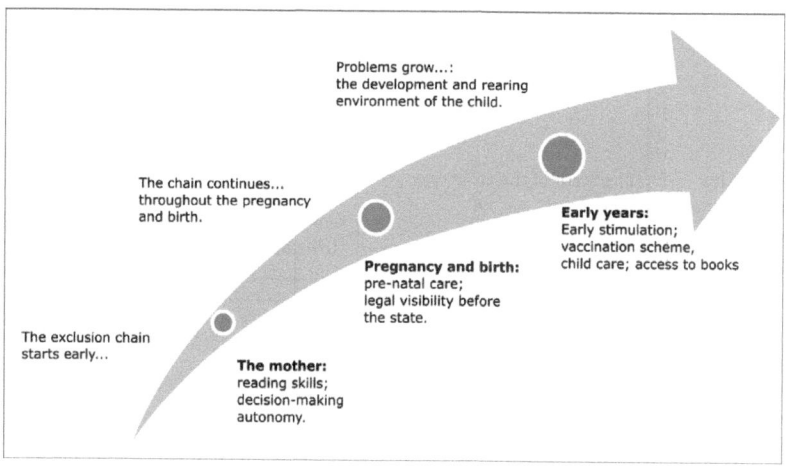

Source: Prepared internally for this article.

The indicator includes 11 partial indicators (see table 1). Their choice was based on the following criteria (Ben-Arieh and Gross-Manos, 2011):
- Indicators that are inputs rather than outcomes
- The child and the mother as an observation unit
- Short-term indicators with long-term effects
- Susceptible of being modified by public policy

- Use of a highly reliable database, potentially replicable in other countries

Table 1. Variables included in the indicator

Variable	Description	Reason for inclusion in the indicator
Reading capacity of the mother	The mother has completed over three years of education? yes, no	The education and autonomy of the mother as a protective or positive factor that increases the chances of a better early development for the child. Beyond a "mere" protection against risk (Ben-Arieh and Frones, 2007; Walker et al., 2011: 7)
Autonomy of the mother	Who makes the decisions related to the health care of the mother? The mother, husband, the mother and other person, and others	
Prenatal care	Number of prenatal controls received by the mother during her latest pregnancy: 0, 1–3, and +4	Prevention of injuries and death of the mother, early detection of problems, and prevention of transmission of diseases before birth (World Vision, 2011)
Legal visibility before the state	The birth of the child was registered? yes, no	The registration of the child in the official registry makes it visible before the state for the "recognition of the rights and obligations of Colombians before society and family" (UNICEF and National Registry of Civil Status, 2003)
Child care	In the past week, did the mother leave the child at the care of another child under 10 years? yes, no	Fewer learning opportunities and an inadequate interaction between the person providing the care and the child contribute to a deterioration in potential development in children, as reflected by cognitive results (Walker et al., 2011: 6)
	Is the child registered with the growth and development program? yes, no	
	Who does the child live with? mother, mother and father	
Early stimulation	Number of early stimulation activities (reading stories or looking at books with images, listening to stories, singing songs, going out for walks or	

	to play) in which the child participated in the past week: 0, 1, 2-3, 4-5	
Access to books	The child had access to books during the past week at: home, library/play center/community center, both, no access	
Breastfeeding	Breastfeeding period (months): 0, 1-6, 7-24, and + 24 The *World Health Organization* (WHO) recommends breastfeeding during the first six months of life, as it is an "unparalleled way of providing adequate sustenance for the healthy growth and development of infants" (WHO, 2001)	
Vaccination	Did the child receive the third dose of the DPT vaccine? yes, no	Vaccination safeguards against preventable diseases and disabilities in children, and it is one of the most cost-effective public health interventions (UNICEF, 2009)

Source: Prepared internally for this paper.

The Growth and Development Program is defined as "the set of activities, procedures and interventions targeted at this sector of the population, to guarantee a periodic and systematic attention to disease. This includes early detection, diagnosis, and treatment, prevention of after-effects, and reduced susceptibility to disability and death" (Ministerio de Salud y Protección Social, 2000, p. 6).

IV. Data and methodology for the development of the indicator

The information for the development of the indicator comes from ENDS 2010, which provides extensive information on the sexual and reproductive health of mothers as well as information on the socioeconomic characteristics of the general population. This facilitates the monitoring and evaluation of relevant baselines in the design and review of policies pertaining to the mother–child dyad. In the case of Colombia, this survey has been applied by Profamilia every five years since 1990. The survey is national in scope and is applicable to both urban and rural areas. It is organized by department, region (Atlantic, Eastern, Bogota, Central, Pacific and Amazonia, and Orinoquía), and subregion. ENDS 2010 uses a multistage sample, stratified in conglomerates, of 51,447 homes located in urban and rural areas of 258 municipalities and includes 53,521 women of reproductive age (13–49) and 17,756 children under the age of 5 (0–60 months).

Regarding the sample, it must be noted that the information on prenatal care, birth, and the postpartum period was only collected for the mother's youngest child, which necessarily reduced the sample size ($n=14,325$). Other variables that were eliminated include the following: whether the child was left under the supervision of another child under the age of 10, values related to prenatal care, number of months the child was breastfed, and whether the child has received the third dose of the DPT vaccine. Lastly, the sample included 12,067 live children between the ages of 6 and 60 months who live at home, and for whom full information was obtained. PCA is used for the development of the indicator and to generate the weight assigned to the variables identified in the survey. This was done using polychoric correlations. Although PCA is an adequate method when continual variables are available, when variables are categorical (such as those included in the indicator, e.g., who makes the decisions related to the health care of the mother), it has been proven that PCA underestimates the expected variance. Kolenikov and Angeles (2009) describe a technique to incorporate categorical variables into the PCA using polychoric correlations (e.g., the correlation between two categorical variables). Polychoric PCA is based on the premise that categorical variables are obtained from latent continual variables that follow a bivariate normal distribution, and using the maximum likelihood method, it calculates the correlation between latent variables (Olsson, 1979). After obtaining the polychoric correlations matrix, the PCA is calculated as usual. Polychoric PCA not only makes a more accurate estimation of coefficients than regular PCA but also guarantees that the coefficients of the ordinal variables follow the order of their categories (Moser and Felton, 2009). The *polychoric* and *polychoricpca* commands of version 12 of STATA were used for the estimation of the polychoric correlations and the PCA.

Following the methodology proposed by Osorio *et al.* (2013, 2014), after performing the polychoric PCA, the main components are selected, based on Kaiser's (1960) criterion, along with the components of values over 1. The VARIMAX criterion is used to facilitate the interpretation of the components to rotate the correlations matrix (Kaiser, 1958). The indicator is calculated as a weighted average of the chosen components. The weight of each component is calculated as the division of its own characteristic value between the sum of all the values of the components chosen. Lastly, the scale of the indicator is adjusted to values between 0 and 1, where 0 is the worst case scenario, that is, total social exclusion, and 1 is the best case scenario, that is, that the child, from birth to infancy, will have the conditions required for an adequate development in terms of the variables under consideration.

V. Results

Table 2 shows the description of the variables included in the indicator. All the estimations were made using the *svy* command of STATA, version 12, which allows for the consideration of the design of the survey weighing the results with the sample weights.

Table 2. Description of the variables included in the indicator*

Department	Reading capacity of the mother	Autonomy of the mother	Prenatal care	Legal visibility before the state		Child care			Early stimulation	Access to books	Breastfeeding	Vaccination
	+3 years of education (%)	Mother decides her own health care (%)	+4 visits (%)	The child is registered (%)	The child is never left under the care of a child <10 (%)	The child is registered with the growth and development program (%)	The child lives with the mother and the father (%)		The child participates in 4–5 early stimulation activities (%)	The child has access to books outside the home (%)	The child is breastfed from 7 to 24 months (%)	The child received the third dose of the DPT vaccine (%)
Antioquia	90.3	83.2	92.1	99.4	95.5	85.7	61.9		48.8	1.4	60.5	85.2
Atlántico	95.0	79.0	94.5	99.3	95.9	78.8	79.3		34.5	0.2	66.8	93.3
Bogotá	96.8	87.1	93.9	99.7	96.7	69.0	66.3		56.7	2.5	61.0	92.3
Bolívar	92.0	74.4	90.7	98.3	96.3	78.6	70.7		34.1	0.7	73.5	84.5
Boyacá	89.9	83.2	88.8	99.6	92.0	80.0	69.4		50.4	2.4	66.7	90.3
Caldas	89.1	82.6	91.7	100.0	92.4	89.5	62.9		41.0	0.9	48.3	96.3
Caquetá	85.1	80.5	85.2	97.7	88.6	91.0	67.8		27.3	0.6	67.4	86.9
Cauca	82.1	68.6	84.0	99.0	94.7	92.2	66.6		42.9	1.1	78.7	92.6
Cesar	86.2	65.1	90.2	97.6	97.5	81.5	76.6		38.9	0.0	66.9	90.1
Córdoba	81.2	72.0	85.4	95.4	95.4	76.1	78.0		36.9	3.8	67.1	83.6
Cundinamarca	92.0	81.3	90.8	100.0	94.8	71.9	70.3		46.3	0.0	55.4	90.2
Chocó	81.1	78.4	68.9	95.2	86.5	56.7	61.0		22.3	0.5	78.8	78.3
Huila	88.1	73.1	93.4	100.0	95.3	87.4	72.7		39.9	0.3	67.2	95.7
La guajira	74.9	64.2	81.9	95.1	96.3	64.2	73.5		29.0	0.4	76.5	80.1
Magdalena	90.9	70.9	88.5	97.0	96.3	77.1	74.3		30.5	0.2	73.2	84.0
Meta	91.0	88.2	89.3	99.1	95.0	74.0	69.2		36.1	1.9	59.2	88.4
Nariño	80.0	59.5	86.0	98.7	93.0	91.1	58.6		47.8	1.0	84.0	95.0

A Social Exclusion Indicator

Norte de Santander	83.4	77.2	86.6	99.0	94.3	73.8	73.3	38.4	1.7	64.1	87.7
Quindío	92.1	84.4	96.4	100.0	97.9	95.6	60.9	45.2	3.0	51.2	95.2
Risaralda	88.0	76.0	93.2	99.6	98.5	87.1	62.0	45.6	1.2	50.7	95.6
Santander	91.0	84.0	90.6	99.1	95.5	76.3	71.7	35.4	0.2	66.8	93.0
Sucre	85.6	76.4	88.2	97.9	96.2	82.8	69.0	30.7	2.5	67.6	85.8
Tolima	90.0	84.9	91.8	99.5	93.3	86.6	62.8	47.3	0.3	52.9	91.2
Valle	94.2	84.5	94.3	98.9	97.2	83.6	65.1	46.5	0.8	63.0	91.5
Arauca	89.4	82.8	88.5	100.0	93.7	84.9	63.5	37.0	1.5	67.4	94.9
Casanare	92.3	81.5	85.5	99.7	95.4	67.3	67.7	37.2	1.1	69.6	96.0
Putumayo	85.0	64.9	83.3	99.6	96.8	92.8	67.3	47.1	1.6	74.2	93.9
San Andrés y Providencia	99.3	87.2	91.3	99.3	97.6	66.4	62.6	48.7	2.0	61.7	81.5
Amazonas	82.5	66.6	70.1	98.8	85.0	71.1	77.5	42.8	1.6	80.2	93.0
Guainía	72.6	61.0	66.6	95.8	93.8	55.8	74.5	33.3	0.0	63.1	84.8
Guaviare	86.2	84.8	91.1	100.0	97.4	83.1	66.0	51.5	0.3	60.9	91.4
Vaupés	85.8	63.9	54.3	98.4	84.7	65.0	70.8	31.6	1.3	67.4	88.6
Vichada	78.1	70.2	59.3	94.8	97.2	55.2	75.3	36.4	1.4	65.7	87.8
Colombia	**90.3**	**79.8**	**90.6**	**99.0**	**95.5**	**79.0**	**68.0**	**44.1**	**1.4**	**64.4**	**89.9**

*Proportions of categories that reflect better living conditions and access to social services.

VI. Selection of the components and the variables represented by each component

Five principal components (PC) are selected, based on the PCA using polychoric correlations and Kaiser's criterion (PC1, PC2, PC3, PC4, and PC5). These components account for 69.5% of the total variance (table 3).

Table 3. Values of the rotated correlations matrix

Component	Characteristic value	Proportion of the variance explained
PC1	2.235	0.203
PC2	1.743	0.362
PC3	1.415	0.490
PC4	1.198	0.599
PC5	1.054	0.695

Table 4 shows the correlations between the PC and the categories of variables included in the analysis. The results indicate that the variables that most strongly correlated with the first component (PC1) include whether the child has legal visibility before the state, whether he or she is enrolled in the growth and development program, and whether the child has received the third dose of the DPT vaccine. This first component highlights the importance of variables that reflect the presence of factors that jeopardize the quality of life for children.

The variables, related to early stimulation and access to books, are represented in the second component (PC2). These variables indicate positive factors that influence the various child-rearing styles practiced by parents. In addition, they attest to the importance of access to public services such as libraries that, by making books available to children, promote early stimulation.

In addition to a variety of prenatal controls, the education of the mother, the duration of breastfeeding, and child care are grouped in the third component (PC3). These variables reflect the importance of the mother's education—as a protection factor—and its relationship with prevention of disease during pregnancy (prenatal controls), breastfeeding, child care, and vaccination practices as integral to the quality of life for infant children. Counterintuitively, an increased duration of breastfeeding has a negative correlation with the indicator. This can be attributed to the fact that poorer mothers do not have access to complementary food resources, leaving them with no choice but to continue breastfeeding their children for longer periods.

The autonomy of the mother may be understood as the capacity to make both personal decisions as well as those related to home affairs, based on the power the woman has over others, her access to information, her command over material resources, and the freedom to act based on her desires (Fotso et al., 2009). The autonomy of the woman to make decisions regarding her health care is represented in the fourth component (PC4).

Lastly, whether the child is being raised by a single mother or by both a mother and a father is represented in the fifth component (PC5). An overview of the variables that are more highly correlated in each component is presented in figure 2.

Table 4. Polychoric correlations matrix

Variables	PC1	PC2	PC3	PC4	PC5
Prenatal care					
0 visits	−0.6	−0.336	−0.668	−0.256	−0.283
1-3 visits	−0.357	−0.175	−0.412	−0.132	−0.175
4+ visits	0.594	0.282	0.662	0.225	0.263
Reading capacity of the mother					
< 3 years of education	−0.292	−0.42	−0.613	−0.281	0.28
> 3 years of education	0.292	0.42	0.613	0.281	−0.28
Mother autonomy (decides her own healthcare)					
Single mother	0.207	0.072	−0.228	0.915	0.041
Single husband	−0.198	−0.153	−0.148	−0.315	0.305
Mother and another person	−0.069	0.016	0.308	−0.652	0.155
Someone else	−0.171	−0.034	0.471	−0.816	−0.582
Legal visibility before the State					
no	−0.622	−0.339	−0.278	−0.182	−0.11
yes	0.623	0.338	0.278	0.182	0.11
Child at the care of another child under 10 years					
no	0.081	0.098	0.721	−0.054	0.022
yes	−0.081	−0.098	−0.721	0.054	−0.022

Registered with the growth and development program					
no	−0.84	−0.123	−0.263	0.068	−0.077
yes	0.84	0.123	0.263	−0.068	0.077
Who does the child live with?					
mother	−0.001	−0.003	0.05	−0.045	−0.998
mother and father	0.001	0.003	−0.05	0.045	0.998
Early stimulation (# of activities)					
0	−0.193	−0.976	−0.212	−0.066	−0.061
1	−0.145	−0.737	−0.216	−0.05	−0.033
2–3	−0.069	−0.446	−0.018	−0.006	−0.021
4–5	0.199	0.896	0.171	0.04	0.048
Access to books					
no access to books	−0.115	−0.944	−0.035	−0.052	−0.038
access to books at home	0.125	0.699	0.065	0.059	0.041
access to books in a library / play center / community center	0.025	0.555	−0.078	−0.048	0.018
access to books at home and outside the home	−0.011	0.957	−0.085	0.017	−0.01
Breastfeeding period (months)					
0	−0.3	−0.033	0.715	0.685	−0.087
1–6	−0.299	−0.009	0.606	0.474	−0.065
7–24	0.171	−0.011	−0.274	−0.254	0.043
+25	0.458	0.055	−0.477	−0.343	0.062
Vaccination (DPT3)					
no	−0.696	−0.091	0.218	−0.009	0.035
yes	0.696	0.091	−0.218	0.009	−0.035

Figure 2. Variables represented by each component

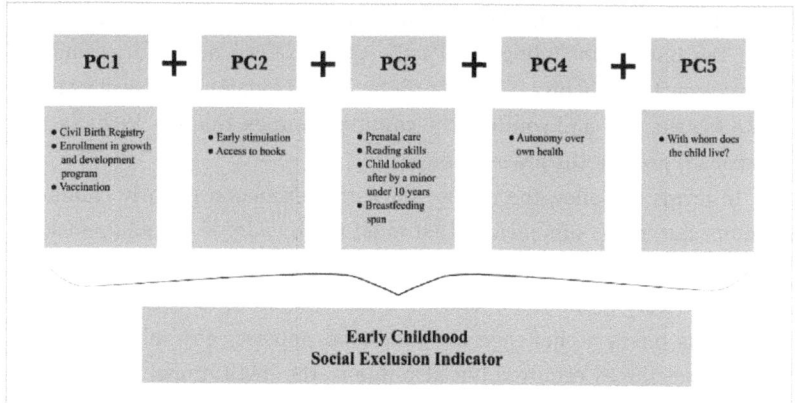

VII. Sorting the departments with the indicator

Figure 3 shows the sorting of Colombian departments (states) as per the composite early childhood social exclusion indicator. Although the indicator is not an instrument that evaluates public policies for childhood, it allows for the identification of relative differences between departments based on certain key variables for adequate development and with regard to access to key social services during a child's early years. Bogota, San Andres y Providencia, Antioquia, Quindio, and Boyaca are among the departments with a lower level of social exclusion, while the departments with a greater degree of social exclusion for children include Vaupes, Chocó, La Guajira, Guainia, and Vichada.

Table 5 shows each department's rating in each PC as well as in the global indicator, with the latter determining the relative ranking of each department. There is a significant heterogeneity in the performance of certain departments. For example, the components that correspond to a greater degree of relative economic development, such as PC2 (early stimulation and access to books) and PC4 (decision-making autonomy of the mother), are more favorably represented in the wealthier departments of the country (Bogota, Antioquia, and Valle), whereas PC3, which relates to various prenatal controls in addition to breastfeeding, is clearly deficient in the poorest departments (La Guajira, Cordoba, Chocó, and Guainia).

These results reflect a double reality: *geographic inequality* and the *concentration of the deficit* in the distribution and access to goods, services, and resources proposed in the indicator. In effect, taking the distribution of the indicator by departments, it is apparent that those departments located along the border, including the Pacific coast (Chocó and Cauca) and the Atlantic coast (La Guajira, Sucre, Cordoba, and Magdalena), as well as those located in the east and south of the country (Vaupes, Guainia, Vichada, and Amazonas) present the lowest indexes.

In terms of policy, the results show that exclusion in early childhood encompasses many dimensions that must be considered by policy-makers, which range from the education and the decision-making autonomy of the mothers to early stimulation activities such as access to books. Without a doubt, this poses a challenge for childhood policies, not only due to the financial resources required but also due to the institutional coordination within the state to integrate programs across different areas and agencies that correspond to departmental needs.

Figure 3. Social exclusion in early childhood by department

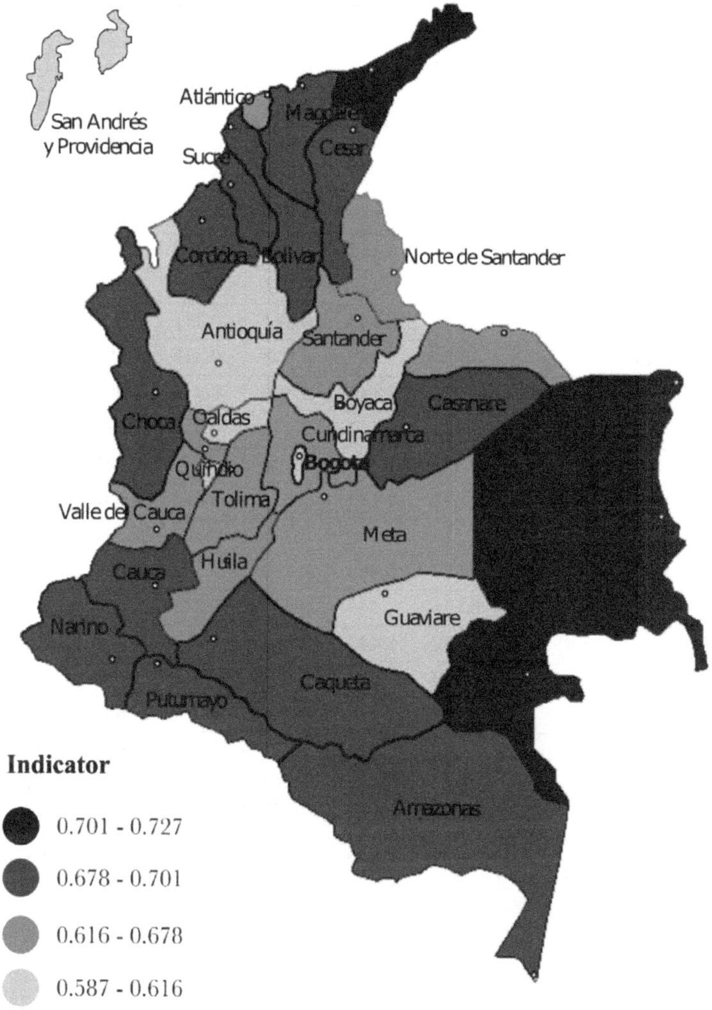

Indicator
- 0.701 - 0.727
- 0.678 - 0.701
- 0.616 - 0.678
- 0.587 - 0.616

Source: Prepared internally for this paper.

Table 5. Social exclusion in early childhood by PC

Department	PC1	PC2	PC3	PC4	PC5	Weighed Average
Bogota	**0.804**	**0.523**	**0.368**	**−0.302**	**0.641**	**0.727**
San Andrés y providencia	0.773	0.525	0.357	−0.296	0.620	0.719
Antioquia	0.807	0.488	0.356	−0.312	0.624	0.710
Quindío	0.846	0.440	0.344	−0.304	0.617	0.707
Boyacá	0.817	0.488	0.387	−0.320	0.659	0.707
Guaviare	0.825	0.473	0.376	−0.317	0.649	0.706
Caldas	0.828	0.449	0.357	−0.296	0.624	0.705
Risaralda	0.817	0.461	0.341	−0.322	0.616	0.701
Huila	0.846	0.458	0.371	−0.355	0.675	0.699
Valle	0.826	0.443	0.354	−0.312	0.636	0.698
Cundinamarca	0.798	0.469	0.368	−0.315	0.658	0.698
Atlántico	0.822	0.441	0.358	−0.330	0.698	0.696
Tolima	0.823	0.447	0.370	−0.304	0.626	0.696
Arauca	0.832	0.444	0.386	−0.320	0.626	0.688
Meta	0.802	0.437	0.379	−0.298	0.657	0.687
Santander	0.820	0.439	0.386	−0.323	0.667	0.685
Norte de Santander	0.793	0.463	0.389	−0.345	0.677	0.680
Casanare	0.806	0.446	0.394	−0.325	0.638	0.678
Putumayo	0.832	0.447	0.367	−0.384	0.637	0.676
Cesar	0.803	0.430	0.352	−0.368	0.685	0.673
Caquetá	0.817	0.411	0.396	−0.321	0.648	0.667
Sucre	0.800	0.420	0.370	−0.348	0.652	0.664
Cordoba	0.765	0.438	0.381	−0.343	0.694	0.663
Bolívar	0.799	0.421	0.362	−0.362	0.654	0.662
Cauca	0.835	0.433	0.388	−0.393	0.638	0.662
Nariño	0.839	0.453	0.389	−0.418	0.601	0.660
Magdalena	0.792	0.409	0.361	−0.364	0.671	0.656
Amazonas	0.787	0.447	0.438	−0.384	0.672	0.644
Vichada	0.709	0.440	0.434	−0.369	0.649	0.616
Guainia	0.726	0.440	0.437	−0.415	0.661	0.608
La guajira	0.741	0.370	0.391	−0.385	0.670	0.605
Chocó	0.709	0.374	0.434	−0.331	0.590	0.591
Vaupes	**0.750**	**0.406**	**0.476**	**−0.404**	**0.608**	**0.587**

VIII. Limitations

To improve our analysis of the quality of life for children and, more concretely, of the social exclusion reflected by the indicator, it would be necessary to consider feeding practices, punishment practices, sexual violence, access to early education, and the voice of the children. ENDS 2010 takes into account these additional variables not addressed by the previous surveys; therefore, we will have to wait for the 2015 data to appreciate a more fully developed index. Our work will continue to examine how other variables like sex, ethnicity, age, and variations between urban and rural settings affect the indicator and to relate it to other indicators that reflect the quality of life in early childhood to procure recommendations for more robust public policies.

IX. Conclusions

The indicator developed constitutes a stepforward in the empirical investigation on the quality of life during early childhood for a developing country that may be replicated in other countries in the Andean region and Latin America in general. Its main use is that it provides a quantitative analysis that broadly reflects, by considering the mother–child dyad, minimum elements that may be altered by public policy in the short term and that shall guarantee the quality of life in the long term, precisely where and when the social exclusion chain starts, that is, during pregnancy, birth, or the first five years of life.

The indicator includes variables that are seldom used in empirical research of childhood welfare in developing countries, such as early stimulation and the decision-making autonomy of the mother. Likewise, the indicator suggests a temporal perspective that incorporates children's life cycle and development, emphasizing the access to and use of key social goods and services and the availability of resources at the appropriate time, and, on a preventive basis, as elements of public policy for the benefit of children.

The findings show the geographic concentration of social exclusion in childhood throughout various regions of the country. The index shows dramatic geographic variation: Those departments concentrated on the border, which encompasses the areas along the Pacific coast (Chocó and Cauca) and the Atlantic coast (La Guajira, Sucre, Cordoba, and Magdalena), and the eastern and southern borders (Vaupes, Guainia, Vichada, and Amazonas) produce the lowest indexes.

These results reflect the complex nature of childhood policy in Colombia, which must necessarily incorporate the varying needs of the child, mother, material resources, and the environment as they relate with state institutions. This makes institutional coordination ever more complicated. The geographical inequalities suggest the need for public spending allocation criteria that take into account the concrete needs of childhood, the economic status of the household, and the territorial environment.

X. Bibliography

Aguado, Luis Fernando and García, Carlos Alberto, 2008, "Monitoreando el bienestar de la niñez en Colombia,"*Revista de Ciencias Sociales*, vol. 14, No. 2.

Aguado, Luis Fernando *et al.*, 2008, "Un índice de carencias en la niñez. Una aproximación por Departamentos para Colombia,"*Revista de Estudios Regionales*, vol. 85.

Ben-Arieh, Asher, 2007, "Measuring and Monitoring the Well-Being of Young Children Around the World," *Paper Commissioned for the EFA Global Monitoring*.

Ben-Arieh, Asher, 2008, "The Child Indicators Movement: Past, Present, and Future," *Child Indicators Research*, vol. 1.

Ben-Arieh, Asher and Frønes, Ivar, 2007, "Indicators of Children's Well Being: What Should Be Measured and Why?, "*Social Indicators Research*, vol. 84.

Ben-Arieh, Asher and Gross-Manos, Daphna, 2011, "Taxonomy for Child Well-Being Indicators: A Framework for the Analysis of the Well-Being of Children," *Childhood*, vol. 18.

Bloom, Shelah S. *et al.*, 2001, "Dimensions of Women's Autonomy and the Influence on Maternal Health Care Utilization in a North Indian City," *Demography*, vol. 38, No. 1.

Brooks, Anne-Marie and Hanafin, Sinéad, 2005, "Measuring Child Well–Being: An Inventory of Key Indicators, Domains and Indicator Selection Criteria to Support the Development of a National Set of Child Well–Being Indicators".

CEPAL and UNICEF TACRO, 2010, *Pobreza infantil en América Latina y el Caribe*, CEPAL and UNICEF, in http://www.cepal.org/publicaciones/xml/6/42796/Libro-pobreza-infantil-America-Latina-2010.pdf.

Fotso, Jean-Christophe *et al.*, 2009, "Maternal Health in Resource-Poor Urban Settings: How Does Women's Autonomy Influence the Utilization of Obstetric Care Services?," *Reproductive Health*, vol. 6, No. 9.

Kaiser, Henry Felix, 1958, "The Varimax Criterion for Analytic Rotation in Factor Analysis," *Psychometrika*, vol. 23, No. 3.

Kaiser, Henry Felix, 1960, "The Application of Electronic Computers to Factor Analysis," *Educational and Psychological Measurement*, vol. 20.

Kilburn, Rebecca and Karoly, Lynn, 2008, "The Economics of Early Childhood Policy: What the Dismal Science Has to Say About Investing in Children," *RAND Labor and Population*.

Kolenikov, Stanislav and Ángeles, Gustavo, 2009, "Socioeconomic Status Measurement with Discrete Proxy Variables: Is Principal Component Analysis a Reliable Answer?," *Review of Income and Wealth*, vol. 55.

Logan, Cassandra *et al.*, 2007, "Conceptualizing a Strong Start: Antecedents of Positive Child Outcomes at Birth into Early Childhood," *Child Trends Research Brief*, vol. 10.

Minujin, Alberto, 2013, "Estrategias regionales de medición de pobreza en niñez. Informe Final de Investigación. Equidad para la Infancia América Latina."

Ministerio de Salud y Protección Social, 2000, *Norma Técnica de Detección de las Alteraciones del Crecimiento y Desarrollo en menores de 10 años*, Bogotá, Ministerio de Salud y Protección Social.

Moore, Kristin Anderson *et al.*, 2008, "A Microdata Child Well-Being Index: Conceptualization, Creation and Findings," *Child Indicators Research*, vol. 1, No. 1.

Moser, Caroline and Felton, Andrew, 2009, "The Construction of an Asset Index: Measuring Asset Accumulation in Ecuador," in Addisson, Tonny *et al.* (eds.), *Poverty Dynamics Interdisciplinary Perspectives*, Oxford, Oxford University Press.

O'Hare, William and Gutiérrez, Florencia, 2012, "The Use of Domains in Constructing a Comprehensive Composite Index of Child Well-Being," *Child Indicators Research*, vol. 5, No. 4.

OECD, 2008, *Handbook on Constructing Composite Indicators: Methodology and User Guide. Methodology*, París, OECD.

OECD, 2009, *Doing Better for Children*, OECD Publishing.

Olsson, Ulff, 1979, "Maximum Likelihood Estimation of the Polychoric Correlation Coefficient," *Psychometrika*, vol. 44, No. 4.

Osorio, Ana María *et al.*, 2013, "Measuring Intermediary Determinants of Early Childhood Health: A Composite Index Comparing Colombian Departments," *Child Indicators Research*, vol. 6, No. 2.

Osorio, Ana María *et al.*, 2014, "Community Socioeconomic Context and Its Influence on Intermediary Determinants of Child Health: Evidence from Colombia," *Journal of Biosocial Science*.

Saltelli, Andrea, 2007, "Composite Indicators Between Analysis and Advocacy," *Social Indicators Research*, vol. 81, No. 1.

Solar, Orielle y Irwin, Alec, 2010, "A conceptual framework for action on the social determinants of health," Discussion Paper 2 (Policy and Practice), Geneva, *http://www.who.int/sdhconference/resources/Conceptualframeworkforactionon SDH_eng.pdf.*

UNICEF, 2007, *Estado Mundial de la Infancia 2007: la mujer y la infancia. El doble dividendo de la igualdad de género*, New York, retrieved from *http://www.unicef.com.co/publicacion/estado-mundial-de-la-infancia-2007-la-mujer-y-la-infancia-el-doble-dividendo-de-la-igualdad-de-genero/.*

UNICEF, 2014, *El estado mundial de la infancia 2014: Todos los niños y niñas cuentan. Revelando las disparidades para impulsar los derechos de la niñez*, New York.

Valenzuela, Carmen and Benguigui, Yehuda, 1999, "Atención integral en salud materno infantil y sus componentes," in Benguigui, Yehuda *et al.* (eds.), *Acciones de salud materno infantil a nivel local: según las metas de la Cumbre Mundial en Favor de la Infancia*, OPS.

World Vision, 2011, "The Best Start: Saving Children's Lives in Their First Thousand Days," India, World Vision.

CHILD POVERTY AND INEQUALITIES AT THE GEOGRAPHIC LEVEL: A SPATIAL ANALYSIS. MEXICO 2010

Héctor E. Nájera Catalán[1]

> I. Introduction. II. Theories on child poverty and space III. Conceptual considerations on poverty and the severity of material deprivation. IV. Description of variables and methods. V. Descriptive analysis of the variables. VI. Results. VII. Discussion and conclusions. VIII. Bibliography. IX. Annexes.

I. Introduction

Enormous progress has been made in recent decades in terms of measuring global poverty. These exercises have been extended and adapted to estimate child poverty at the global, regional, and national levels (Gordon *et al.*, 2003; Roelen and Gassmann, 2012; Cornia and Danzinger, 1997; Minujin *et al.*, 2006). Although the central question continues to be how to scientifically determine the prevalence of child poverty, research has started to incorporate questions on the dynamics of child poverty, the difference between measuring its prevalence and its intensity, the relationship between poverty and life cycle, and, in general, on the causes and effects of poverty at the personal and social dimension (Minujin and Nandy, 2012; Vandecasteele, 2011; Kamerman *et al.*, 2010).

With respect to the factors associated with poverty, the existing empirical studies tend to employ various theoretical approaches in the analysis of socioeconomic or demographic factors at the individual or home level. In the case of childhood poverty, it is known that living in an indigenous home, being part of a home with many dependants, living in a family led by a woman, and living in a single-parent household are clear predictors of child poverty (Ridge, 2002; Bradshaw, 2006; UNICEF-CEPAL, 2010; Kamerman *et al.*, 2010). Although it is known that a rural environment is a reliable

---

[1] Senior Research Associate. Townsend Centre for International Poverty Research. University of Bristol, United Kingdom. pthen@brsitol.ac.uk.

predictor, very little is known about the relationship between poverty and environment.

Poverty maps have shown that general and childhood poverty follow a geographic pattern in most countries (Dorling et al., 2007; Berthoud, 2004; UNICEF-CEPAL, 2010; Coneval, 2011a,b). The empirical theories and analysis on the distribution of poverty posit questions such asthese: Why is poverty more prevalent in certain areas? Is it exclusively due to the fact that those areas have persons with certain characteristics or is there another cause? Are spatial factors exclusively endogenous or are there exogenous public policy factors associated with poverty? Little and slow progress has been made to answer those questions due to both the lack of data and the methodological difficulties involved in an analysis of that kind (Ravallion, 1996). However, using an economic model, studies based on the geographic poverty traps approach have proven that consumption in the home is related both to individual factors and to characteristics of the context (Jalan and Ravallion, 2002; Aassve and Alpino, 2007). Other examples have explored the effect of poverty on one's attitude toward life and the physical and mental health of the children (Caughy et al., 2003; Brooks-Gunn, 1997).

The purpose of this document is to explore the relationship between child poverty and geography in Mexico. It posits the following questions: What is the geographical distribution of child poverty at the municipal level? Is there a nonseasonal geographical link between childhood poverty and certain contextual factors? Where is this relationship stronger?

The document is organized as follows: First, it briefly describes and discusses poverty theories, with an emphasis on childhood and geography. Then it establishes some conceptual considerations on poverty and material deprivation. After describing the data and the methods used in the study, the results are presented. Lastly, it discusses the scope and limitations of the study.

II. Theories on child poverty and space

The purpose of measuring and explaining the reasons for poverty has been present since the pioneering study by Rowntree (1901), which provided one of the first theories on the relationship between life cycle and poverty. For Rowntree, child poverty was virtually inevitable. Only children born to relatively affluent parents could avoid falling into poverty during childhood.

The relationship between the position of the head of the household in society and the subordinate nature of childhood continues to prevail in the explanations for child poverty. However, it may be anchored in different theoretical frameworks, leading to different or even opposing explanations and policies. These traditions or schools are often classified into two groups: individual and structural (Alcock, 2006; Spicker, 2007; Townsend, 1979; Ridge and Wright, 2008). The explanations is related with understand poverty as a product of cultural deficits or of skill-deficits of the person (human capital). Child poverty is then the product of the individual failings of parents. Said failures are transmitted from one generation to the other. It virtually ignores the structure of other inequalities between households, and there is a greater concern for producing intergenerational rather than intragenerational mobility (Gordon, 2011).

Those with a structural-institutional approach propose that social inequalities, generated by the institutional order, produce different patterns and modalities of *access to resources in time* (Townsend, 1979). Thus, society and its institutions generate and perpetuate unequal patterns in terms of their access to resources and opportunities, which affects population groups such as children, women, the young, people with varying skills, indigenous people, and certain classes in the socioeconomic structure, among others (Townsend, 1979, 1993).

With respect to the tension between both theories, Altimir (1979) underlines that the central characteristic of a theory on poverty must be the explanation of the reasons underlying the acquisition of different amounts of (human, social, and cultural) capital, and not the description of a certain empirical normality: The less the capital there is, the greater the chances of being poor. Precisely, Townsend (1993) argues that the main cause lies with the (national and international) institutional order, which determines in an unequal manner the access to resources in time, and child poverty is a result of two processes, the first of which is the unequal distribution of resources and opportunities between households. The second process is the result of an institutional order that is unable to produce policies to fight child poverty in a context of significant social inequality.[2]

---

2   Please note that methodologically speaking, under this tradition it is necessary to first show the production of inequality and then its relationship in the individual level. Townsend (1979) follows an approach of this kind, and Boltvinik and Hernández-Laos (2001) for the case of Mexico.

The international human rights' framework has made it possible to reinforce the structural/institutional dimension of the study of child poverty and to place child poverty in a primary level, where the child is the holder of rights, and not merely an economic dependent (Minujin *et al.*, 2006; Gordon *et al.*, 2003; Pemberton *et al.*, 2005). It has also allowed incorporating the state as an obligor, and a responsible party in relation to poverty, which involves a very different perspective from the social justice standpoint (Townsend, 2009). Child poverty is then the product of failures and breaches of obligations by the state, given that it is incapable of rectifying the processes that give rise to social injustices.[3]

1. Theories on poverty areas

One of the central concerns of human geography is the study of the relationship between the distribution of resources and social justice (Smith, 1994), that is to say, how social systems produce differentials between areas, which in turn affect people's outlook on life.

The literature highlights three major explanations on why poverty is concentrated in certain areas (Bird *et al.*, 2011; Powell *et al.*, 2002; Townsend, 1979; Taylor, 2008). The first one argues that the concentration of poverty is a reflection of the fact that the areas are inhabited by persons with similar characteristics (e.g., low education, unemployed). A second group, based on the economic tradition, establishes that the composition of human capital combined with the comparative advantages of certain areas (natural resources, location) produce differentials throughout the space (Fujita *et al.*, 2001). Lastly, structural theories indicate that there are several contextual factors generated by the institutional order that produce differences between regions, states, or sites (Powell *et al.*, 2002; Townsend, 1979). That is to say, persons of similar demographics are more or less likely to face poverty as a result of their place of residence and other economic and social factors.

Contextual factors may be classified in four groups: agroecological (physical characteristics of the environs), economic and regional growth and development, stigmatization and exclusion factors associated with the

---

[3] Although, as pointed out by Sen (2004), a human rights theory is necessary to clarify the mechanisms or processes in which rights are violated, and the way they can be linked to the actions of the state. On the relationship between social justice and rights (see Plant, 2009).

concentration of groups of a certain race, and factors involving isolation and limited access to basic infrastructure (Bird et al., 2011). Clearly, some of these factors overlap with those proposed by the economic theory; however, there are decisive differences with respect to the mechanisms with which poverty is produced or perpetuated. In economic theory, the economic growth and development, the level of production, and the human capital of the area are the main factors to explain the spatial distribution of poverty. On the other hand, under institutional theories, the explanation focuses on how the social order structures growth, development, and the provision of basic infrastructure. A historical review of the regional development process and the divergence processes seems to support this view, where there is a relationship between the bias introduced by regional policies in the distribution and provision of the initial conditions of basic infrastructure and the historical pattern of divergence of the regional development (Unikel, 1975; Garza, 1983; Asuad, 2000; Vilalta, 2010).

From the perspective of the areas of poverty developed by Townsend (1979), environmental deprivation is the product of unequal social systems that, through economic and social policies, introduce a bias in the distribution of resources to certain areas.[4] These differences result in precarious environments that produce and reinforce other inequalities, such as low-quality educational systems, inadequate infrastructure for economic development, and environments that hinder development at the personal and community level. These are factors that affect people's command over and access to resources over a prolonged period of time.

III. Conceptual considerations on poverty and the severity of material deprivation

Poverty is defined as the lack of resources over time, which results in material and/or social deprivation (Gordon, 2006). Measuring poverty is a complex matter because it requires high-quality longitudinal data that retrieve information on the different sources of income and the access to different goods and services (Gordon, 2010). Part of the contemporary debate on measuring poverty is related with the juncture or the intersection of the set of basic needs (material deprivation) with that of income (Boltvinik, 1999; Alkire and Foster, 2011). Measurement exclusively based

---

4   In English, the term is *environmental deprivation*.

on unmet basic needs is a direct method of measurement that has advantages with respect to the indirect method (i.e., income) because the effective access to goods and services is more accurate than income in measuring a person's standard of living (Boltvinik, 1999).

For children, it has been noted that direct measurements more accurately determine their relative welfare, because it does not require assumptions on the distribution of income within the home, and it draws a connection between material deprivation and various human rights (Minujin et al., 2006; Gordon et al., 2003).

Severity, on the other hand, refers to different degrees of poverty or material deprivation. However, other concepts such as intensity and depth are used as alternatives or surrogate names for the concept of severity (Delamonica and Minujin, 2007; Alkire and Roche, 2011; Foster et al., 1984; Gordon et al., 2003). These three concepts coincide in that there are different degrees of material deprivation, but they differ in terms of the *space* where deprivation is measured.[5]

In this document, severity is understood and measured as multiple deprivation, based on the premise that deprivations are cumulative, and severity is related to the number of deprivations. The concepts of depth and intensity of deprivation will not be used in the document, although we recognize the importance of reaching consensus with regard to their meaning and measurement. As for thresholds, it is assumed that in the "continuum" of the recognition of rights or the satisfaction of basic needs, there are different thresholds that reflect the degree of deprivation ranging from acute to mild (Gordon et al., 2003).

IV. Description of variables and methods

1. Dependent variable

The dependent variable is an indicator of material deprivation among children based on four dimensions derived from the human rights framework (chart 1). It was calculated from the 2010 National Population and Housing Census (CNPV 2010), which is representative for the 2,456

---

[5] Although in some cases it refers to multiple deprivation (a sum of deprivations), in others, it refers to the thresholds used, which may identify situations more or less extreme (water inside the house, or water inside the land, for example).

municipalities of Mexico (INEGI, 2010). The sample used included 3 million children aged between 0 and 12 at the time of the census.

The indicator is based on both Gordon *et al.* (2003) and the adaptation of this work by UNICEF-CEPAL (2010). Based on Gordon (2010) and Gordon and Nandy (2012), we chose to use thresholds that ensure a *reliable, valid, and cumulative* measurement of poverty.[6] These thresholds are much less restrictive than those used by UNICEF-CEPAL (2010) and moderately less restrictive than those used by Coneval (2010) to measure poverty in Mexico. However, other measurements using more severe thresholds were devised for analysis.[7] Due to space limitations, results are based on only the valid and reliable measurement. The indicators used for the construction of both measurements are shown in chart 1.

Chart 1. Thresholds used for the material deprivation index

Dimension/Right	Indicator/Threshold
Education	School absenteeism
Minimum social protection floor	No access to social security or no access to health services
Essential services	Lack of tap water inside the home
	Lack of independent Water Close connected to the water supply
	Use of inadequate/dangerous fuels
	Lack of adequate means to process garbage
Home habitability	Dirt floor
	Walls with material other than brick, block, stone, quarry, cement, or concrete
	Roofs with material other than brick, block, stone, quarry, cement, or concrete
	Overcrowding (+2.5 per room)

Source: Prepared internally for this paper.

---

6 Reliability refers to the internal consistency of the measurement, validity to its relationship to a factor (deprivation), whereas cumulative implies that two deprivations represent a situation rather than a deprivation (Gordon, 2010).
7 The author may be consulted regarding this analysis. In general, regardless of the threshold used, the conclusions of the study stand. This is due to the high correlation between different measurements of deprivation, which affect incidence but not its distribution in space.

The childhood deprivation index varies between 0 and 4, because it uses the four dimensions and not the disaggregated indicators for the estimate. Following Gordon (2010), we have concluded that the dimensions of the index are cumulative, and therefore, the degree of deprivation increases as the number of material or social deprivations increases. For the statistical analysis at the municipal level, we considered the typical level of deprivation experienced by a child in a given municipality.[8]

2. Explanatory variables

A. Contextual deprivation

Based on Townsend (1979), we created a *contextual deprivation* variable. This is an exogenous variable that largely depends on social and urban policy. As has been studied in Mexico, the current enjoyment of urban environments is correlated with the allocation of resources and to the local effectiveness of the government. As shown in the study by Coneval (2011a,b), there are serious problems in the management of resources at the local level, which is also related to the problems of "good" governance and corruption (Cabrero, 2003; Palavicini, 2012).

The calculation is based on data from the survey on the conditions of the housing context of the sample of the 2010 CNPV. It uses information on basic services such as public lighting, public sewage and drainage, pavement, signage, sidewalks, public green space, ramps for persons with mobility problems, and public telephones. There are three degrees for the qualitative assessment of each item: whether it exists throughout the entire area, whether it exists only in some parts, or whether it is missing altogether. The decision was made to use simple weighing: 0 if it is missing, 1 if it exists partially, and 2 if it exists throughout, dividing the sum of the three between the total. To assess the internal consistency of the index, Cronbach's alpha coefficient was calculated as 0.84 (annex).

The data are not available for all municipalities, because information was collected only from 5,000 residents. The following data sets were

---

[8] As shown in the descriptive analysis, there is a high "local" correlation between incidence and severity of deprivation among children. Therefore, in order to avoid repetitive analyses, results will be presented and discussed by considering only this variable. The results on incidence appear in the annex. The conclusions do not change in any of the two cases.

considered in our analysis: data from the 2010 CNPV sample, information on the characteristics of sites with fewer than 5,000 residents, municipal data, a selection model of Heckman, and a prediction based on a Geographically Weighed Regression (RGP). Using this information, we estimated the values for the municipalities that lacked data (annex 1). In the selection model of Heckman (1979), the "selection" variables (the reasons for a certain piece of information to be missing from the sample) were the demographic density of the municipality and access to a road. The prediction variables were based on access to amenities, such as the existence of a hospital, the number of doctors per capita, and the percentage of residents with access to information technologies (Internet and telephone). This process made it possible to include 2,454 municipalities in the analysis (the annex IX shows the resulting map).

B. Economic and educational development

From the economic perspective of poverty areas, the aggregated level of local human capital is a determining factor of the variation of poverty in the space. This is because, under standard economic theory, the returns of observable variables such as education are related to productivity. However, in this perspective, there is scant discussion of the origin of the differences in human capital at the spatial level. These differences, at least in the case of Mexico, are the result of the way in which urban and regional development policies affected the development of the educational system, the role of the elites in the stratification of the educational system (public *vs.* private), and the existing relationship between poverty at the home level and the high probability of school abandonment (Escalante *et al.*, 2011; Villa, 2007; Arnaut *et al.*, 2010). This means that the educational level at the local level may be conceptualized from many different perspectives; however, from the statistical standpoint, all of the intermediations and interrelationships are very difficult to model, and they are beyond the scope of this paper. However, their implications are briefly considered in the interpretation of the results. As a proxy to the educational level of the area, we used the average years of schooling, which were based on the 2010 CNPV.

The rate of participation in wage employment (formality) is used as a second control variable. This variable is used as an approximation of the local economic development, and its calculation was also based on the CNPV.

3. Methods

Spatial or geographic analyses produce better results to the extent that they distinguish the individual effect from the contextual one. Various alternatives are proposed in the literature, which allow one to partially handle this problem. For example, multilevel (hierarchical) models, unlike the traditional regressions based on fixed effects, allow the simultaneous incorporation of contextual and individual variables (Goldstein, 2011; Rabe-Hesketh and Skrondal, 2012). From the geographic standpoint, they have the limitation of using discrete units and of being unable to explore nonseasonal relationships at the spatial level (Fotheringham et al., 2002).[9]

RGP allows analyzing whether the relationships between the variables fluctuate across the geographic space (Fotheringham et al., 2002; Brunson, 1998). It offers a set of local regression coefficients, which may be mapped to display the relationships of interest. They have the advantage of using non-discrete areas in a series of windows that are adjusted based on the proximity of the observations.

If there were access to the specific location of the children, it would be possible to directly use an RGP with individual and contextual variables. However, this kind of information is not available. Therefore, it is necessary to use aggregated values for each area, and therefore, it is not possible to distinguish the effect of the variables of the home. This results in problems that are typical in geographic analyses, such as that of the Modifiable Area Unit Problem (MAUP) (Openshaw, 1981). The consequence is that there may be effects in the estimation due to the number of areas used and the type of aggregation (small to larger units). There is no solution available to the MAUP; however, it has been observed that RGP tends to mitigate its negative effects (Fotheringham et al., 2002).[10]

This paper focuses on presenting and analyzing the results of the RGP, because its results require a lot of space, and the central questions of the research of this paper are restricted to the analysis based on the RGP. However, at first, we explored the presence of contextual seasonal discrete

---

9   In addition, they are computationally intensive; they require random samples or weight adjustments for complex samples (Rabe-Hesketh and Skrondal, 2006). Another option is the Conditional Autoregressive models (CAR models); however, they also operate with other discrete areas (Jin et al., 2005).

10   Morenoff (2003) proposes a stage-based modeling that partially integrates RPG with multilevel analysis. This approach has been applied by Chen and Truong (2012).

effects, using a "hurdle-multilevel model" based on a negative binomial distribution (William et al, 1995; Cameron and Trivedi, 2013).[11]

The RGP uses the severity of child deprivation at the municipal level as a dependent variable and contextual deprivation, the educational level, and the formal employment rate as explanatory variables. Given that incidence and severity are highly correlated at the local level (areas with high incidence have high severity and vice versa), we only present the results for one model. The inference of the study is in terms of the association of variables, instead of effects; a possible interpretation of the relationship is proposed at the theoretical and conceptual level.

V. Descriptive analysis of the variables

1. Material deprivation among children

Table 1 shows the distribution of material deprivation among children. Approximately one in every 10 children in Mexico does not suffer material deprivations. A little over a third of the child population has one or two deprivations and approximately two out of every five children have three or more deprivations. These data suggest that child poverty in Mexico must be characterized from the multiple deprivation perspective, where future questions must be posited over the pattern of overlap and the interrelationships of the dimensions.

Table 1. Child deprivation index, children (0–12 years), Mexico, 2010

Total deprivations	Millions	%
0	3.2	13
1	5.4	21
2	6.5	25
3	9.2	36
4	1.4	5
Total	25.7	100

Source: Estimations based on the National Population and Housing Census (INEGI, 2010).

---

11 To estimate this model, we used Mplus 7.1 (Muthén and Muthén, 2012). We considered the complex structure of the Population and Housing Census sample (including weights, sectors, and primary sampling units). We found that contextual effects exist, and therefore, it is plausible to proceed to RGP-based analysis.

2. Distribution of child poverty, municipalities, Mexico

Map 1 shows the distribution of the severity of child deprivation in Mexico at the municipal level in 2010.[12] It can be seen that in the north, center, and west of the country, children tend to present a lower degree of severity with respect to the children in the south, particularly the children in the southwest (Chiapas, Guerrero, and Oaxaca) and the municipalities that are near the southern border. However, a high severity is evident in a significant portion of the northwest region (obscure region of the Western Sierra madre). This pattern coincides with the findings of the UNICEF-CEPAL (2010) study, suggesting that between 2000 and 2010, the geographic distribution of child poverty at the municipal level has not seen substantial changes in Mexico (the same cannot be said of the degree of severity, as it is necessary to make a comparative work).

Map 1. Severity of material deprivation among children (2010). Municipalities, Mexico, Natural Breaks

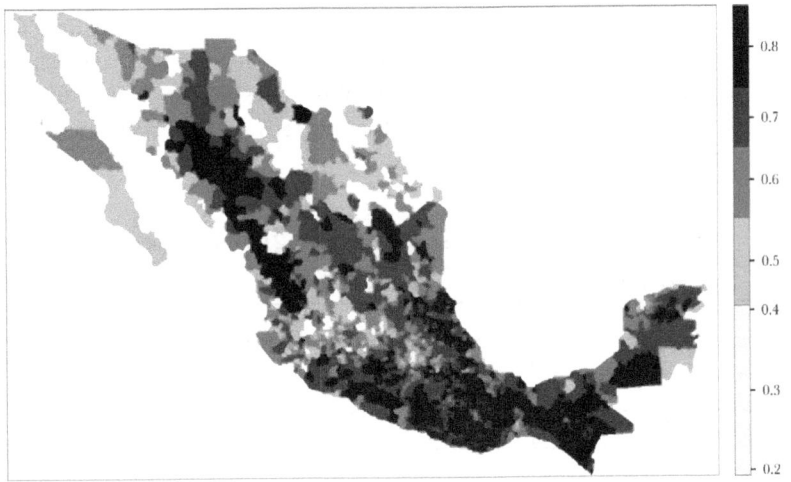

Source: Prepared internally with information from INEGI (2010).

In map 1, it can be seen that visually there are clusters of municipalities with very similar severity values. This can be analyzed formally with Moran's

---

12   In this case, we use the average and not the number of deprivations, since four maps would need to be used to represent the same idea.

statistic index, which is analogous to Pearson's coefficient of correlation, and can only be applied to geographic analysis (Vilalta, 2005). In this case, the correlation is based on the distance and the value of the neighboring municipalities. Graph 1 shows the spatial autocorrelation dispersion diagram, considering their first-degree spatial backwardness (i.e., the value in neighboring municipalities). Moran's index suggests that, in effect, municipalities with similar material deprivation severity values among children tend to be close to each other throughout the Mexican territory.

Graph 1. Dispersion diagram. Spatial severity versus backwardness

Morans's I. 0.69***

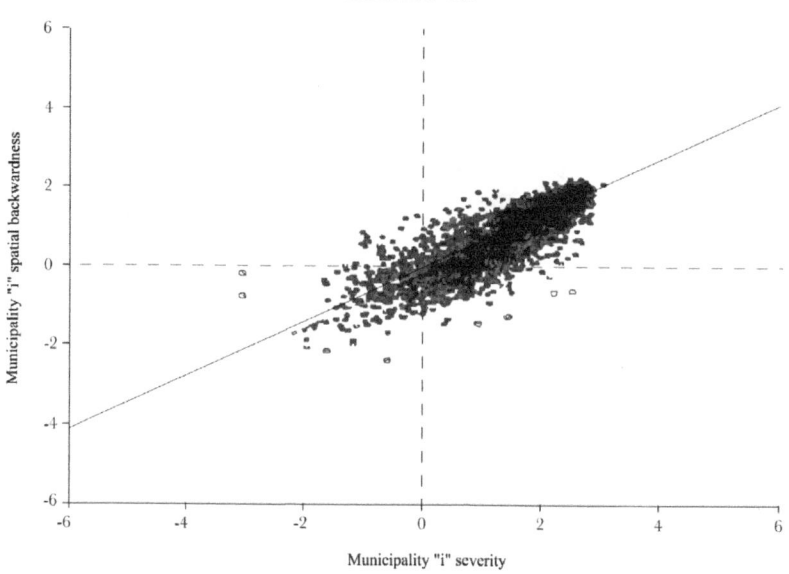

To find out the location trends of the groups of municipalities with similar values, we calculated Local Indicators of Spatial Association[13] (Anselin, 1995). Map 2a shows the clusters of municipalities with a high spatial correlation. However, because the municipalities vary in size, the visual interpretation may turn out to be wrong. Maps 2a and 2b show that in the southeast of the country, there are two large groups of municipalities with high incidence and high severity of deprivation among children. One is located in the areas of Oaxaca and Guerrero and the other in Chiapas. In turn,

---

13 For that purpose, we used the free GeoData software of the University of Illinois.

it is possible to detect another group in the area of the Yucatán peninsula (southeast). On the other hand, in the northwest, it is clear that there is another cluster of municipalities with high severity of child poverty. The groups of municipalities with low incidence and severity tend to be located in the northeast and the center of the country.

Map 2a. Cluster of Municipalities with high/low severity of deprivation among children

Map 2b. Cartogram (map 2a)

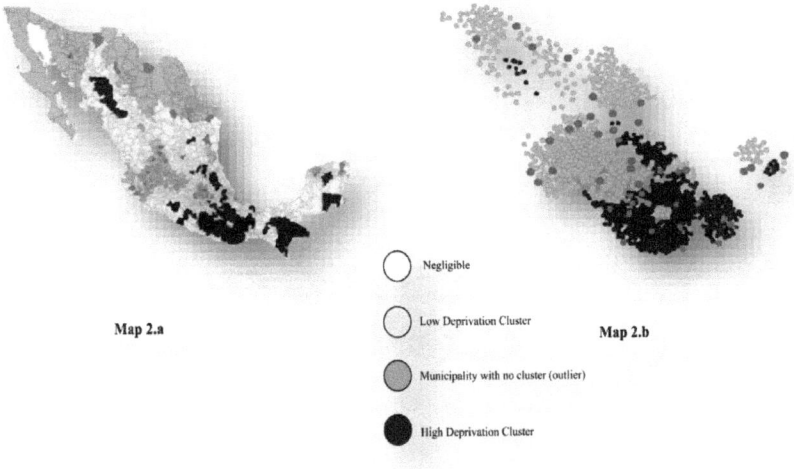

Source: Prepared internally with information from INEGI (2010).

3. Descriptive analysis of the explanatory variables

Table 2 presents the basic descriptions of the three explanatory variables. Based on these data, it can be stated that there are no municipalities in Mexico with full contextual deprivation (minimum=0.1) nor municipalities without contextual deprivation (maximum=0.9). That is to say, in all municipalities, there is some kind of shortcoming in one of the indicators. In average, the population has approximately 6.5 years of schooling, with the maximum being 13.5 and the minimum being 2 years. The average wage employment rate (formality) is 45%; however, it is highly variable (0.21).

Table 2. Explanatory variable descriptions

	Average	Minimum	Maximum	Std. deviation
Contextual deprivation	0.3	0.1	0.9	0.1
Schooling (years)	6.5	2.0	13.5	1.5
% of wage employment	45	03	92	21

Source: Internal information, INEGI (2010).

Similar to the measurement of material deprivation among children, graph 2 shows the dispersion diagrams considering the spatial lag of each variable. The three of them show a high positive and significant spatial autocorrelation. The maps of each variable are shown in the annex.

Graph 2. Spatial autocorrelation dispersion diagrams of the explanatory variables

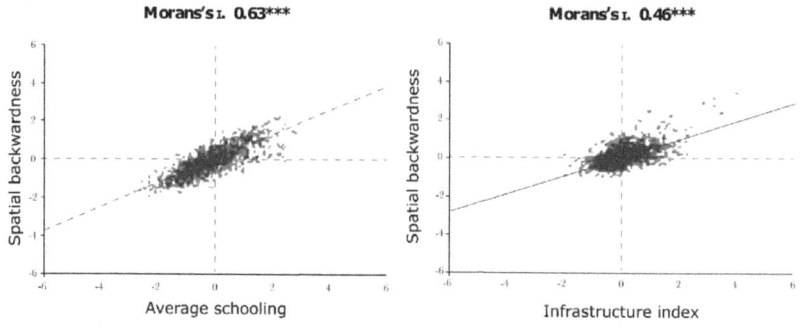

VI. Results

The results of the RGP-based model are presented below. It uses the severity of deprivation among children as a dependent variable and contextual deprivation, the educational level, and the formal employment rate as explanatory variables. Partial models were estimated to evaluate the adjustment of the final model.[14] RGP is highly sensitive to local multicollinearity issues (Brunson et al., s.f.; Wheeler and Tiefelsdorf, 2005). The spatial analysis of the local condition number suggests that no evidence of greater local correlation exists among the variables (annex 5). The RGP, the maps, and the significance tests for the local coefficient were performed for 2,454 municipalities using the R package of the "GWmodel" software (Lu et al., 2014).

Table 3 presents the results of the RGP. To assist in the interpretation, coefficients were centered to the median and then rescaled. The RGP may be interpreted in a similar way to quantile regression, where there is a coefficient to the median, and a series of coefficients for different cuts in the distribution. The signs of the three explanatory variables, considering the regression to the median, are as expected: Lower severity is associated with positive changes in the provision of infrastructure, increases in average schooling, and the formal participation rate.

However, the relationship is not seasonal (i.e., it varies in certain areas of the territory), although it is negative in at least 75% of the municipalities. Minimum, maximum, and quartile values show that there are clusters of municipalities where the association tends to be stronger compared to the other areas. For example, in 25% of the municipalities, 10% increases in the wage employment rate are associated with decreases ranging between 15 and 45% in severity. Positive changes of 10% in the infrastructure index (10% improvements in the provision of infrastructure) are associated with decreases ranging between 15 and 3% for 25% of the municipalities. As to education, similar associations are observed in accordance to an increase of one year of schooling.

These relationships, although illustrative of the global results of the analysis, require significance tests. However, in the context of the RGP, there is a hypothesis test per variable per municipality. One of the characteristics of the RGP is that both coefficients and their corresponding significance tests may be visualized with maps. Due to the amount of tests, if the P-value is not adjusted, there will likely be a "false discovery rate," because it is probable that some of the coefficients will be randomly significant (Holm, 1979). There are different procedures to adjust the tests in the context of the RGP

---

14 We used R square, Akaike's Information Criterion (AIC), and the Bayesian Information Criterion (BIC) to compare the models.

(Byrne *et al.*, 2009). In this case, they were adjusted with the Benjamini and Yekutieli (2001) method.

Table 3. Model 1. Dependent variable: Severity of deprivation among children at the municipal level

	AICc:	-10746.9	
	BIC/MDL:	-8881	
	R square	0.89	
	Adjusted R square	0.87	
	Coefficients		
Variable		Minimum	Maximum
Constant		51	81
Wage employment % (10% changes)		-45.2	13.4
Contextual deprivation (10% changes)		-14.9	4.1
Municipal educational level (school year)		-10.9	1.4
	Low Quartile	Medium Quartile	High Quartile
Constant	62	66	68
Wage employment % (10% changes)	-15.5	-8.9	-3.0
Contextual deprivation (10% changes)	-3.1	-1.8	-.6
Municipal educational level (school year)	-5.2	-3.7	-1.9

Source: Internal estimates.

Map 3a shows the coefficients of the contextual deprivation variable. The grayer areas are those where the relationship tends to be more strongly negative, and the clear areas are those where the relationship is weakened. In combination with map 3b (adjusted *P*-value), it can be seen that the relationship is significant in four large areas:

- The northwestern border (Baja California, Tijuana, Mexicali, and Ensenada).
- The northern region (Chihuahua—Chihuahua capital, Coahuila—the area of its capital, Torreón, Nuevo León and Tamaulipas—Tampico).
- West and center (Jalisco—Puerto Vallarta and Guadalajara, Guanajuato and the central metropolitan area—including the capital of the country). Municipalities of the Oaxaca region (tourist municipalities up to the capital) and the western area of the de Yucatan peninsula—the cities of Merida and Campeche.

Map 3a. Coefficients of the contextual deprivation variable. Natural Breaks

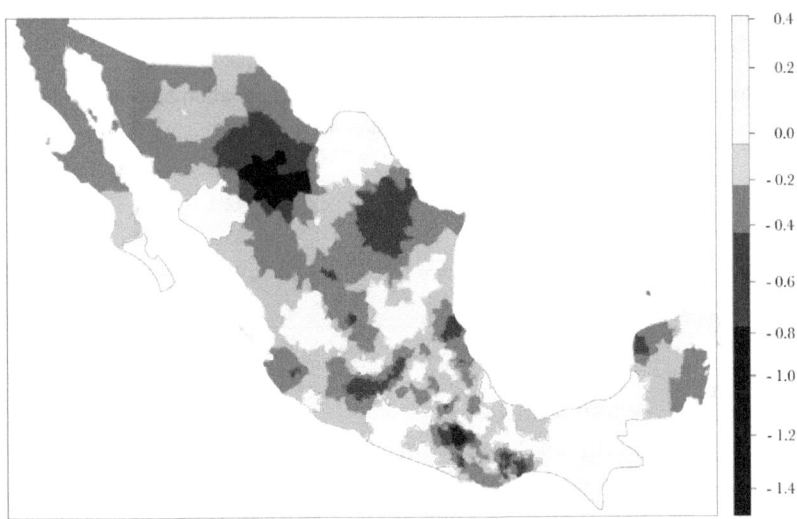

Map 3b. Map 3a hypothesis test adjusted P-value

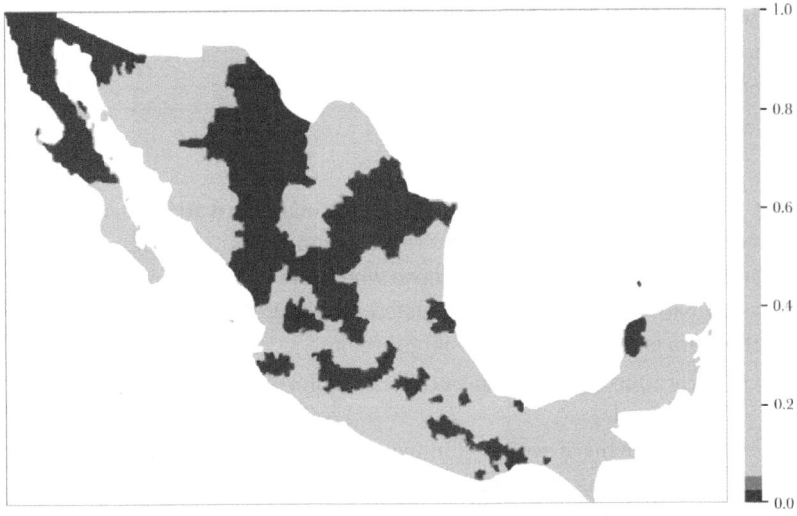

All these areas are characterized for being the capitals of the states or for having a high economic development, with a relatively higher basic provision of infrastructure and facilities compared to the rest of the municipalities of the country. This means that, after controlling per educational level and formal employment rate, the severity of deprivation among children has a negative relationship with the areas that have been historically favored by social policies in terms of the provision of basic infrastructure and, therefore, they cannot be understood without referring to inequality processes induced by regional and local policies for the elemental provision of an adequate environment for people. Although this suggests that there are differences between municipalities and areas, the same cannot be said with respect to the inequalities within the municipalities, which requires spatial analyses with disaggregated and more specific data for each city.

Maps 4a and 4b show the coefficients of the average schooling variable and the adjusted significance tests, respectively. The gray areas indicate those where the regression slope is more negative. As can be seen, the relationship tends to be stronger in the north than in the south, and particularly the southwest, where the relationship is virtually 0 or positive. Map 4b shows that the relation is significant throughout the country, except for the border between Chihuahua and Durango (mountain region with small towns), the state of Guerrero and Michoacán, and part of the border between Tamaulipas and San Luis Potosi and the area of the southern border of Chiapas.

Leaving aside areas with very low population density in the north of the country, the areas where the educational level is not significant correspond to municipalities with a very low educational level, high contextual deprivation, high rates of informality, and highly severe deprivation among children. This suggests that even when the educational level is a good predictor of severity among children, positive changes in this variable are not necessarily associated with a lower severity. Two hypotheses emerge from these results. First, a necessary condition for changes in education to be followed by negative changes in the severity of deprivation among children (at the ecological level), the population needs to attain at least a minimum average years of schooling. Second, it is also necessary that the said increases occur in the neighboring municipalities, because there seems to exist a strong spatial relationship with respect to the educational level of the neighboring areas. These two conditions require both a complex statistical analysis and, more importantly, a consistent theoretical discussion that explains exactly how that relationship occurs in space.

Map 4a. Coefficients of the average schooling variable. Natural Breaks

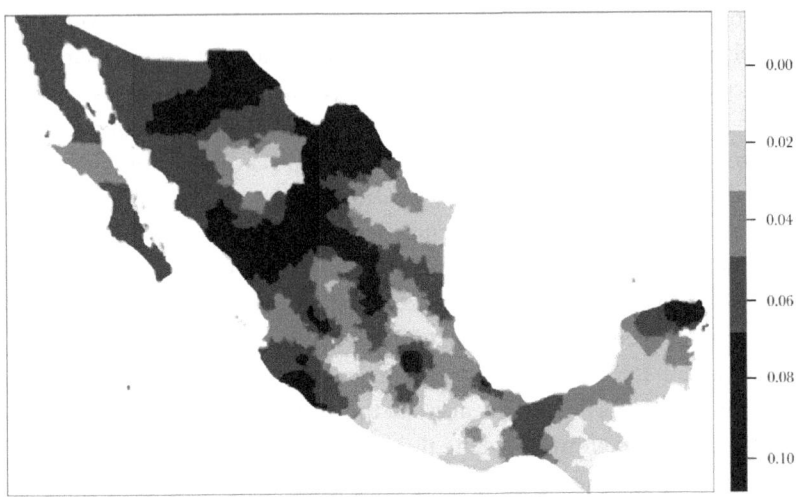

Map 4b. Hypothesis test adjusted P-value

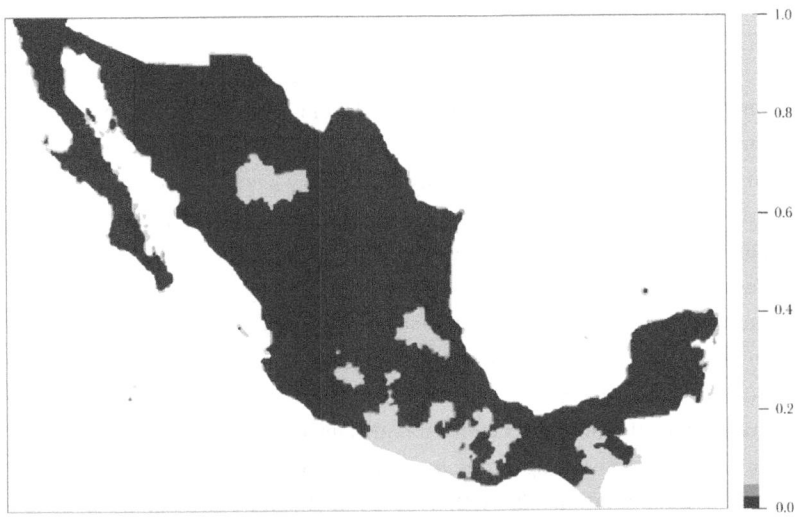

Map 5a shows the coefficients of the relationship between the formal participation rate and the severity of deprivation among children. As can be seen, the relationship tends to be stronger in the northeast and center than in the northwest and southwest. As shown in map 5b, these relationships seem to hold in the indicated areas. The municipalities in the northeast form an important area of formal employment; therefore, in this area of the country, there is a relationship between employment conditions and the severity of deprivation among children. This is possible because of the relationship between a greater proportion of adults and the young in jobs with some benefits and perks and their transmission to the children at the household level. The same pattern is observed in the area near the city of Chihuahua, which has a relatively higher rate of formal employment than the neighboring areas in the west. The area that starts in the Bajio (Jalisco, Guanajuato) and goes through the cities of Queretaro and San Luis Potosi all the way to Nuevo Leon shows a corridor in which changes in the formal employment rate are associated with a lower severity of deprivation among children.

With respect to the small areas in the southwest (Oaxaca) they also correspond to the tourist cities of the Pacific coast (particularly Huatulco), where compared to the neighboring areas, the formal employment rate is significantly higher. This relationship is also observed in the southern region of the golf, in the area of the city of Coatzacoalcos. On the southeast, the cities of Campeche and Chetumal make up another area where the relationship is significant and negative. However, the model excludes Merida, and it includes an area with low rates of formal employment. This relationship is difficult to interpret, because it is not entirely consistent with what was observed in the remaining areas of the country.

Map 5a. Formal employment rate coefficients. Natural Breaks

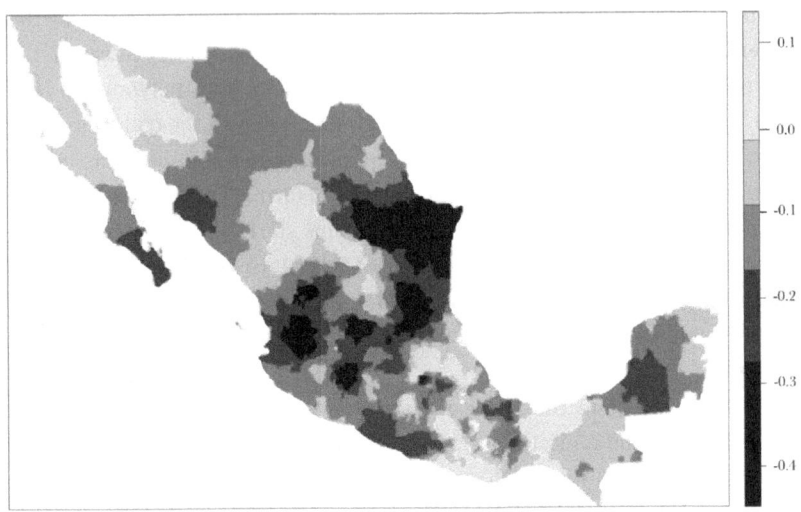

Map 5b. Hypothesis test adjusted P-value

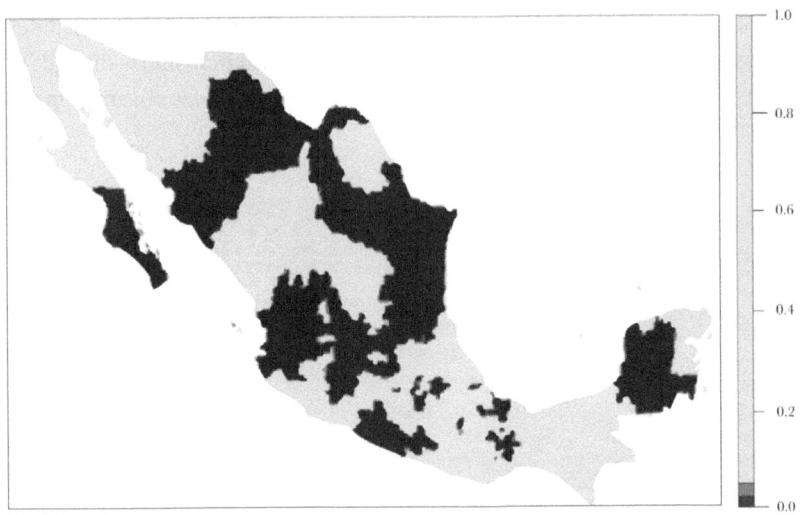

VII. Discussion and conclusions

The core purpose of this paper is to move forward in the analysis of the relationship between geographical inequalities and child poverty from the standpoint of social justice. This subject, although present in international literature, seems to have permeated very little into the analysis of poverty and inequality in Latin America (e.g., Aassve and Alpino, 2007; Dorling et al., 2007; Jalan and Ravallion, 2002).

The article shows that child poverty is spatially concentrated in Mexico, that the said distribution is not random, and that it can be understood by considering the existing literature on the role of the institutions in the creation of geographic patterns of inequality.

There is a negative relationship between the severity of deprivation among children at the municipal level and a better provision of basic infrastructure. A core question derived from this finding is: Why do some municipalities have better contexts than others? Literature on the subject has shown that these inequalities resulted not only from the regional development process of the country but also from recent failures of the local governments in the provision of basic infrastructure (Coneval, 2011a,b; Garza and Schteingart, 2010; Garza, 1983), which cannot be separated from administrative problems of the local governments (Palavicini, 2012).

As a hypothesis, it can then be proposed that two children would have very different probabilities of being poor because of the municipality and the region where they were born. From the standpoint of social justice and of the eradication of poverty, it is vital to incorporate the spatial approach, because it is possible to think that individual programs will have partial and unequal effects becauseof the context, which, as previously mentioned, can be modified with institutional efforts.

The educational level and the formal employment in the area seem to be crucial in the reduction of the severity of material deprivation among children, particularly in the areas with levels above the national average. However, this regularity needs to be analyzed from a contextual approach. To what extent are the differentials in educational achievement and the formal employment rates between different areas produced by institutions? Literature has shown, although with different methodological approaches, that the economic and educational divergences between the regions have a strong institutional component (Garza, 1983; Esquivel and Messmacher, 2002; Asuad, 2000; Vilalta, 2010).

From the technical–methodological standpoint, different approaches are required. From the qualitative area, studies are required to understand the relationship between people and space in Mexico. It is necessary to use estimates for small areas to create deprivation measurements with a greater geographical breakdown to explore intra-urban inequalities (Rao, 2005). It will also be important to use multilevel models with random effects for contextual factors to obtain a better assessment of the individual and contextual effect, and of how the latter varies, using discrete areas. Lastly, it is necessary to have better indicators at the contextual level, which improve the identification and specification of statistical models.

VIII. Bibliography

Aassve, Arnstein and Alpino, Bruno, 2007, "Dynamic Multi-Level Analysis of Households' Living Standards and Poverty: Evidence from Vietnam," *Institute for Social and Economic Research (ISER). ISER Working Paper 2007-10*.

Alcock, Peter, 2006, *Understanding Poverty*, Palgrave Macmillan Limited.

Altimir, Oscar, 1979, "La dimensión de la pobreza," *Cuaderno de la CEPAL*, Santiago de Chile, No. 27.

Alkire, Sabina and Foster, James, 2011, "Counting and Multidimensional Poverty Measurement," *Journal of Public Economics*, vol. 95, No. 7-8.

Alkire, Sabina and Roche, José Manuel, 2011, "Beyond Headcount: Measures Components of Child Poverty," *OPHI Working Paper No. 45*.

Anselin, Luc, 1995, "Local Indicators of Spatial Association. LISA," *Geographical Analysis*, vol. 27, No. 2.

Arnaut, Alberto *et al.* (ed.), 2010, *Educación. Los grandes problemas de Mexico*, vol. 7, El Colegio de Mexico.

Asuad, Normand, 2000, "Aspectos básicos que debe atender una política de desarrollo regional y urbano en Mexico en el corto, mediano y largo plazo," *Revista Investigación Económica*, vol. 60, No. 23.

Benjamini, Yoav and Yekutieli, Daniel, 2001, "The Control of the False Discovery Rate in Multiple Testing Under Dependency," *The Annals of Statistics*, vol. 29, No. 4.

Berthoud, Richard, 2004, *Patterns of Poverty Across Europe*, Bristol, Policy Press.

Bird, Kate *et al.*, 2011, "Spatial Poverty Traps. An Overview," *ODI Working Paper 321, CPRC Working Paper 161*, Chronic Poverty Research Centre.

Boltvinik, Julio, 1999, "Métodos de medición de la pobreza. Conceptos y Tipología," in *Socialis, Revista Latinoamericana de Política Social*, No. 1, Argentina.

Bradshaw, J. (2006), 'A review of the comparative evidence on child poverty', Technical report, Joseph Rowntree Foundation.

Boltvinik, Julio and Hernández-Láos, Enrique, 2001, *Pobreza y distribución del ingreso en Mexico*, Siglo XXI Editores.

Brooks-Gunn, Jeanne et al., 1997, *Neighborhood Poverty, Volume 1: Context and Consequences for Children*, Russell Sage Foundation.

Brunson, Chris et al., 1998, "Geographically Weighted Regression," *Journal of the Royal Statistical Society Series*, vol. 47.

Brunson, Chris et al., s.f., *Living with Collinearity in Local Regression Models*, National Centre for Geocomputation, National University of Ireland.

Byrne, Graeme et al., 2009, *Multiple Dependent Hypothesis Test in Geographically Weighted Regression*, National Centre for Geocomputation.

Delamonica, Enrique Ernesto and Minujin, Alberto, 2007, "Incidence, Depth and Severity of Children in Poverty," *Social Indicators Research*, vol. 82, No. 2.

Cameron, Adrian and Trivedi, Pravi, 2013, *Regression Analysis of Count Data*, Cambridge University Press.

Cabrero, E. (2003), 'Políticas de modernización de la administración municipal. Viejas y nuevas estrategias para transformar a los gobiernos locales', Technical report, Documentos de Trabajo del CIDE, No. 128, Centro de Investigación y Docencia Económicas.

Chen, Duan-Rung and Truong, Duan-Rung, 2012, "Using Multilevel Modeling and Geographically Weighted Regression to Identify Spatial Variations in the Relationship Between Place-Level Disadvantages and Obesity in Taiwan," *Applied Geography*, vol. 32, No. 2.

Coneval, 2011a, *Pobreza municipal 2010*, Consejo Nacional para la Evaluación de la Política de Desarrollo Social.

Coneval, 2011b, *El Ramo 33 en el desarrollo social en Mexico: evaluación de ocho fondos de política pública*, Consejo Nacional para la Evaluación de la Política de Desarrollo Social.

Coneval, 2010, *Metodología para la medición de la pobreza multidimensional*, Consejo Nacional para la Evaluación de la Política de Desarrollo Social.

Cornia, Giovanni Andrea and Danzinger, Sheldon, 1997, *Child Poverty and Deprivation in the Industrialized Countries 1945–1995—A UNICEF International Child Development Centre Study*, Nueva York, Oxford University Press.

Dorling, Daniel et al., 2007, *Poverty, wealth and place in Britain, 1968 to 2005*, Joseph Rowntree Foundation and The Policy Press.

Escalante, Pablo et al. (ed.), 2011, *Historia mínima de la educación en Mexico*, El Colegio de Mexico.

Esquivel, Gerardo and Messmacher, Miguel, 2002, "Sources of Regional (non) Convergence in Mexico," *Technical report, Paper presented at the Wider/Cornell/LSE Mexico Conference on Spatial Inequality in Latin America*, Institute of Public Policy and Development Studies, Universidad de las Américas, Puebla.

Fotheringham, A. Stewart et al., 2002, *Geographically Weighted Regression: The Analysis of Spatially Varying Relationships*, John Wiley & Sons.

Foster, J.; Greer, J. & Thorbecke, E. (1984), 'A Class of Decomposable Poverty Measures', Econometrica 52(3), pp. 761-766.

Fujita, M.; Krugman, P. & Venables, A., ed. (2001), The Spatial Economy: cities regions and international trade, The MIT Press.

Garza, Gustavo, 1983, "Desarrollo económico, urbanización y políticas urbano-regionales en Mexico (1900-1982),"*Demografía \y Economía*, vol. 17, No.2.

Garza, Gustavo and Schteingart, Martha, 2010, *Desarrollo urbano y regional, Los grandes problemas de Mexico*, Colegio de Mexico.

Goldstein, Harvey, 2011, *Multilevel Statistical Model*, Wiley.

Gordon, David, 2011, "Consultation Response: Social Mobility & Child Poverty Review," *Policy Response Series No. 2*, Poverty and Social Exclusion in the UK.

Gordon, David, 2010, "Metodología de medición multidimensional de la pobreza a partir del concepto de privación relativa," in Mora, M. (coord.), *La medición multidimensional de la pobreza en Mexico*, El Colegio de Mexico-Coneval.

Gordon, David, 2006, "The Concept and Measurement of Poverty," in Pantazis, Christina *et al.* (eds.), *Poverty and Social Exclusion in Britain*, Bristol Policy Press.

Gordon, David *et al.*, 2003, *Child Poverty in Developing World*, The Policy Press, UNICEF.

Gordon, David & Nandy, Shailen. (2012), Measuring Child Poverty and Deprivation: Measurement, concepts, policy and action'Global child poverty and well-being', The Policy Press. University of Bristol, , pp. 57-102.

Heckman, James, 1979, "Sample Selection Bias as a Specific Error," *Econometrica*, vol. 47, No. 1.

Holm, Sture, 1979, "A Simple Sequentially Rejective Multiple test Procedure," *Scandinavian Journal of Statistics*, vol. 6, No. 1.

INEGI, 2010, *Muestra del Censo Nacional de Población y Vivienda 2010*, Mexico, INEGI.

Jalan, Jyotsna and Ravallion, Martin, 2002, "Geographic Poverty Traps? A Micro Model of Consumption Growth in Rural China," *Journal of Applied Econometrics*, vol. 17.

Jin, Xiaoping *et al.*, 2005, "Generalized Hierarchical Multivariate CAR Models for Areal Data," *Biometrics*, vol. 61, No. 4.

Kamerman, Sheila B. *et al.*, 2010, *From Child Welfare to Child Well-Being*, Springer, Netherlands.

Lu, B. Harris *et al.*, 2014, *Gwmodel. R-package*.

Minujin, Alberto *et al.*, 2006, "The Definition of Child Poverty: A Discussion of Concepts and Measurements," *Environment and Urbanization*, vol. 18.

Minujin, Alberto & Nandy, Shailen (2012), Global child poverty and well-being: Measurement, concepts, policy and action, Policy Press.

Muthén, Linda K. and Muthén, Bengt O., 1998–2012, *Mplus User's Guide*, 7a. ed., Los Angeles, Muthén & Muthén.

Morenoff, Jeffrey, 2003, "Neighborhood Mechanisms and the Spatial Dynamics of Birth Weight," *American Journal of Science*, vol. 108, No. 5. Caughy, Margaret O'Brien *et al.*, 2003, "When Being Alone Might Be Better: Neighborhood Poverty, Social Capital, and Child Mental Health," *Social Science & Medicine,* vol. 57, No. 2.

Openshaw, S. & Taylor, P. J. (1981), The modifiable areal unit problem., in N. Wrigley & R. Bennett., ed., 'Quantitative Geography: A British View.', Routledge and Kegan Paul, London, pp. 60-90.

Palavicini, E. (2012), 'Local Economic Development in Mexico', PhD thesis, The London School of Economics and Political Science.

Pemberton, Simon A. *et al.*, 2005, "The Relationship Between Child Poverty and Child Rights: The Role of Indicators," in Minujin, Alberto (eds.), *Human Rights and Social Policies for Children and Women: The Multiple Indicator Cluster Survey (MICS) in Practice*, Nueva York, New School University.

Plant, Raymond (ed.), 2009, *The Neo-liberal State*, Oxford University Press.

Powell, Martin *et al.*, 2002, "Towards a Geography of People Poverty and Place Poverty," *Policy & Politics*, vol. 29, No. 3.

Townsend, Peter, 1979, *Poverty in the United Kingdom. A Survey of Household Resources and Standards of Living*, University of California Press.

Rabe-Hesketh, Sophia & Skrondal, Anders. (2006), 'Multilevel Modelling of Complex Survey Data', Journal of the Royal Statistical Society. Series A (Statistics in Society) 169(4), pp. 805-827.

Townsend, Peter, 1993, *The International Analysis of Poverty*, Harvester Wheatsheaf.

Rabe-Hesketh, Sophia and Skrondal, Anders, 2012, *Multilevel and Longitudinal Modeling Using Stata*, 3a. ed., Stata Press Books, Stata Corp LP.

Rao, J. K., 2005, *Small Area Estimation*, New Jersey, Wiley.

Ridge, Tess, 2002, *Childhood Poverty and Social Exclusion: From a Child's Perspective*, The Policy Press.

Ridge, Tess and Wright, Sharon, 2008, *Understanding Inequality, Poverty and Wealth: Policies and Prospects*, Bristol, Policy Press.

Roelen, Keetie and Gassmann, Franziska, 2012, "Multidimensional Child Poverty in Vietnam," in Minujin, Alberto and Nandy, Shailen (eds.), *Global Child Poverty and Well-Being*, Bristol, The Policy Press.

Rowntree, Seebohm, 1901, *Poverty: A Study of Town Life*, Macmillan and Co.

Sen, Amartya, 2004, "Elements of a Theory of Human Rights," *Philosophy & Public Affairs*, vol. 32, No. 4.

Smith, David, 1994, *Geography and Social Justice: Social Justice in a Changing World*, Wiley-Blackwell.

Spicker, Paul, 2007, *The Idea of Poverty*, The Policy Press.

Townsend, Peter, ed. (2009), Building decent societies, Palgrave Macmillan.

Taylor, Marilyn, 2008, *Transforming Disadvantaged Places: Effective Strategies for Places and People*, New York, Joseph Rowntree Foundation.

UNICEF-CEPAL, 2010, *Pobreza infantil en Latinoamérica y el Caribe*, UNICEF-CEPAL.

Unikel, Luis, 1975, "Políticas de desarrollo regional en Mexico,"*Demografía y Economía*, vol. 9, No. 2.

Vandecasteele, Leen, 2011, "Life Course Risks or Cumulative Disadvantage? The Structuring Effect of Social Stratification Determinants and Life Course Events on Poverty Transitions in Europe," *European Sociological Review*, vol. 27, No. 2.

Villa, Lorenza, 2007, "La educación media superior ¿igualdad de oportunidades?,"*Revista de Educación Superior*, vol. 36, No. 1.

Vilalta, Carlos, 2010, "Evolución de las desigualdades regionales: 1960-2020," inGarza, Gustavo y Schteingart, Martha (eds.), *Desarrollo urbano y regional. Los grandes problemas de Mexico*, El Colegio de Mexico, t. II.

Vilalta, Carlos, 2005, "Sobre cómo enseñar autocorrelación espacial (2005-03),"*Technical report*, Tecnológico de Monterrey, Campus Ciudad de Mexico.

Wheeler, David and Tiefelsdorf, Michael, 2005, "Multicollinearity and Correlation Among Local Regression Coefficients in Geographically Weighted Regression," *Journal of Geographical Systems*, vol. 7, No. 2.

William, Gardner *et al.*, 1995, "Regression Analyses of Counts and Rates: Poisson, Overdispersed Poisson, and Negative Binomial Models," *Psychological Bulletin*, vol. 118, No. 3.

IX. Annexes

1. Reliability of the thresholds used (light thresholds)

Indicator	Average interitem correlation	Alpha
Floor	0.288	0.784
Roof materials	0.265	0.764
Wall materials	0.266	0.765
Access to water	0.274	0.772
Fuel	0.249	0.749
Garbage collection	0.259	0.759
Sanitation	0.256	0.756
Education	0.332	0.792
Minimum social protection floor	0.293	0.788
Overcrowding	0.282	0.780
Test scale	0.277	0.793

2. Reliability of the contextual deprivation index

Indicator	Average interitem correlation	Alpha
Paved streets	0.316	0.7874
Existence of sidewalks	0.3089	0.7815
Drainage and sewage	0.3697	0.8243
Traffic island or areas for pedestrians	0.3163	0.7873
Public green space	0.3668	0.8225
Public telephone	0.3753	0.8278
Ramps	0.3822	0.8319
Public lighting	0.3402	0.8048
Signage	0.3421	0.8062
Test scale	**0.3464**	**0.8267**

3. Infrastructure and facilities index Mexico. Municipalities. Natural Breaks. 2010

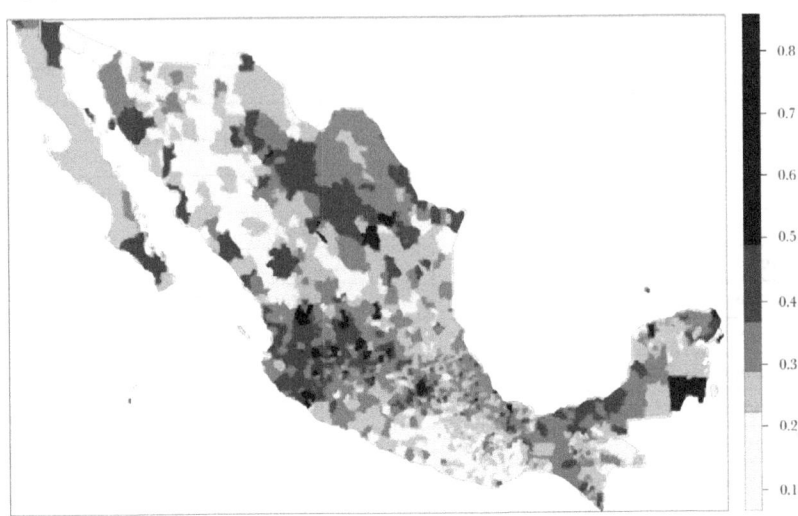

4. Percentage of wage workers. Mexico. Municipalities. Natural Breaks. 2010

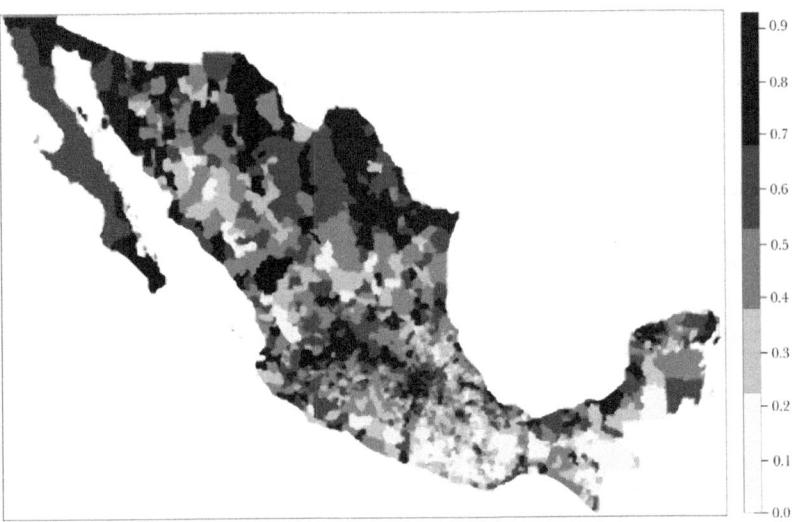

5. Average schooling. Mexico. Municipalities. Natural Breaks. 2010

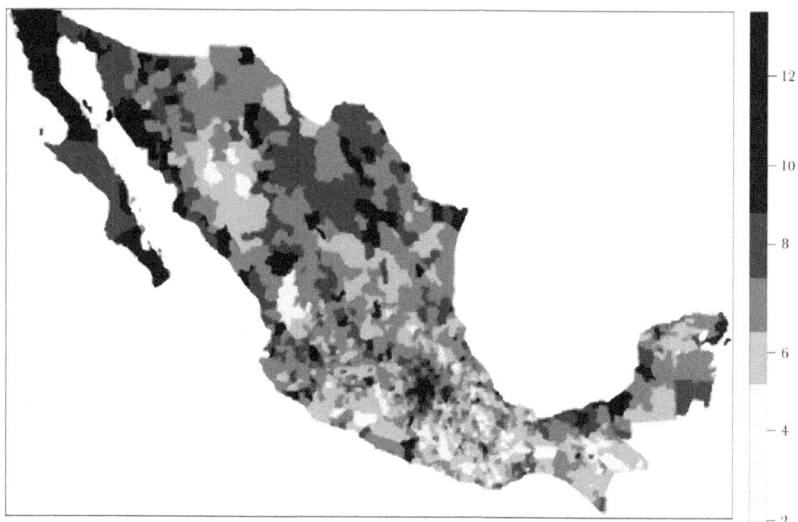

6. Local collinearity analysis (Local Condition Number)

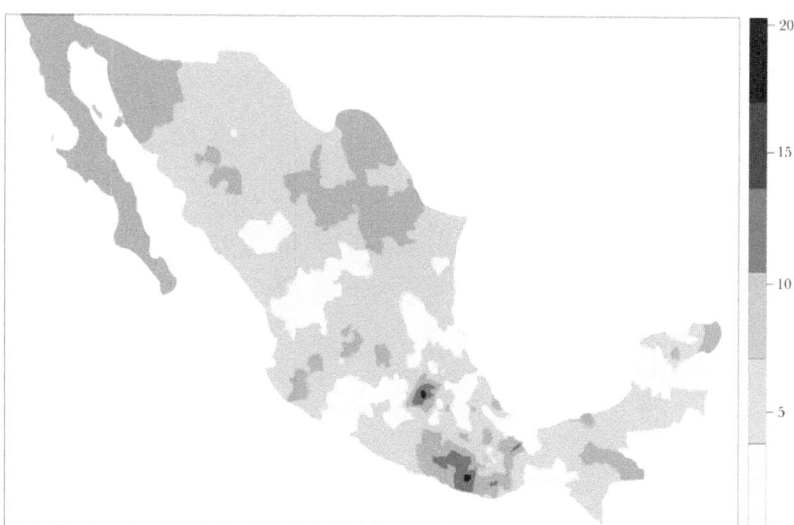

FAMILY POVERTY, TEENAGE WORK, AND SCHOOL DESERTION. AN OVERVIEW OF A COMPLEX RELATIONSHIP BASED ON THE CASE OF LIMA (PERU)

Robin Cavagnoud[1]

I. Introduction. II. Methodology. III. A typology of teen employment. IV. The school issue in this typology of teen employment. V. Briseyda: A representative example of a social path to de-schooling. VI. Life path and socioeconomic vulnerability of the families. VII. Conclusion. VIII. Bibliography.

I. Introduction

Teen employment is a widespread phenomenon in the low-income areas of Lima, the capital of Peru. Based on the results of the National Household Survey (Enaho) conducted by the National Institute of Statistics and Informatics (INEI), the number of children and teenagers between 6 and 17 years who work in the metropolis of Lima–Callao in 2008 is approximately 213,200, of which, 179,300 are between 14 and 17 years, that is to say, one teenager out of every five.[2] The prevalence of teen employment in Lima is evident in activities such asstreet vending, or vending in the markets of low-income neighborhoods, the "small" services performed on the street (shoe-shining, windshield washing, and car guarding), household occupations (washing and laundry, taking care of small children or elderly persons), the construction sector, and driving light vehicles, all of them related to the informal sector of the economy[3] (Alarcón, 1991; Cavagnoud, 2011).

---

[1] Sociologist, Professor in the Department of Social Science of Pontificia Universidad Católica del Peru (PUCP). E-mail: *rcavagnoud@pucp.pe*.
[2] At the national level, 29.8% of Peruvian children and teenagers between 6 and 17 years old performed an economic activity in 2008, as well as 40% of the teenagers between 14 to 17 and 21.9% of the children between 6 and 13. The employment rate of children and teenagers between 6 and 17 is lower in the urban areas of the country (14.2%) than in rural areas (47%) (INEI, 2009).
[3] The number of teenagers that are legally present in the job market (from 14 years of age, under Peruvian law, and in compliance with ILO Convention 138) and of labor regulations that seek to protect them is extremely low.

Performing an economic activity is not necessarily perceived by teenagers as a negative experience. Working can be a strategy to counter poverty, to meet the economic needs of the home (Bonnet, 1998; Schlemmer, 1996), and, sometimes, to escape from a very tense family environment (Invernizzi, 2001) Working can also be a synonym of independence, of personal development, and of learning a series of skills (Liebel, 2003). Based on these premises, the educational issue and, at the forefront, the conciliation of the economic activity of teenagers with their attendance to school remaina constant. The existing works on the allocation of time between a job and school show that a greater productive activity of the teenagers has consequences on their accumulation of schooling. They indicate that even when the school attendance rate is not affected, there are more negative results related to school lag and learning (Rodríguez and Vargas, 2006). However, little is known about the factors for school desertion of certain working teens.

This article goes further than the debate on child employment in Latin America (Cussianovich, 1997; Rausky, 2009) and proposes to address the school path of working teens, both those who reconcile economic activities and school attendance and those who, on the other hand, only focus on their work and have abandoned school, as a result of which they are in the situation of breaching the obligation to study (which is made compulsory until the age of 16 in Peru). First, one could think that the economicfamily problems of a teenager and his or her introduction to work would be the cause for his or her abandonment of school. However, not all working teenagers who live in Lima are outside the educational system, and a large majority (around 80%, according to INEI) actually reconcile school attendance and an economic activity due to the fact that schools operate in "shifts" (morning, evening, and night). The deliberate or involuntary decision to abandon school takes place in a struggle between the duress of one's social environment and his or her margin of individual freedom, as shared between the aspirations and the strategies conceived by his or her family. Why do de-schooled working teens find themselves in this situation? When and how does this transition between school inclusion and exclusion intervene? Is the time burden of teen employment the fundamental reason for leaving school? Is it also a consequence of the type of economic activity performed? Or would it be more convenient to consider the global situation of each teenager and his or her family history, beyond the teenager's status as a worker, to understand why he or she abandoned school?

This article seeks to analyze the de-schooling that affectcertain group of working teenagers as a *complex* phenomenon that can only be explained by analyzing their personal stories, by way of assessing the interaction of multiple micro- and macro-sociological factors that produce this situation. First, it will present a typology of teen employment in Lima, based on the degree of participation of the teenagers in the resources of their home, and the significance assigned to work. Although this allows finding the types of occupation in which school attendance disappears to give way to full-time employment, it does not indicate the specific factors leading to school desertion. Only a case study such as that proposed below with the example of a de-schooled teenage worker (Briseyda) can facilitate a finer analysis with respect to the chain of factors that leads to abandonment. Lastly, the paper will approach the context of poverty and precariousness that is present in the life path of de-schooled teenage workers and their families.

II. Methodology

The cases considered in this paper come from an investigation performed in the Lima–Callao metropolis on a sample of 42 schooled and de-schooled teenage workers between 12 and 17 years of age, which analyzes the reasons behind the natureof their school attendance. The survey, which includes in-depth interviews, life stories, and observations, was developed around four economic categories that facilitated integrating a varied set of activities:

- Extra-familial household work performed by teenagers in a private space outside their own home (13 teenagers—12 girls and one boy, nine cases of schooling and four of de-schooling).
- Sales and services performed by teenagers in roofed markets and stores (13 teenagers—seven girls and six boys, eight cases of schooling and five of de-schooling).
- Street vending, and other street services such as the sale of candy and food, carrying packages in the markets, shoe-shining, cleaning windshields, or entertainment activities (10 teenagers—two girls and eight boys, eight cases of schooling and two of de-schooling).

- Recyclable waste collection, classification, and sale (six teenagers—one girl and five boys, three cases of schooling and three of deschooling).

The teenagers in this qualitative survey were found with the assistance of local associations and NGOs that work in different areas of Lima and Callao. To interview each of these teenagers, it was necessary to establish a rapport through a series of informal meetings with their family and at their workplace. To the extent possible, an interview was conducted with their parents to find out more details about their family history.

III. A typology of teen employment

Teen employment in Lima encompasses cases as diverse as that of a 14-year-old girl who takes care of two children near her home every morning to make some money and that of a 16-year-old boy who cleans windshields all day long in a busy corner to feed his younger siblings. To deal with that heterogeneity, we propose a typology of teen employment based on the survey performed.

1. Nonpaid help in family-owned micro-companies (category 1)

In this first group, teenagers receive no salary, except a few soles sometimes as a tip from their parents for their contribution to the operation of the family-owned micro-company. In return for their assistance, their parents cover their basic needs, such as nurturing, clothes, and school enrollment. The activity of these teenagers is part of the operation of the micro-company of their parents, supporting the growth of the family business. They thus obtain a secondary benefit: To guarantee that their basic needs and, particularly, their schooling, are covered, because all these teenagers continue to study and work with one of their parents the rest of the day. The latter may be small formal (merchants at a fixed location) or informal (street vendors) local business owners. The choice by these teenagers to perform this type of activity is related to the structure of the micro-entepriceand the staffing needs of these economic structures. Parents are present at the workplace most of the time, but variations in demand require the support that the teenagers provide outside their school hours. Therefore, the teenagers do not refer to this partial economic activity as a job, but rather as a family assistance they provide to their parents. From this perspective, the work of the teenagers and their contribution is accompanied by a positive value. Their participation does not interfere with their attendance to school, and parents make an effort to not hinder the educational continuity of their children.

2. The search for a "daily": In search of financial autonomy (category 2)

The first characteristic of this category is related to income and its distribution. Teenagers who start in an economic activity to obtain income, regardless of how variable it may be, receive a financial retribution from the person they work for, and who is not necessarily a member of their family. Unlike teenagers in the first category, these teenagers get an income of a few soles a day, which, accrued throughout the week, serves as a "daily." This income is not shared with their parents or siblings. It is basically used to cover personal expenses and, first, school-related needs, such as purchasing school materials or making photocopies. The economic activities performed by the teenagers here do not take place in the family environment, and they are found in their neighborhood, based on opportunities that arise. Considering the disadvantaged conditions of their family lives (insufficient money to pay the bills, professional instability of their parents, parents working in low-paying jobs, or their health problems), their earnings allow them to have their own personal budget to gain autonomy, no matter how relative it may be, from their parents. The representation these teenagers make of their job, then, has a double intent: to obtain a "daily" and, this way, help their parents by avoiding asking them for money for their expenses. The shared characteristic of these teenagers is continuing, without exception, their school education.

3. Work outside the family environment as a contribution to the budget of the household (category 3)

In this group, teenagers receive income of up to several tens of soles a week (between 8 and 25 dollars). The weight of the earnings is distinct from the earnings of the first two categories. An important feature is that the income received is shared with the family, particularly with the mother, who then uses the money to pay the bills of the household (especially water and electricity) and to buy food for all the members of the family. However, they do not give up the entirety of their earnings; instead they keep a part of it for personal expenses (e.g., clothes, school-related needs, and consumer goods). Hence, we must talk about it as their contribution to the bills of the household, understanding it as a complementary——contribution to the needs of the family.

Another feature is that the activity assumed outside the family environment does not correspond to a personal inclination toward a specific job, but to an adaptation to the jobs available in the neighborhood, which do not fit into the category of "structured" employment. The relative importance of the income of these teenagers compared to those of the first two categories means that they spend more hours in the workplace. These teenagers then show signs of de-schooling. To keep attending school, under some conditions, is opposed to their work and the number of hours used in the accumulation of capital.

4. Work for family subsistence (category 4)

The earnings of the teenagers in this category are between 8 and 28 dollars a day for an economic activity performed five to six days a week, on average. These earnings are a daily contribution to the family, great part —or even entirely—delivered to the mother, who manages the budget of the household. We cannot talk about it as a useful economic complement for the operation of the household unit, but rather as the generation of a core capital for the subsistence of the family. The money obtained is used by the mother to purchase food for every member of the family and to purchase basic goods, such as clothes or school materials, for the younger siblings. The full-time engagement of these teenagers is accompanied by the absence of the father from the home and by the inactivity of the remaining adult members. Mothers are the first to be affected, as they cannot work outside of the home for reasons that range from their lack of schooling to health or administrative problems (not having identity documents). However, their status as the only adult in the home confers on them the administration of the family budget supplied by the economic activity of their teenage children. Faced with the urgency of the situation, these teenagers seek quick and fruitful sources of income (street vending, classification of garbage). Their role as the main economic actor in the family involves, without exception, a rupture with their schooling.

5. Work as an alternative life project (category 5)

The shared element among working teenagers in this category is not the division of their income, or sharing of their income with other family members, but their progressive school failure, which leads them to replace school attendance with full-time employment. These teenagers experience difficult family situations, considering the conditions of poverty, but unlike the previous category they are not the main economic actors in the home. At least one of their parents works full time, and the sharing of their income with their parents is not a condition to meet the essential needs of the family. Unlike the second category, we cannot talk about obtaining a "daily," because the income obtained is greater, and it reflects the search of independence of each teenager to take care of their personal expenses (food, transportation, and buying personal objects). The transversal characteristic of these working teenagers is their abandonment of school. This shared feature is identical to that of the group of teenagers of the fourth category but with the difference that they are not in charge of meeting the basic needs of the family. Although they may have started to work in their early teenage years, while simultaneously attending school, their path shows that they replaced school with full-time employment. These teenagers express the same need of finding an alternative socialization space to school and a productive role in their family.

IV. The school issue in this typology of teen employment

The classification of teen employment in Lima, as established above, yields very different categories in terms of the relationship of the teenagers with the school. The two first groups and a part of the third show a situation of reconcilement between the economic activity and school attendance, whereas the last two indicate an antagonism between work and school.

1. The reconcilement of work and school

In the first three categories, it is possible to note a rigorous organization of time and the concern of each teenager to prevent the work schedule from reducing school hours. This strict administration corresponds to a positive representation of the school, which is seen as an essential value in the daily life of the teenagers, and as an internalized referent that stimulates them to attend their classes. This positive value granted to education and the school system was widely spread in Peru during the second half of the twentieth century, both in cities and in rural areas. Literacy is in constant growth in the country, and it goes hand in hand with the increase in years of schooling throughout the generations, and with the generalization of primary school (Pasquier-Doumer, 2002). This shows the weight of the school institution as a primary socialization space for children, regardless of their sex, their place of residence, or their social status. For the teenagers in the first two categories and part of the third, school is more significant than work, and faced with the question of what do they prefer—only working or only studying—they all answer that, if they had the chance to choose, they would choose school, without a doubt. The association betweenschool attendance and the perspective of a social status above that of their parents is also a recurrent feature. This perception of education as a tool of social mobility grants to the school a considerable value. Likewise, it motivates them to continue their school path, despite the need of having to work to mitigate the precarious status of their families.

Most working teenagers who live in urban areas in Peru continue to attend school, combining their economic activity with their studies. Without a doubt, the Peruvian school system, organized under a scheme of double "shifts," which teaches half the students in the morning and the other half in the evening, allows children and teenagers to attend school and work at the same time.

2. The marginalization of the school

Unlike the first two categories of teenage work, the following three, and particularly the last two, are distinguished by a rupture with school continuity. In the third category of teen employment "as a contribution to the family budget," de-schooling examples have various underlying reasons (such as lack of motivation to attend school and a wish to devote more time to their job to help the family). In these cases, we see that the interests are so diverse that school and work endure an insurmountable clash, ruling out any possibility of reconcilement. The desire to obtain earnings leads to de-schooling, marginalizing the school, which does not provide any immediate benefit and presents itself as a waste of time for teenagers. In the fourth category of teenage employment "for the subsistence of the family," the absence of the father in the domestic unit, combined with the inactivity of other members of the home, creates a situation in which the teenagers become the only economic actor of the family. In this case, the main reason to abandon school is not directly related to their economic activity, but rather the direness of the family situation, which allows us to understand the decisions made by the teenagers. In this context, work is not the direct cause of de-schooling, but rather a means to face inevitable family conditions that reduce the possibilities of the teenagers to improve their situation. The cases reveal a similar family organization scheme in that sense, with the economic activity they perform being a response to obtain the vital minimum for themselves and for the people related to them by kinship. Finally, in the last category of teen employment "as an alternative life project," teenagers start to work full time as a response to an event that makes it impossible for them to continue studying (recent migration, motherhood, accident, and lack of support from their parents).

With respect to the type of economic activity, the classification of teen employment shows that no type of activity is more affected than others by school desertion, to the extent that each economic category of the survey features both schooled and de-schooled teenagers. This applies both to household services performed by the teenage girls in their neighborhood and to vending activities in a fixed location or in the street (in the market or as street vendors) or to the occupations linked to waste recycling. Then, it is not the type of economic activity that generates school abandonment, but the purpose of the work in question, a phenomenon that depends on the family situation of the teenager, the intensity of the effort involved in performing the activity, the useful character of their service, their earnings for the family budget, and the skills and (social and economic) capital available to the teenager. Although it is true that most de-schooled teenagers work outside of family micro-companies, this is but a visible symptom that does not reflect the true reasons of school desertion.

3. The challenge of complexity

The categories of teen employment allow us to place the types of situation in which the cases of de-schooled teenagers emerge, based on the sense assigned to their economic activity. This combines both objective and subjective dimensions, which vary between the notions of work/identity (Schibotto, 1990) and work/subsistence (Alarcón, 1989). The de-schooling of teenagers involved in a job is a complex process, as it is characterized by a combination of elements that are in constant evolution. This realization shows, first, that the very frequent association between work and school desertion does not work to the extent that it does not seek to problematize the living situation of each teenager, that is to say, the combination of their near and far living conditions, his or her interpretation of them, and his or her reaction as an individual. This encourages a focus based on a biographical approach, which would be better adapted to conceive the complexity of the social status of each teenager as a de-schooled worker, and to contemplate the analysis of their situation. This is what we propose now with the case of Briseyda to understand the interweaving of the factors at play in her path outside school.

V. Briseyda: a representative example of a social path to de-schooling

1. From helping the family to full-time employment

Briseyda is a 15-year-old teenager, born in Lima, who works selling glass at her aunt's store. Her work consists of talking to the clients to determine their needs and of going to their homes to measure the windows. She has worked in the store for one year, Monday through Friday, 8:00 a.m. through 8:00 p.m. and one Sunday every two weeks, for a weekly wage of 30 dollars. She uses this income to cover her personal expenses and to help her mother on a regular basis with a portion of the expenses of their home. Briseyda lives with her mother, Teresa, 46 years old, her 17-year-old sister (who finished junior high school but has not continued studying), her 12-year-old sister (who studies and does not work), and their 7-year-old brother. Her parents split seven months ago. Her father seldom sees his children, and he helps his former partner by giving her 7 dollars a week that he obtains from his job as a cab driver.

At home, Briseyda's mother assumes the responsibility of the head of the family; she supports the home and pays the water and electricity bills. Her two older daughters work to help her, but it is she who guarantees the functioning of the family. She works at a street stall selling food (coffee, sandwiches, soup, and meals) at a residential neighborhood, which is a cause of some problems with local authorities, who bar the presence of street vendors in public spaces.

Briseyda used to help her mother in this family-owned micro-company (since she was seven) in the morning, then she went to school in the evening, but she stopped when she abandoned school and changed activities to work at her aunt's store. Teresa now works alone and complains about being tired from transporting the goods she sells and her work tools (pans and stove). Briseyda left school one year before the interview, when she finished her second year of junior high. Before, she had repeated one year of primary school, which is the reason she finished that school period one year behind.

Two weeks after Briseyda decided to abandon school, she started working at her aunt's store. "I was already missing a lot [of schooldays]; I would go one day, and not go the next day. My grades were suffering and I knew my professors were going to flunk me to repeat the year. My mother wanted me to approve, but it was not possible .... I simply saw no future in school. Then I decided to work." Splitting her time between helping her family in the morning and school in the evening eventually led her to exclusively do the economic activity at her aunt's store. This decision was warranted by the economic conditions of her family. "Because [money] was scarce at home, I think my mom did not think it was such a bad decision." When Briseyda was still attending school, she would do her homework at night, and she would normally have the assistance of her older sister, who preferred to study full time, and not skipping school, getting engaged in a parallel economic activity.

Since Briseyda was seven, she used to get up early to assist her mother in the street stall. During this period, her father still lived at home, but he would only partially help his children with their food and school expenses, which were borne by the mother. He lived in the family home, but he would go every night to sleep at the house of his partner. "My father never cared too much for us, and he thinks that, since we are older now, we can make it on our own. My mother used to tell him 'when are you going to help us?'" Briseyda also talks about the violence of his father against her sisters, her mother, and herself. In this case, alcohol issues influence and create an environment of discomfort and emotional instability in each member of the family that is a subject of the violence and physical domination. "My mom says he is a drunkard .... He used to yell a lot, also to me and my sisters. He would hit my mom very hard." Since he left, the contact between the father and the rest of the family is sporadic. Teresa wishes to take legal action and sue him for alimony, but since she has no ID documents, she cannot start the proceedings, which causes her a feeling of exclusion before justice.

2. A combination of factors toward school demotivation

The precarious conditions of Briseyda's family are evident. The employment of their mother as a street vendor falls into the category of sub-employment. She has to face the authorities, who bar her from exercising her activity, already penalized by the irregularity of the clientele. Likewise, the family home has no sanitary services, and the kids need to go to the bathroom outside, on the sandbank, which exposes them to attacks by rodents. This situation of poverty also affects Teresa because of the impossibility of her older daughter to choose to follow higher education, despite the fact that she finished school with excellent results. The cost of higher education or of a short professional training is too high for her resources, which creates a feeling of frustration in the mother, who does not see her daughter developing the academic skills she showed in school to their full extent.

Briseyda started working with her mother at seven, when the last child of the family was born. For seven years, she combined her participation in the family stall with attending school in the evenings. However, this organization of time could not be overcome without setbacks, since Briseyda had to repeat one year of primary school. This event represented for her a source of demotivation, and it, coupled with the difficulties faced by her family, incited her to abandon her schooling to devote herself to a full-time economic activity. Being one year behind, after repeating one year in primary school, repeating a second year meant that Briseyda would meet younger classmates than she already had. This aspect is generally assumed as an embarrassment for teenagers when they compare themselves with the other students, and it does not contribute to their school integration the following year. Faced with this school failure, Briseyda's escape was to get engaged in a full-time economic activity, made possible by her aunt's business.

However, the reason behind Briseyda's decision was not exclusively her demotivation with her school failure. Two factors need to be mentioned. First, the inherent needs of her family status in poverty played a role without discussion in her school rupture. "She [Briseyda] used to study, but since she was helping me a lot at the business, she could not attend school regularly. She repeated one year and then, little by little, she dropped out. Because of that, she told me she was going to work and study. She had a lot of homework, and little by little she increasingly neglected school, and then she started to work only." This comment by her mother reveals the path that separated Briseyda from school, and her difficulties in assuming the transition from primary to secondary learning.

Second, the constant references Briseyda made during the interview to the violent and alcoholic demeanor of her father illustrate the problem and the atmosphere that prevailed in the family, as well as a search of well-being of each member to find emotional stability. It is evident that this type of situation has consequences on the ability of a teenager to concentrate at school. Both factors explained her leaving school, and her choice to be exclusively engaged in her work as an alternative life project to school and its long-term benefits. To this regard, Briseyda does not even perceive the advantages of schooling in the case of her 17-year-old sister, who is restricted to only working after getting good results in her secondary studies.

The cost ocontinuing studies after school, be it at a college or a professional institute, cannot be assumed by her sister other than through the accumulation of a capital that will allow her to face that commitment to a higher education or a professional training. It is possible that the situation of her older sister pushed Briseyda to drop out, by having an unfavorable assessment of the cost and the benefits of getting an education in the long term. The significant precariousness of the family situation and the tensions derived from it, the negative attitude of Briseyda's father, the discouraging example that her sister represents in terms of the usefulness of school after its completion, and the lack of opportunities that schooling involves are the main reasons that explain that she dropped out of school to pursue a full-time job.

VI. Life path and socioeconomic vulnerability of the families

1. The social space of high precariousness

Briseyda's case study is representative of the schedule of teenager workers toward de-schooling. It reveals a series of intrafamilial factors that explain the situation: a significant number of siblings, combined with the rank as the eldest child (or circumscribed to the position of the eldest child) among the siblings, a monoparental family structure, along with the absence of the father as the main actor to support the family economy, the difficulty in getting access to stable resources by the mother, the dispersion of interests linked to her economic activity with respect to school interests, and others. These micro-sociological factors are not sufficiently significant if they are not related to the vulnerability of the highly precarious households.

In Briseyda's case, there are recurring signs of poverty in her family: insufficiency of economic resources, unhealthy home without drinking water or electricity. The coercions of the environment are offset by her economic activity, which mitigates the effects of poverty. The lack of "skills" by Sen (2000) is an approach to poverty that is very visible in this example. The insufficiency of skills of the mother opposes to the work of her teenage children, and particularly of Briseyda. However, this appropriation of skills is hindered by the delusion of school attendance, which becomes impossible due to the lack of time outside the work schedule.

The ability to overcome the economic difficulties of the family is then followed by the inability to return to school. It is evident that not all the teenagers in low-income neighborhoods of Lima who belong to a poor family are workers, and therefore, not all of them are in a situation of school desertion. Despite this, there are circumstances in which poverty weakens the capacities of a family to the point of not having enough good, combined with a series of factors such as monoparentality and a large number of siblings.

Teenage, represented herein by Briseyda, involves specific behavioral models linked to the social environment, dominated by the extreme needs of her family. The association between childhood and poverty involves an early clash with hardship. Faced with the context of poverty, which exercises a daily pressure on monoparental families, many teenagers organize themselves, or with their siblings, to take on an economic activity that gradually becomes more important than schooling.

2. The struggle for food

Most of the families living in the outskirts of Lima have lunch at community kitchens, which are community centers offering meals for less than 1 dollar and that focus on the relationship networks in low-income neighborhoods. Families buy their lunch and save a portion for dinner, which they may complement with a piece of bread cookies or tea. Very few households can afford to buy breakfast, lunch, and dinner with their own income. As a result, teenagers try to help support the family budget by working, seizing opportunities in their environment such as collecting waste for sale or selling candy in the streets. Under these conditions, school becomes a secondary concern in the daily lives of the teenagers who play the role of "elders," or it becomes a social space of reduced usefulness, given that it does not respond to their most immediate needs. Therefore, the degree of socioeconomic vulnerability of the family of a teenager with a tendency to destitution is a determining factor that attempts against the schooling future of the teenager. The transition from school to full-time employment becomes internalized and is a social standard in the most marginalized and excluded social sectors. This transition becomes legitimate for teenagers, and particularly for those who play the role of an elder in a monoparental home with a large number of siblings.

3. The cost of the school system

In the context described above, an essential element is the relative cost of school in Peru. The enrollment fee, paid at the beginning of the school year, is approximately 15 dollars per student, plus 35 to 43 dollars for school materials (books, notebooks, and pencils). This represents a restriction for the schooling of the children of poor and numerous families, and especially for teenagers who already cover a great deal of the needs of the younger siblings. The cost of schooling is a constraint, every year, in the life of the teenagers. The large number of family members makes it very difficult to assume the school expenses of every child. Therefore, it is the income from the job of the teenagers that makes it possible to cover the school expenses of the younger ones, as well as to have a regular schooling. Enrollment fees and the purchase of school materials have not been questioned by political authorities, despite the fact that they represent a fundamental factor for exclusion in the educational sphere. The cost of school reveals a significant impact on the social inequalities during childhood. The parents, who cannot assume the school expenses of (all) their children, put some of them (especially the oldest ones) in an unfavorable position in the long term. The question of immediate investment in formal education and the school projects is never posited as such for mothers, because the benefits of school are unquestionable and shared as a collective value. Therefore, the de-schooling of the elder children is not experienced as a desirable status by the mother, or as a deliberate decision, but rather as an imposed circumstance, derived from the extreme socioeconomic vulnerability of the home.

VII. Conclusion

Working teenagers who dropped out of school belong to families "in the edge," which are pushed by an accident (death, health problems, and absence of the father) to a situation of deeper precariousness that touches on subsistence. The accumulation of economic (low and irregular income) and social (decomposition of family ties, the destructuring of the home) disadvantages ends up breaking the uncertain balance of the family budget, and it pushes the elder children to drop out of school. Although the age factor plays a prominent role in this sense, by exposing teenagers to the risk of school desertion to a higher extent than their younger siblings, in the studied cases it is possible to see a family path that evolves from a situation of "tolerable" precariousness to a status of subsistence that no longer is tolerable. The combination of factors that explain their de-schooling converges toward this degradation of daily life, where school attendance becomes superfluous or impossible to reconcile with the urgency of the needs of the household.

VIII. Bibliography

Alarcón, Walter, 1989, "El trabajo infantil como estrategia de supervivencia familiar,"*Socialismo y Participación*, No. 48.

Alarcón, Walter, 1991, *Entre calles y plazas. El trabajo de los niños en Lima*, Lima, Acción Laboral para el Desarrollo-IEP-UNICEF.

Bonnet, Michel, 1998, *Regards sur les enfants travailleurs. La mise au travail des enfants dans le monde contemporain. Analyse et étude de cas*, Lausanne, Page Deux.

Cavagnoud, Robin, 2011, *Entre la escuela y la supervivencia. Trabajo adolescente y dinámicas familiares en Lima*, Lima, FT-IEP-IFEA.

Cussianovich, Alejandro, 1997, "Infancia y trabajo: dos nudos culturales en profunda transformación," in *Niños trabajadores. Protagonismo y actoría social*, Lima, IFEJANT.

INEI, 2009, *Peru: niños, niñas y adolescentes que trabajan, 1993-2008*, Lima, INEI.

Invernizzi, Antonella, 2001, *La vie quotidienne des enfants travailleurs: stratégies de survie et socialisation dans les rues de Lima*, París, L'Harmattan.

Liebel, Manfred, 2003, *Infancia y trabajo*, Lima, IFEJANT.

Pasquier-Doumer, Laure, 2002, "La evolución de la movilidad escolar intergeneracional en el Peru a lo largo del siglo XXI,"*Boletín del Instituto Francés de Estudios Andinos*, vol. 31, No. 3.

Rausky, María Eugenia, 2009, "¿Infancia sin trabajo o Infancia trabajadora? Perspectivas sobre el trabajo infantil," *Rev.latinoam.cienc.soc.niñez juv*, vol. 7, No. 2.

Rodríguez, José and Vargas, Silvana, 2006, *Escolaridad y trabajo infantil: patrones y determinantes de la asignación del tiempo de niños y adolescentes en Lima Metropolitana*, Lima, PUCP-CIES.

Schibotto, Giangi, 1990, *Niños trabajadores. Construyendo una identidad*, Lima, Manthoc, IPEC.

Schlemmer, Bernard, 1996, *The Exploited Child*, París, Zed Books, IRD.

Sen, Amartya, 2000, *Repenser l'Inégalité*, París, Seuil.

PRODUCTION AND REPRODUCTION OF CHILD POVERTY IN LATIN AMERICA. AN ANALYSIS CENTERED ON THE EDUCATIONAL DIMENSION

Jorge A. PAZ[1]*

> I. Introduction. II. The addressed issue. III. Data used and methodology. IV. Results. V. Final considerations. VI. Bibliography. VII. Graphs Appendix.

I. Introduction

The main weapon used by national states in Latin America to fight poverty is the so-called Conditional Transfer Programs (PTC). These are interventions targeted at the socially vulnerable population, which hand their beneficiaries a sum of money in exchange for a (verifiable) commitment to make their children (NyN) attend school and to systematically control their health and nutrition.[2] The conditionality implies, precisely, that the economic aid granted is subject to compliance with these controls. Today, virtually all the countries in the region have one or more PTC in effect.[3] Although the history of such programs in Latin America goes back to the 1980s (Lavinas, 2013), it could be said that the first of its kind was Mexico's Education, Health and Nutrition Program (Progresa), which started in August 1997.

There are various premises, or rather axioms, held by the PTCs, many of which are not explicitly recognized, but it is clear that they work as a motivation, sustain their validity, and are the justification for the resources

---

1 Researcher with the National Scientific and Technical Research Council (Conicet) in the Institute of Labor and Development Economics Studies (IELDE) of Universidad Nacional de Salta (Argentina). The author expresses his gratitude to Cristian Herrera and Daniel Vasquez for their valuable comments to a previous version of this document. Also the questions and suggestions of the participants of the "Child Poverty, Public Policy and Democracy" International Seminar, held in Mexico City in February 19-21, 2014. Any errors and omissions are the exclusive responsibility of the author and the statements involve no liability for the institutions represented by the author.
2 Conditions that mainly include keeping the vaccination schedule.
3 The *Oportunidades* program (formerly Progresa) in Mexico, the *Bolsa Familia* program in Brazil, the *Asignación Universal por Hijo* program in Argentina (and, more recently, *Progresar*) are examples of PTC in the region.

applied to execute them. The first of them is that it is morally correct to provide the poorest and the most vulnerable with an assistance that will allow them to subsist. A second axiom—derived from the preceding one—is that the PTC is the most effective social policy instrument to achieve this.[4] A third axiom is that PTCs not only relieve poverty today but they contribute to break the intergenerational reproduction of poverty and economic inequality. In turn, the latter axiom is based on a couple of hypotheses that schooling involves learning, and learning leads to increased welfare. The first hypothesis is related to children who attend school due to the assistance provided by the PTCs; the second one, to the adult stage of the children who join the labor market and obtain higher income due to their increased education. Acknowledging these premises, the problem then consists of providing equal opportunities to all the population, providing those who have less with the human capital required to face economic life, and waiting for the results in a few generations.

This paper goes further than discussing the possibility and efficiency of the PTCs in reducing poverty today in Latin America and seeks to research the potential in providing equal opportunities to impact the gap in educational results between poor and nonpoor children. If the said impact occurs, the challenge would then be to calibrate the current PTCs and to expect that, within one or two generations, the said interventions start to yield results. Education, as can be seen, is one of the focuses of PTC, and schooling is one of its main goals. That is also what the Millennium Development Goals propose and also what is sought by everyone who agrees in one way or another on the conceptual framework of the equalization of opportunities (IOP).

There is plentiful discussion on the equalization of opportunities (IOP) and literature on the subject abounds today (Ferreira and Gignoux, 2011). However, here we posit that acting in favor of IOP often causes the connection between IOP and equality of outcome (IRE) to be blurred, and it also blurs the processes that generate exclusion, inequality, and poverty, and which go way beyond the variables that are regularly observed and monitored (income, meeting basic needs, etc.) and which are used to identify opportunities. That is important because, as it was said before, the basic

---

4   In the words of Carlos Auyero: "Maximum focalization to minimize spending" (García, 2014).

purpose of the existing PTCs in ALC is the IOP under the seldom questioned belief (Paz, 2010) that IOP leads to IRE, after one or two generations.[5]

Thus, this paper seeks to reveal how the differences in living standards in opportunity variables (precarious housing and overcrowding) lead to differences in the level and the distribution of variables of outcomes, such as the scores obtained by children and/or by the interruptions to a process that the prevailing economic trend calls "accumulation of human capital." It will also emphasize variables that can be altered with the instruments provided by the democratic system, and many of which appear as rights that are guaranteed by the constitutions of the countries. But after this is completed, we will see what would happen if IOP took place in these variables to realize, surprisingly, that a good portion of the differences found could not be mitigated even with these measures, and that deeper actions, aimed at a longer term, would be required to achieve the IRE.

To achieve these goals, we analyze the Math and Language scores obtained by sixth-grade children in countries in Latin America and the Caribbean (ALC). We attempt to show that the intergenerational transmission of poverty and inequality through (in this case) education goes way beyond the IOP, thus revealing one of the many processes in which the rights of the children contemplated in the Convention on the Rights of the Child (CDN) are violated. A second goal is to identify relevant variables that allow us to list public policy actions, in the style of Conditional Transfer-Programs (PTC), aimed at breaking—or reducing the intensity of—the cycle of reproduction of poverty and inequality. For that purpose, it will be necessary to separate the opportunity restrictors (in this paper, "endowments") from others that operate independently, which cause identical opportunities to generate different results.

This paper has been structured according to the following plan: In the following section, we present the problem under review, proposing the conceptual base framework and the extensions made to address the problem of the reproduction of poverty and inequality. In Section III, we discuss the data, and we describe the methodology we used to handle them. In Section IV, we explain the results obtained. Section V presents, as final

---

5   The work of James Heckman (one of them is mentioned here: Heckman *et al.* 1996) addresses the issue, even though the results are provisional due to the lack of relevant data.

considerations, the public policy options that arise from the results obtained in the previous sections.

II. The addressed issue

This paper posits that the intergenerational transmission of poverty and inequality operates through two mechanisms: (a) poverty and inequality itself, which put children from poor homes at a disadvantage compared to those who come from nonpoor homes; (b) the way in which the educational process that serves populations in different socioeconomic sectors is generated. The first problem is the main focus of the IOP paradigm, according to which the playing field is not level; a major part of the solution is to provide poor children with the same opportunities provided to nonpoor children.

Here we argue that, due to some reason that is less intuitive than the above premise, children from poor and nonpoor households experience their educational process differently. We will call that "different experiencing" here: a different capacity to transform input into outcome, or opportunities into results (O→R), appealing to the concept of educational production function explained below in this same section. The idea is subtle, but simple: It may be so that more poor children than nonpoor children attend public schools, that those children are the children of parents with less education, that they repeat courses more frequently, that they work inside and outside their homes, and so on.[6] But it may also be the case that, due to some mechanism (or a set of mechanisms), children who are classified as "poor," who attend the same schools as nonpoor children, with parents of similar educational levels, and so on, are less likely to transform that input into an outcome of a similar "quality" to that obtained by children classified as "nonpoor." This internal segregation process may be generating inequalities that are harder to fight with the traditional public policy tools (e.g., the PTCs). A first challenge would then be to find out the weight of those processes in generating educational gaps and/or inequalities.

Unfortunately, the data available do not reveal the "invisible" mechanisms of the reproduction of poverty and economic inequality, which occur in parallel to the differences in opportunities for the children population. One theory could be that this is due to the conduct of the various

---

6   That is to say, that they face different opportunities.

actors involved in the educational system, the parents, teachers, directors, the state, and to aspects that are often contained in the curriculum. All of them, in one way or the other, produce and reproduce poverty and inequality schemes from within the system. Hanna and Linden (2009) discuss an example of how these discrimination processes are produced within the system in a group of children from India, whereas a great deal of chapter 5 of Banerjee and Duflo (2011) is devoted to explanations and contributions on these mechanisms that are not apparent in the quantitative information available.

As will be seen below, it is likely that these processes operate differently with children in different quality education sectors, so that those who tested poorly will show a different treatment from those who surpassed the average score of the group. It is easier to understand this idea by resorting to an analogy with labor segmentation. Let's assume that there is a labor market with two segments: a low segment and a high segment. For a worker who earns a lower salary of the secondary (disadvantaged) segment, crossing into the primary segment (the advantaged segment) may be an achievement (earning, e.g., social security payments and the status of a worker with a formal wage). But, what would be the position of this worker in the distribution of the income of this job? The second goal of the worker, earning a higher salary, may be very complicated.

1. Education and economy: Conceptual framework

The idea expressed in the educational production function, the main conceptual tool of this paper, is closely related to the concept of human capital, or the "canonical model" as it will be known here (Becker, 1964; Schultz, 1961; Heckman *et al.*, 1996; among others), and it may be expressed as follows: A person may learn to obtain certain skills and abilities that have a market value. Acquiring these skills and abilities takes time (time that is taken from other activities that may provide welfare) of other actors (parents, private teachers, etc.) and involves various inputs that may be purchased in the market or which are provided by the state as public services (education and health are the most common examples). The knowledge acquired is advantageous to the individual: It allows him or her to recoup what he or she invested during the process (the costs), which is the net "earning" derived from the human capital invested.

In the case of the preceding paragraph, it is shown that the result of the human capital investment process is the salary or compensation that the owner of the human capital sells in the market. If the said compensation is higher than the compensation, the same individual would have obtained without investing in that capital; the investment is not profitable, making the investment in human capital a key mechanism to extract people who perhaps would have otherwise been poor from their destitute situation, or of redistributing income to those who do not have any other asset than their innate skills and time.

It is useful to express the ideas above as a function to make it easier to understand them and to analyze their consequences and ramifications. The above concepts then can be written as follows:

$$R = \gamma H + X\beta + \varepsilon \quad [1]$$

where (an example in parentheses) R is the result variable (income in the labor market), H is the human capital accumulated by the individuals (years of education), and X is the other determinants (occupation performed).

The key for this paper is in γ and β, which represent parameters of conversion of the skills, dexterities, and/or abilities (expressed in H and X) into results. In economic literature, γ and β represent "prices" of the "endowments" (H and X, respectively).

Last, ε is a term of error that includes all the factors that are impossible to observe and that affect the results.

A. The education production function

The problem in the preceding case consists of defining H, which is the human capital variable that is of particular interest for this study. Under Hanushek and Woessmann (2011), we will assume that H is determined by family factors (F), by the quality and quantity of the inputs provided by the school (qS), the individual skills and abilities (D), and other relevant factors (Z), in addition to those that cannot be observed with the information available. As variables, the above can be written as

$$H = \lambda F + \phi(qS) + \eta D + Z\pi + \mu \quad [2]$$

This expression is what is called the "education production function." As correctly posited by Hanushek and Woessmann (2011), H is not directly observable, and it needs to be measured in some way to reveal its effect on other variables. The literature has suggested in this case that we should concentrate on the measure of educational performance, such as various test scores (Language and Math are most commonly used). The main advantage of these measures of H is to measure variations in knowledge and in the personal skills that transform knowledge into practical skills.

B. Differences in achievement

As has been said, the most frequently used examples of investment in human capital are the actions of people who seek to expand their educational level and their health benefits. From an individual economic perspective and in terms of expression [1], that would imply a higher H to improve R; from a more social perspective, it would mean more people obtaining access to higher Hs to improve the Rs they would have obtained if they did not have those higher human capital endowments. It may be argued that this is one of the goals of the conditions in the Conditional Money Transfer Programs (PTC): improving the distribution of the labor income of future generations by promoting school attendance or enrollment today and vaccinating the children population (higher Hs).[7]

But, although school enrollment partially reflects the educational achievement of various countries, it does not adequately show what happens within the system: the way in which children are educated and the results they obtain from that process where inputs of various kinds intervene (professor work hours, materials computers, etc.), reflected in the educational production function described in expression [2]. Here, we propose an axiom and a hypothesis: (a) not all the students obtain the same Rs, and they largely depend not only on the endowments (F, qS, etc.) but also on the conversion of the endowments into results (of the λ, ϕ, etc.); (b) the value of the parameters (λ, ϕ, etc.) depends on the socioeconomic sector of origin of children and their position in the distribution of scores.

Within this conceptual framework, the IOP would provide the children population with identical benefits, that is to say, to remove any barriers derived from an origin other than talent. This would lead to the equalization

---

[7] An elaboration of this idea may be found in Paz (2010).

of results in the labor market and to "fair" differences that are based on talent, effort, and dedication. Since no longitudinal design is available enabling us to observe compensation for children who are subject to such treatment and controlled, here we analyze academic performance as a variable affecting their future labor position and compensation.

III. Data used and methodology

1. Data

The data are taken from the Second Regional Comparative and Explanatory Study (SERCE), performed by the Latin American Laboratory for Assessment of the Quality of Education (LLECE).[8] The databases available include information on the academic performance (scores) of third- and sixth-grade students in 16 countries in Latin America and the state of Nuevo Leon (Mexico). The areas analyzed here are Language (reading and writing) and Math, and we chose to exclusively work with sixth-grade students.[9]

In addition to strictly pedagogical aspects, the databases include information on the directors, the teachers, and the parents, which provides the opportunity to analyze school and social factors that are probably associated with the academic performance of the students. All the data correspond to the 2005–06 period, depending on the school calendar of each country, and since it comes from a single source, the information is strictly comparable.

The dependent variable used in this paper, indicative of the academic "result," is the standardized average score, a measure of performance with an average score of 500 and a standard deviation of 100. The socioeconomic sector was captured with variables that allow us to identify homes with structural deprivations such as availability of electric power and drainage in the homes where the children live.

---

[8] The SERCE study is part of the global actions of the Regional Bureau for Education for Latin America and the Caribbean (OREALC) of the United Nations Educational, Scientific and Cultural Organization (UNESCO). The SERCE is the largest study of the quality of education in Latin America and the Caribbean.

[9] This decision was made because we considered that school desertion occurs more frequently in that grade and because the processes analyzed herein start to generate the dissimilar results that are the subject of this document.

The explanatory variables, many of them representative of different opportunities for children in the region, respond to the clustering (a) directly attributable to the child: age, sex, ethnic origin, course repetition, and labor status (works/does not work); (b) corresponding to the home where the children live: education of the mother; and (c) related to the educational institution: area of residence, public or private dependency, and characteristics of the faculty.[10]

2. Methods

To understand the relationship between the goals of the investigation and the methods applied, we reformulate the former in three sets of questions to be answered: How do the opportunity variables impact the scores of the children in the region? Is this effect similar among poor and nonpoor children? To answer these questions, we estimate a least-squares (MC) multiple regression, allowing us to evaluate the relationship of each independent variable on the Language and Math grades and for each child in different socioeconomic sectors.

Do the estimated coefficients (the β are representative of the O→R process) similarly impact students with low grades and those with higher grades? To obtain an answer to this question, we estimate a quantile regression (RC) and evaluate the stability and robustness of the β estimated.

What are the effects of inequality of opportunities and the conversion of opportunities into results on the academic results of poor and nonpoor children? In this case, two types of breakdowns are applied: the traditional Blinder–Oaxaca (Blinder, 1973) and Oaxaca (1973) for the values obtained in (a) and that of Machado–Mata (Machado and Mata, 2005) for the values computed in (b).

The RCs were estimated with the approach proposed by Koenker and Bassett (1978). This model involves that the nth percentile of the grades (in this case), conditioned by a set of control variables or opportunities (education, type of school, gender of the professor, etc.), is linear. With which, for a sample of a given size, the percentile is defined as the solution to a problem of optimization that may be resolved with linear programming. In

---

10 Many other variables could have been included, but we need to consider that, as they are incorporated, cases or observations are lost. Therefore, we chose the most economic model, from the perspective of the use of the information available.

this study, we estimated two RCs, one per each socioeconomic sector of the children, with the understanding that the traditional regression approach offers a partial image of the relationship between the grades and their determinants.

The Machado–Mata approach is similar to that of Blinder–Oaxaca, but it is based on the RC and not the parameters (β) obtained with MCO. It consists of estimating a counterfactual distribution of the grades, assuming that the opportunities are the same in both groups. Thus, we intend to determine what the grades of poor children would be if they had identical opportunity values as nonpoor children. If the difference in results is solely from the fact that poor and nonpoor children have different opportunities, then the counterfactual distribution would be equal to the distribution observed.

IV. Results

1. Poverty in ALC

The first step of this study consisted of obtaining an indicator that would allow us to stratify the homes of the sixth-grade children in ALC countries.[11] Graph 1 shows the percentage of children who live in homes without water and electricity services. Please note that, although the intervention measures based on the canonical model submitted and discussed in Section II treat the region as a homogeneous whole (Paz, 2010), it is possible to see a range of situations that clearly define and differentiate ALC from other, more developed, regions of the world.

The services of the household, as well as the quality of the materials it is built with, are frequently used as indicators to identify poor homes, both in the more traditional studies (Feres and Mancero, 2001) and in the recent contributions to multidimensional poverty [Comisión Económica para América Latina y el Caribe (CEPAL)-United Nations Children's Fund (UNICEF), 2010; Alkire and Foster, 2008; Delamónica and Minujin, 2007; Gordon *et al.*, 2003; among others]. Although the database available provides information on several of these indicators, only drainage and electric power

---

11 We also tested the highest educational level of the father, which is an indicator of the income generation capacity of the population (Mincer, 1974). The correlation between family income and the educational level of the head of the home is analyzed in Deaton (1997). The arrangement does not differ.

were used, because these services are the foundation for the others, and their absence excludes the access to many others.[12] With data from other studies, we were able to verify that the arrangement of the countries that results from using an alternative measurement of poverty (economic poverty, for example) is not modified in substantial terms [Comisión Económica para América Latina y el Caribe (CEPAL), 2013].

The indicator selected allows differentiating at least three large groups of countries: those with high poverty (such as Guatemala and Nicaragua), those in the intermediate level (such as Brazil, Paraguay, and Ecuador), and those with low poverty (such as Chile, Uruguay, and Cuba). As can be verified in brief, this indicator produces a similar arrangement of countries to that generated by the grades of the students, which suggests a correlation between poverty and the academic performance of children.

2. Grade level and distribution

In academic performance, Cuba leads the rest of the countries in the region (graphs 2a and 2b), particularly in Math.[13] It is followed by Uruguay, Nuevo Leon (Mexico), and Costa Rica, whereas a third group may include Mexico, Chile, Argentina, Brazil, and Colombia, which score as the regional average. Lastly, there are the lowest-performing countries: Peru, El Salvador, Paraguay, Nicaragua, Guatemala, Panama, and the Dominican Republic. The latter is placed, similarly to Cuba, at the top of the distribution, removed from the rest of the countries.[14]

Given the goals of this study, we are more interested in the grade differences in Language and Math by socioeconomic sector of origin of the children, than in their level. Graphs 3a and 3b show that the status of the home of origin of the children of ALC establishes important and significant differences in the grades obtained in international tests. The gaps range between 4.7 (Uruguay) and 63.3 (Peru) SERCE points in Language and between 0.7 (Cuba) and 64.7 (Peru) SERCE points in Math. Given that the

---

12   For example, it is not possible to have access to a computer if there is no electricity in the home.
13   This classification is based on the visual inspection derived from the data of graphs 3a and 3b and it matches the proposal of other studies based on this data source (for example Treviño et al., 2010).
14   Please note that this classification, while arbitrary, may be applied to the average score of the countries in Language. The correlation of the grades obtained by the students in the two disciplines reviewed was very strong.

standard deviations computed for complex samples are below 3 (and almost always below 2), the differences obtained are highly significant, and it is not possible to reject the hypothesis that establishes differences between the groups.

Opening by discipline (Language and Math) does not change the arrangement of the countries in any substantial form. Cuba and Nicaragua appear as the countries with the smallest gaps in both disciplines; Uruguay and the Dominican Republic are countries with small gaps; Colombia, Chile, Argentina, and others have medium gaps; Peru, Brazil, and Mexico have the greatest gaps. Those graphs indicate the way in which educational results are analyzed and interpreted, given the significant heterogeneity of the situations presented by the region.

Lastly, another area of interest in this descriptive introduction is the focus on distributions rather than on mean values. In graph 4a and 4b, it is possible to see the Kernel densities obtained for the grades in Language and Math. An alternative to the graphic approach is to compute the values of table 1, which shows percentiles 5, 25, 50, 75, 95, and 99 of grades in the disciplines of Language and Math.

The densities extend the analytical panorama and allow us to infer that the differences by socioeconomic sector of origin of the children occur not only in the average, but that they generate different masses, although with considerable overlap. It can also be seen that the greater gaps between socioeconomic sectors appear with students with better performance (located on the right side of the Kernel distributions) and that the dispersion is greater between children who come from a socioeconomic sector classified here as "high."

To summarize, the socioeconomic differences in performance are amplified as performance increases, which implies that the children from the lower socioeconomic sectors face a "glass roof" of sorts in terms of academic performance, despite which there are also important and significant differences in children at the lowest end of the grades.

3. Different opportunities

Table 2 shows the mean values of the variables included in Language and Math in the academic performance test for children of ALC. The ratio of students repeating courses is higher among those who live in poor homes, compared with those who live in nonpoor homes. The former also have a significantly higher incidence of workers, both inside and outside their homes, their mothers have a lower educational level, and they also have a greater percentage of speakers of indigenous languages. On the other hand, poor children who go to schools where there is a higher proportion of male teachers have less job stability and a lower educational level. In turn, the children who live in poor homes live in countries with lower income per capita than those who live in nonpoor homes.

Given that the aforementioned factors are related to academic performance (as will be proven below), it is logical to think that the average grades of children who live in poor homes are lower than those of the children who live in nonpoor homes: in Language 486 points *vs.* 521; in Math 481 *vs.* 515 (these values can also be seen in table 1).

If we resort to the IOP paradigm, a public policy alternative may be to provide poor children with endowments identical to those of nonpoor children: reducing course repetition and child employment, improving the educational level of their mothers and their teachers, promoting job stability for the latter, and economic growth, among other things. This reduces structural poverty to zero. The question is, if this were to happen, would the performance gap between poor and nonpoor children be closed?

4. Conditional analysis

To answer the question in the preceding paragraph, first it is necessary to know how each opportunity impacts the grades, independently from the rest. Then, we must consider whether or not the said impact differs between socioeconomic sectors.

A. Considerations for the median regression (tables 3a and 3b)

In very general terms (an inference that is valid for Language and Math, and for children from homes of both sectors), the average sixth-grade student has a lower academic performance the older he or she is, if he or she speaks a foreign or indigenous language, and if he or she has a male teacher. The educational level of the mother, the teacher's age, his increased dedication to school, academic training, and job stability significantly improve the performance of children in ALC. The general economic status, expressed in the GDP level per capita, also has a net positive effect. These findings apply to median students (percentile 50 of the distribution of the grades).

If children are classified as "poor" and "nonpoor" (columns 2 and 3, tables 3a and 3b), it can be seen that the Language grade is more sensitive to the education of the mothers among poor children (than among nonpoor children) and to the job stability of the teachers (among nonpoor children, the parameter estimated for this variable is not significantly different from zero). For Math, we find that the education of the mothers has a greater impact on the grades of nonpoor children, whereas the age of the teachers, their gender, and job stability favor the poor. The effect of the GDP of the country, in both cases, is more important for poor children.[15]

B. Different segments of the distribution

Now we will analyze the differential effect of each variable on the different portions of the distribution of the grades by running an RC for the two competencies—Language and Math—and for the two sectors—poor and nonpoor. With this, we attempt to find out whether the parameters considered behave in the same manner among those who obtain different grades in the SERCE in the countries of the region. Thus, a parameter is "neutral" if the difference in the grades between poor and nonpoor children is the same between those who obtain a low grade and those who obtain a high grade. That is to say, we analyze the gap between poor and nonpoor children not only in the average of the grades but also throughout the entire distribution.

The answer to this question for the entire sample can be found in the multiple graphs (graph 5a for Language and graph 5b for Math). Table 4 summarizes these findings differentiating by sector. The graph shows the coefficients estimated $\beta\_i\,(\theta)$, $i=1,...,k$ for $\theta \in (L,M)$ (most of which are neutral to the segment of the distribution they impact) and the confidence intervals (95%) for each of them.

The number of non-neutral parameters in table 4 when differentiating by socioeconomic sector is remarkable. Thus, among the children from poor homes, there are more neutral parameters than among nonpoor children: 31/40 vs. 24/40 (last row, table 4). In addition, the parameters that affect performance grow in absolute value when they go from the low end (left) to the high end (right) of the distribution of the grades. The former implies that

---

[15] This may reflect the resources available to each country for, among other uses, education.

there are less opportunities that generate the equalization of the results[16] among poor children. The latter means that when they are negative, they adversely affect those in the high end of the distribution, and they improve those in the lower end to a greater degree, and when they are positive, they improve those in the higher end of the distribution to a greater degree.

C. Breakdown of the differences

What would happen if poor children were to be placed in conditions identical to those of nonpoor children through public policy actions? In other words, what would happen to the quality of education if the former were provided with homes with electricity and drainage, similar to those where the latter live? Would the differences disappear, or would there still be a need to change public policy? This section proposes an exercise that aims to answer these questions, for which it uses two micro-econometric breakdown techniques: Blinder–Oaxaca and Machado–Mata.

The Blinder–Oaxaca breakdown (table 5) allows us to verify that in 40–42%, the mean gap in the grades is explained with the different endowments (opportunities) for poor and nonpoor children, whereas the rest would be better explained with internal processes for the conversion of opportunities into results. From a conceptual perspective, the above means that even after providing students with identical opportunities, the difference in performance would not be eliminated: For example, in Language, the 34 SERCE point difference between poor and nonpoor children would be reduced to 21 points (table 5), but it would not disappear.

Graphs 6a and 6b show the results of the Machado–Mata breakdown for Language and Math, respectively. The conclusions for both competencies do not differ in substantive terms, so below we provide the most interesting results that can be generalized.

First, the MCO estimate doesn't represent what happens throughout the distribution of the grades. The general gap between poor and nonpoor children increases as the grading scale progresses.[17] This is represented by the "Original" line in the aforementioned graphs. Both the characteristics (the "Carac" line) and the coefficients ("Coefic" and the two "IC 95%" lines)

---

16 It must be noted that, at least in this case, there is no discussion of the actions that generate equal opportunities.

17 The reasons of the O→R process for this behavior for each of the estimated coefficients can be found in Section III.2.

contribute to that behavior. The counterfactual distribution obtained (the "Predicted" line in the graphs), that is to say, the gap that would result if poor and nonpoor children had identical characteristics,[18] yields a smaller gap for all the quantiles. The difference between "Original" and "Predicted" is the part of the gap that could be explained with the opportunities provided to poor and nonpoor children.

If the predicted gap is compared to that obtained by MCO, three things can be verified: (a) that the gap persists even after equalizing the opportunities; (b) that the gap behaves differently depending on the segment of the distribution of the grades; and (c) the gap is greater as the grading scale progresses (the difference between "MCO" and "Predicted" is greater as we move from left to right on the data). Conclusion (c) could be considered a variation of conclusion (b). Lastly, the confidence interval indicates a greater variability of the grades at the ends of the distribution. But, despite this, the estimate for the median is outside the interval in the lowest end of the distribution, between approximately the 10th percentiles and 30th percentiles; therefore, the gap between poor and nonpoor children in the group with the lowest performance is significantly higher than the one found in the average.

V. Final considerations

This paper analyzed the relationship between academic performance, poverty, and the equalization of opportunities in Latin America, in the 2005–06 period, when SERCE data were available. That two-year period is right at the middle of a period of reduction of poverty in the region: 2000–2010/11. But despite the reduction, child poverty continues to be very high, as shown by the detailed study by Comisión Económica para América Latina y el Caribe (CEPAL) (2013). This means that the PTCs are not achieving, at least at the macrolevel, their own goals.

On the other hand, it could be seen that, if poverty is not reduced, the equalization of opportunities in variables that are targeted by the PTCs would not entirely eliminate the academic performance gaps between poverty sectors; therefore, it is feasible that poverty and the inequality that

---

18   The characteristics of the (pooled) average were considered to obtain this line. The methodological alternatives were to take those that correspond to poor NyN or nonpoor NyN.

school differences predict (Heckman *et al.*, 1996) and involve in the long term are reproduced. In other words, those gaps respond to factors that go beyond the social conditioning factors of the children of the region. Poverty not only affects the result (direct effect, or composition, as it was called in this paper) but also affects the process (parameter effect or conversion capacity of opportunities into results). This causes compensation policies to be unable to yield the expected effects, or to be completely effective. In addition, if we take school grades as a proxy of the conditions of the children who enter the labor market, even if poor children had the same opportunities as nonpoor children, they would arrive at a disadvantage. Very few of the former are able to obtain the same grades as the latter. In equal conditions (opportunities), poor children with a better performance obtain a lower grade than nonpoor children with better performance.

Among the policies that would have an effect on the average student, controlling household and external (or market) child work appears as a very important one. In school, it would be important to reduce children who are over their age for the school level and to reinforce work with children from indigenous homes. It would be important to design policies that promote job stability and dedication for teachers. This would help the children from the low-income sectors more, while teacher training would have an equalizing effect, as it would impact the higher sectors. All actions aimed at improving the education of the mothers would also have positive and important effects on the academic performance of the children in general, although the effect on poor and nonpoor children would be ambiguous: It would favor poor children more in Language and nonpoor children in Math.

General economic conditions favor the poorest children more. In other words, it would be necessary to incorporate a component related to the equalization of results among the children to the benefits of countercyclical macroeconomic policies, as well as (and very especially) those that promote growth.

A lot of these actions could be included in the conditions of the existing PTCs (e.g., controlling child labor, the school attendance of the mothers, etc.), whereas others need to be conceived as sector-based policies: labor markets for professors or grant programs aimed at certain demographic groups.[19] But

---

[19] For example, in Argentina, the Ministry of Education implemented school completion programs for adults, although with other purposes, different to the equalization of

all of them share the same goal: equalizing the endowments or opportunities for children. In that sense, they are not very different from the goal of the existing PTCs of the region. What would be the result if the aforementioned actions were effective? It will be a gap of over 20 points between low-performance poor and nonpoor children and of over 40 points for high-performance poor and nonpoor children. That is to say, the glass roof for the poor persists. To select IRE policies and programs, beyond IOP, it would be necessary to consider the neutrality of the opportunities across the distribution of the results. Thus, among poor children, non-neutral opportunities are repeating courses, higher education of the mother, the dedication of the teachers, and the GDP per capita. It would be necessary to consider that the equalization of opportunities in these aspects would generate inequality in results; therefore, it would be necessary to have compensatory measures to prevent the differences between poor and nonpoor children. These compensatory differences should come from the schools, and they should mainly focus on children with grades above the average of the group.

This article reveals that poverty is the result of concrete actions by agents and processes that act in historical structural contexts over the long term (Cimadamore and Cattani, 2008). It is a product of the interaction between specific structures and agents (in this case, the teachers, parents, and directors) that produce and reproduce, at different levels, the conditions that generate and multiply poverty and inequality.

VI. Bibliography

Alkire, Sabina and Foster, James, 2008, "Counting and Multidimensional Poverty Measurement," *OPHI Working Paper No. 7*, Oxford, University of Oxford.

Banerjee, Abhijit and Duflo, Esther, 2011, *Poor Economics. A Radical Rethinking of the Way to Fight Global Poverty*.

Becker, Gary, 1964, *Human Capital. A Theoretical and Empirical Analysis, with Special Reference to Education*, 2nd ed., New York, Columbia University Press.

Blinder, Alan, 1973, "Wage Discrimination: Reduced Form and Structural Estimates," *The Journal of Human Resources*, vol. 8.

---

opportunities for children. In this case, the programs should be targeted at women with children in primary school age, or women at risk of getting pregnant.

Boissiere, Maurice, 2004, "Determinants of Primary Education Outcomes in Developing Countries," *Background Paper for the Evaluation of the World Bank's Support to Primary Education*, Washington, DC, The World Bank.

Cameron, Colin and Trivedi, Pravin, 2009, *Microeconometrics Using Stata*, Texas, Stata Press.

Cimadamore, Alberto and Cattani, David, 2008, "La construcción de la pobreza y la desigualdad en América Latina: una introducción," in Cimadamore, Alberto and Cattani, David (coord.), *Producción de pobreza y desigualdad en América Latina*, CLACSO-CROP.

Comisión Económica para América Latina y el Caribe (CEPAL), 2013, *Panorama social de América Latina 2013*, Santiago, CEPAL, LC/G. 2580.

Comisión Económica para América Latina y el Caribe (CEPAL), United Nations Children's Fund (UNICEF), 2010, *Pobreza infantil en América Latina y el Caribe*, Santiago, CEPAL-UNICEF, LCR 2168.

Deaton, Angus, 1997, *The Analysis of Household Surveys. A Microeconometric Approach to Development Policy*, Baltimore, Maryland, The Johns Hopkins University Press.

Delamónica, Enrique and Minujin, Alberto, 2007, "Incidence, Depth and Severity of Children in Poverty," *Social Indicators Research*, vol. 82, No. 2.

Feres, Juan and Mancero, Xavier, 2001, "El método de las necesidades básicas insatisfechas (NBI) y sus aplicaciones a América Latina,"*Serie Estudios Económicos y Prospectivos No. 7*, Santiago de Chile, CEPAL.

Ferreira, Francisco and Gignoux, Jeremie, 2011, "The Measurement of Inequality of Opportunity: Theory and an Application to Latin America," *Review of Income and Wealth*, vol. 57, No. 4.

García, Diego, 2014, "Entrevista a Carlos Auyero. Primera Parte: La razón clientelar," Austin, http://artepolitica.com/articulos/entrevista-a-javier-auyero-primera-parte/.

Gordon, David et al., 2003, *Child Poverty in the Developing World*, Bristol, The Policy Press.

Hanna, Rema and Linden, Leigh, 2009, "Measuring Discrimination in Education," *National Bureau of Economic Research, Working Paper 15057*.

Hanushek, Eric and Woessmann, Ludger, 2011, "The Economics of International Differences in Educational Achievement," in Hanushek, Eric et al. (eds.), *Handbook of the Economics of Education*, Elsevier B.V.

Heckman, James et al., 1996, "Human Capital Pricing Equations with an Application to Estimating the Effect of Schooling Quality on Earnings," *Review of Economics and Statistics*, vol. 78, No. 4.

Koenker, Roger and Bassett, Gilbert, 1978, "Regression Quantiles," *Econometrica*, vol. 46, No. 1.

Lavinas, Lena, 2013, "21st Century Welfare," *New Left Review*, vol. 84.

Machado, José and Mata, José, 2005, "Counterfactual Decomposition of Changes in Wage Distribution Using Quantile Regression," *Journal of Applied Econometrics*, vol. 20.

Malecki, Christine and Demaray, Michelle, 2006, "Social Support as a Buffer in the Relationship Between Socioeconomic Status and Academic Performance," *School Psychology Quarterly*, vol. 21, No. 4.

Mincer, Jacob, 1974, *Schooling, Experience and Earnings*, New York, NBER.

Oaxaca, Ronald, 1973, "Male-Female Wage Differentials in Urban Labor Markets," *International Economic Review*, vol. 14.

Paz, Jorge, 2010, *Programas dirigidos a la pobreza en América Latina y el Caribe. Sustento teórico e implementación práctica*, Buenos Aires, CLACSO.

Schultz, Theodore, 1961, "Investment in Human Capital," *American Economic Review*, vol. 51, No. 1.

Treviño, Ernesto et al., 2010, *Factores asociados al logro cognitivo de los estudiantes de América Latina y el Caribe*, Santiago, UNESCO's Regional Bureau for Education in Latin America and the Caribbean (OREALC/UNESCO)-Latin American Laboratory for Assessment of the Quality of Education (LLECE).

VII. GRAPHS APPENDIX

Graph 1. Percentage of children living in homes without electric power or drainage

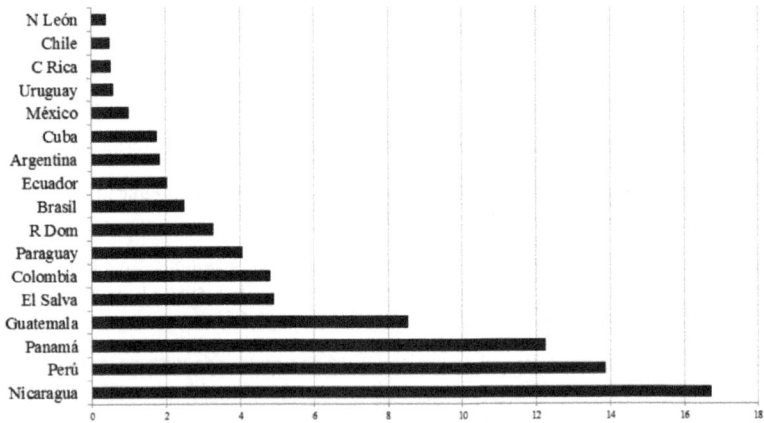

Source: Prepared internally with data from SERCE.

Graph 2. Average grades by country

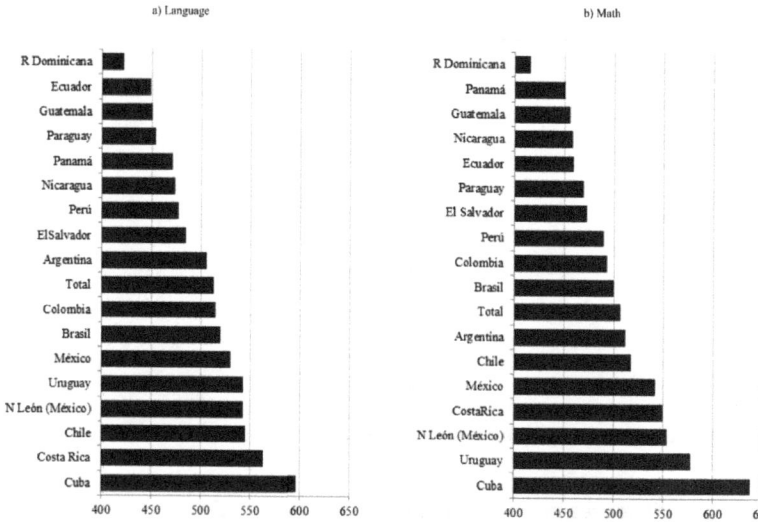

Graph 3. Socioeconomic grade gaps by country

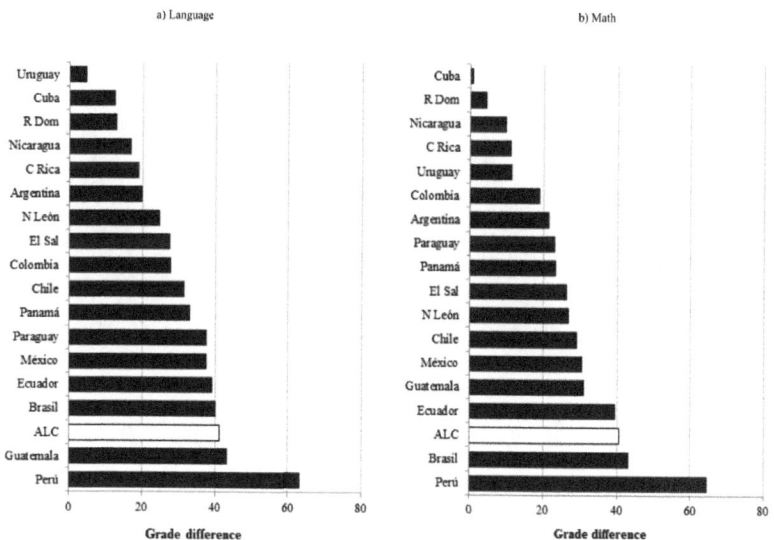

Source: Prepared internally with data from SERCE.

Graph 4. Kernel densities of the grades in relation to the services (electricity and drainage) of the homes: A. Language; B. Math

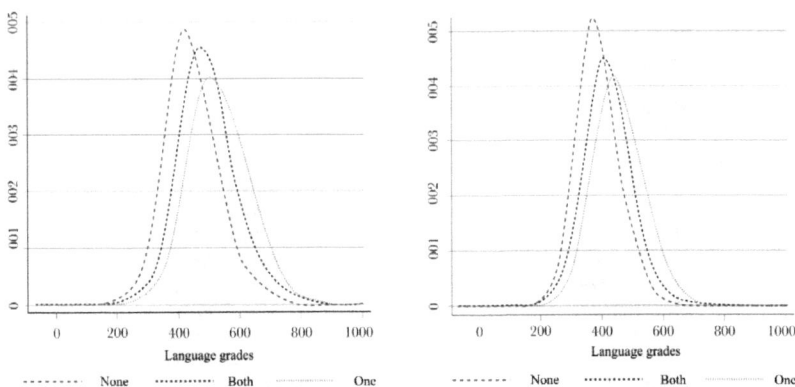

Source: Prepared internally with data from SERCE.

Graph 5a. Differences in the parameters of Language grades for the entire distribution

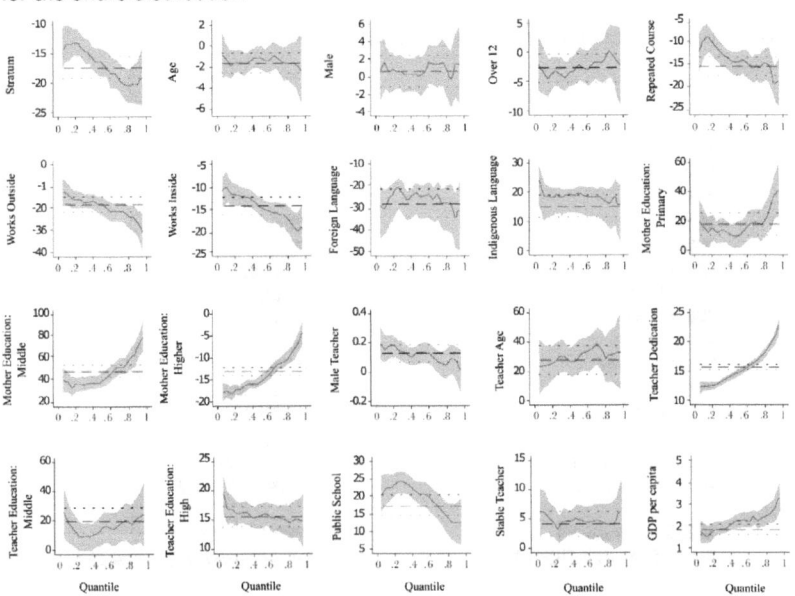

Source: Prepared internally with data from SERCE.

Graph 5b. Differences in the parameters of Math grades for the entire distribution

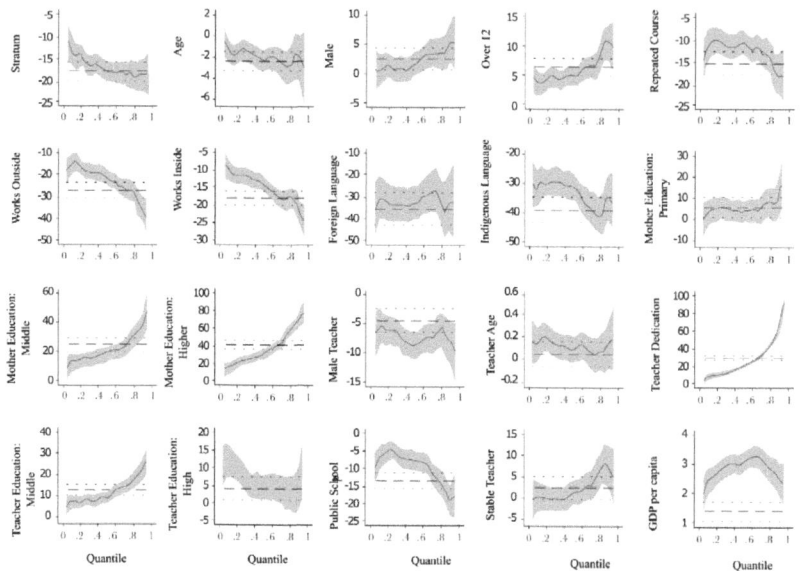

Source: Prepared internally with data from SERCE.

Graph 6a. Machado-Mata breakdown of the difference in grades: Language

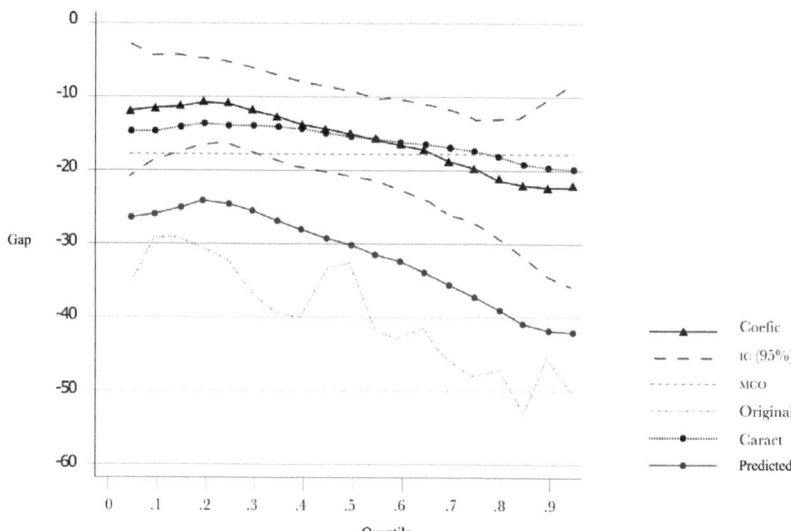

Source: Prepared internally with micro data from SERCE.

Graph 6b. Machado-Mata breakdown of the difference in grades: Math

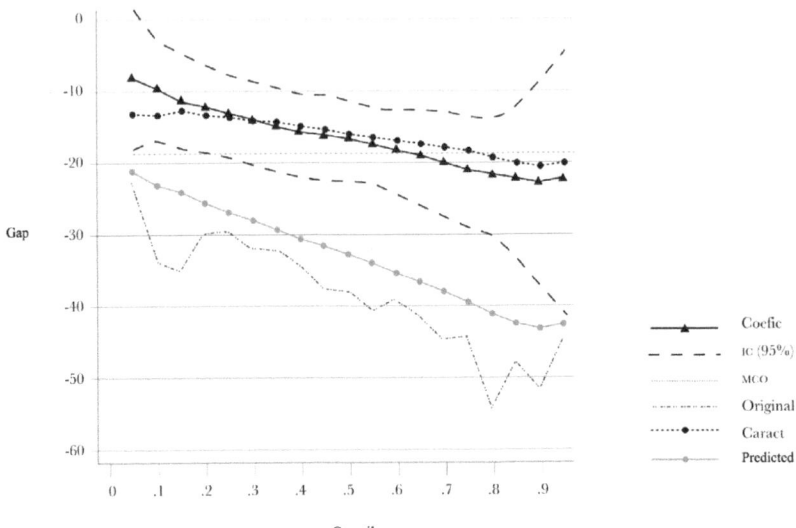

Source: Prepared internally with micro data from SERCE.

VIII. Tables appendix

Table 1. Grades by percentiles in relation to the socioeconomic origin of the children

Competence/services	Grade percentile				
	10	25	50	75	99
Language					
1. None	340.3	384.5	431.5	488.8	668.3
2. One	384.5	431.5	486.9	547.3	724.7
3. Both	413.8	459.4	522.1	595.2	786.9
Difference (3)-(1)	73.5	74.9	90.6	106.4	118.6
Math					
1. None	343.5	392.7	434.2	496.9	660.7
2. One	381.7	427.8	482.6	540.8	734.2
3. Both	406.2	459.5	518.3	582.6	787.4
Difference (3)-(1)	62.7	66.8	84.1	85.7	126.7

Source: Prepared internally with data from SERCE.

Table 2. Sixth-grade student descriptions, several countries in ALC

Variable	Language			Math		
	All	Poor	Nonpoor	All	Poor	Nonpoor
Poor home	0.344			0.345		
Children characteristics						
Average grade	505.701	486.590	521.140	508.209	481.073	515.054
Age	12.095	12.763	12.326	12.100	12.817	12.348
Boy	0.502	0.468	0.517	0.502	0.467	0.518
Under 12	0.329	0.201	0.213	0.330	0.199	0.213
Repeated course	0.244	0.356	0.249	0.244	0.356	0.250
Works outside home	0.091	0.137	0.094	0.092	0.138	0.095
Works at home	0.311	0.416	0.308	0.312	0.416	0.309
Foreign language	0.016	0.012	0.008	0.016	0.012	0.008
Indigenous language	0.056	0.058	0.013	0.056	0.058	0.013
Education of the mother						
Primary	0.343	0.456	0.355	0.343	0.454	0.355
Secondary	0.385	0.346	0.424	0.385	0.346	0.423
Higher education	0.221	0.102	0.192	0.222	0.101	0.192
Teacher characteristics						
Man	0.295	0.369	0.261	0.295	0.371	0.262
Age	40.880	38.256	40.111	40.876	38.239	40.091
Dedication	0.301	0.172	0.132	0.300	0.171	0.131
Stable in the job	0.837	0.753	0.807	0.839	0.752	0.807
Middle education	0.674	0.658	0.630	0.674	0.662	0.632
Higher education	0.168	0.221	0.267	0.168	0.220	0.267
Public school	0.837	0.706	0.756	0.837	0.708	0.757
GDP per capita	5,898.811	6,016.562	6,359.686	5,880.602	6,009.537	6,356.776
Total observations	44,882	15,422	29,460	44,847	15,458	29,389

Source: Prepared internally with data from SERCE.

Table 3a. Determinants of the performance in Language, sixth-grade students, several countries in ALC

Characteristic/variable	Group considered in the RP		
	All	Poor	Nonpoor
	(1)	(2)	(3)
Poor home	−20.119***		
	(1.759)		
Children characteristics			
Age	−0.665	−0.724	−0.225
	(0.533)	(0.710)	(1.162)
Boy	0.025	−0.803	−0.668
	(1.622)	(3.222)	(2.266)
Under 12	−8.186***	−7.125*	−8.098***
	(1.887)	(3.718)	(2.819)
Repeated course	−14.968***	−9.279**	−18.721***
	(2.081)	(3.776)	(3.167)
Works outside	−16.176***	−5.293	−18.301***
	(2.827)	(5.231)	(4.143)
Works at home	−16.869***	−12.772***	−17.084***
	(1.774)	(3.468)	(2.502)
Speaks foreign language	−22.927***	−1.046	−32.419***
	(5.613)	(9.405)	(8.525)
Speaks indigenous language	−37.888***	−33.219***	−45.868***
	(3.120)	(4.626)	(5.633)
Mother studied primary school	4.742	7.537	0.541
	(3.979)	(5.816)	(7.329)
Mother studied secondary school	9.918**	14.016**	5.354
	(4.068)	(6.214)	(7.340)
Mother with higher education	25.548***	25.583***	21.983***
	(4.283)	(7.096)	(7.530)

Teacher characteristics			
Male	−19.548***	−19.944***	−19.834***
	(1.724)	(3.274)	(2.473)
Age	0.222**	0.280	0.226*
	(0.093)	(0.187)	(0.129)
Dedication	8.759***	9.401**	8.753***
	(2.137)	(4.009)	(3.094)
Has job stability	4.807**	11.088***	0.668
	(2.209)	(4.147)	(3.177)
Middle education	25.823***	23.214***	29.294***
	(1.989)	(3.797)	(2.822)
Higher education	39.482***	37.337***	43.076***
	(2.685)	(5.201)	(3.802)
Other characteristics			
Public management	0.770	−1.220	3.409
	(2.226)	(4.242)	(3.178)
Country GDP	6.075***	8.480***	4.851***
	(0.293)	(0.604)	(0.402)
Arranged	451.444***	405.870***	457.902***
	(9.756)	(15.325)	(18.318)
Pseudo R^2	0.052	0.052	0.032
Observations	44,882	15,422	29,460

Note: Significantly different to zero by: ***1%; **5%; *10%. The standard error of the estimate is in parenthesis; its sign is unknown.
Source: Prepared internally with data from SERCE.

Table 3b. Determinants of the performance in Math, sixth-grade students, several countries in ALC

Characteristic/variable	Group considered in the RP		
	All	Poor	Nonpoor
	(1)	(2)	(3)
Poor home	−19.098***		
	(1.998)		
Children characteristics			
Age	−0.907	0.862**	−3.187***
	(0.637)	(0.434)	(0.912)
Boy	0.368	−2.897	1.248
	(1.840)	(1.870)	(2.162)
Under 12	−2.275	3.053	−6.015**
	(2.167)	(2.177)	(2.587)
Repeated course	−17.186***	−11.065***	−18.094***
	(2.359)	(2.178)	(2.938)
Works outside	−9.157***	−11.216***	−8.729**
	(3.208)	(3.013)	(3.944)
Works at home	−11.309***	−14.803***	−8.799***
	(2.014)	(2.014)	(2.391)
Speaks foreign language	−17.172***	−9.664*	−28.565***
	(6.376)	(5.422)	(8.395)
Speaks indigenous language	−29.348***	−24.335***	−41.433***
	(3.547)	(2.695)	(5.335)
Mother studied primary school	11.180**	11.250***	11.289
	(4.535)	(3.394)	(6.950)
Mother studied secondary school	19.500***	12.071***	23.674***
	(4.639)	(3.621)	(6.961)
Mother with higher education	31.106***	29.367***	33.215***
	(4.913)	(4.182)	(7.144)

Teacher characteristics			
Male	−12.389***	−14.133***	−11.767***
	(1.959)	(1.893)	(2.357)
Age	0.583***	0.816***	0.462***
	(0.106)	(0.107)	(0.124)
Dedication	−1.193	−5.658**	0.084
	(2.435)	(2.337)	(2.938)
Has job stability	−4.626*	−0.147	−7.162**
	(2.508)	(2.399)	(3.036)
Middle education	22.360***	15.444***	25.924***
	(2.259)	(2.208)	(2.701)
Higher education	25.737***	18.875***	27.751***
	(3.051)	(3.024)	(3.632)
Other characteristics			
Public management	11.096***	8.687***	12.391***
	(2.530)	(2.465)	(3.031)
Country GDP	7.324***	8.813***	6.197***
	(0.334)	(0.351)	(0.384)
Arranged	421.535***	370.337***	457.238***
	(11.419)	(9.087)	(15.387)
Pseudo R^2	0.052	0.045	0.037
Observations	44,847	15,458	29,389

Note: Significantly different to zero by ***1%, **5%, and *10%. The standard error of the estimate is in parenthesis; its sign is unknown.

Source: Prepared internally with data from SERCE.

Table 4. Neutrality of the parameters to the position of the student in the distribution of the grades

Parameter	Entire sample		Poor		Non poor	
	Language	Math	Language	Math	Language	Math
Arranged	*Non neutral*	*Non neutral*	*Non neutral*	*Non neutral*	*Non neutral*	*Non neutral*
Poverty sector	Neutral	Neutral	NA	NA	NA	NA
Children characteristics						
Age	Neutral	Neutral	Neutral	Neutral	Neutral	Neutral
Boy	Neutral	Neutral	Neutral	Neutral	Neutral	Neutral
Under 12	Neutral	Neutral	Neutral	Neutral	Neutral	Neutral
Repeated course	Neutral	Neutral	Neutral	Non neutral	Neutral	Neutral
Works outside home	Neutral	Non neutral	Neutral	Neutral	Non neutral	Neutral
Works at home	Neutral	Non neutral	Neutral	Neutral	Non neutral	Neutral
Foreign language	Neutral	Neutral	Neutral	Neutral	Neutral	Neutral
Indigenous language	Neutral	Neutral	Neutral	Neutral	Neutral	Neutral
Mother studied primary school	Neutral	Neutral	Neutral	Neutral	Neutral	Neutral
Mother studied secondary school	Non neutral	Non neutral	Neutral	Neutral	Non neutral	Non neutral
Mother with higher education	*Non neutral*	*Non neutral*	*Non neutral*	*Non neutral*	*Non neutral*	*Non neutral*

Teacher characteristics						
Male teacher	Neutral	Neutral	Neutral	Neutral	Neutral	Neutral
Age	Neutral	Non neutral	Neutral	Neutral	Neutral	Neutral
Dedication	*Non neutral*	*Non neutral*	*Non neutral*	*Non neutral*	*Non neutral*	*Non neutral*
Stable in the job	Neutral	Neutral	Neutral	Neutral	Neutral	Neutral
Middle education	Neutral	Non neutral	Neutral	Neutral	Neutral	Non neutral
Higher education	Neutral	Neutral	Neutral	Neutral	Non neutral	Neutral
Other characteristics						
Public school	Neutral	Non neutral	Neutral	Neutral	Non neutral	Non neutral
GDP per capita	Neutral	Non neutral	Non neutral	Non neutral	Non neutral	Non neutral
Neutrals proportion	17/21=0.81	11/21=0.52	16/20=0.80	15/20=0.75	11/20=0.55	13/20=0.65
Both competences		28/42 = 0.67		31/40 = 0.78		24/40 = 0.60

Source: Prepared internally with data from SERCE.

Table 5. Blinder–Oaxaca breakdown of the difference in school performance, sixth-grade students

Scores and breakdown	Language		Math	
Score, nonpoor	521.140 (0.554)		515.054 (0.558)	
Score, poor	486.590 (0.743)		481.073 (0.732)	
Difference	34.550 (0.927)		33.981 (0.921)	
Breakdown				
Opportunities	14.565 (0.528)	42.2%	13.550 (0.516)	39.9%
O→R conversion	20.649 (0.991)	59.8%	18.662 (0.993)	54.9%
Interaction	−0.664 (0.634)	−1.9%	1.768 (0.643)	5.2%
Total		100.0%		100.0%

Source: Prepared internally with data from SERCE.

Part II
Social Policy and Child Protection

HUMAN RIGHTS, HEGEMONY, AND UTOPIA IN LATIN AMERICA: INTERCULTURAL DIMENSIONS OF POVERTY AND INDIGENOUS MIGRATION IN MEXICO AS CASE STUDIES

Camilo Pérez Bustillo[1]

> I ask the political economists and the moralists if they have ever calculated the number of individuals who must be condemned to misery, overwork, demoralisation, degradation, rank ignorance, overwhelming misfortune and utter penury in order to produce one rich man.
> Almeida Garret, in the epigraph of *Raised from the ground* by
> Jose Saramago (Alfaguara, 2000)

I. Introduction. II. Reference frameworks. III. Context of migratory flows in the Mexican territory. IV. Origin and characteristics of indigenous Ecuadorian migration. V. Conclusion. VI. Bibliography.

I. Introduction

This article is dedicated to the memory of Noemí Álvarez Quillay, a 12-year-old Ecuadorian indigenous migrant, born in one of the poorest Quechua-speaking communities of Ecuador, in the district of El Tambo of the Cañar region [*New York Times*, April 2014; Frontera News Service (FNS), April 2014], in the south of the country. Noemi died—supposedly of suicide—under circumstances that remain unclear, in a shelter for migrant minors located in Ciudad Juarez, in northern Mexico, on March 11, 2014, immediately after being aggressively interrogated by Federal Police agents (*id.*). Ciudad Juarez has the unfortunate distinction of being the location where hundreds of unpunished homicides of young women took place, many of them indigenous migrant workers, during the past 20 years, cases that were the basis for a historical ruling by the Inter-American Human Rights Court.

---

1 Visiting Professor, Department of Government and Department of Criminal Justice, New Mexico State University, 2013-15; Professor-Researcher, Graduate Studies for the Defense and Promotion of Human Rights, Universidad Autónoma de la Ciudad de México; CROP Fellow since 2009; he was the first holder of the "Emil Bustamante" regional human rights chair of CLACSO, 2010.

Noemi and the "coyote" (smuggler) who guided her during a 10,000-km odyssey since the start of her journey on February 4, at her place of origin, in the Andean highlands, had been intercepted days before her death by police agents (*id.*). The Ecuadorian government has repeatedly insisted, in a thorough investigation of the case, on the fact that the Ecuadorian consulate was not informed of the presence of Noemi in Mexico until they were notified of her death, in violation of international laws that establish the right to consular assistance in similar conditions.

Noemi had been left with her grandparents since her parents migrated to New York; first her father migrated shortly after she was born, and then her mother, when she was 3 years old. Her parents are undocumented migrants who live and work in the United States, and therefore, it is impossible for them to travel outside the country without losing even the little they have saved during their exile. It is frequent, given the context, that absent families save money and contract massive debts to pay the money that smugglers demand, estimated between 15,000 and 20,000 dollars per person (between 3,000 and 5,000 from Central America), to reunite the families (*id.*).

Noemi died in her second attempt, after the first one failed less than halfway through, in Nicaragua (*New York Times*, 2014). On the second, fatal occasion, she was less than an hour away from the US border when she was intercepted (*id.*). The official version is that her death was a suicide, but many observers question the reliability of the report considering her age, and her hopes and motivations to be reunited with her parents (*id*). Meanwhile, the causes of her death continue to be investigated. There is little empirical basis to trust the effectiveness of such investigations by the Mexican authorities, given the recurring pattern of impunity of thousands of cases of serious human rights violations (murders, kidnappings, forced disappearances, rapes, extortions, and mugging) against migrants while in transit through Mexican territory in recent years (Amnesty International, 2010; Centro Pro/WOLA, 2011).

Human Rights, Hegemony, and Utopia in Latin America   141

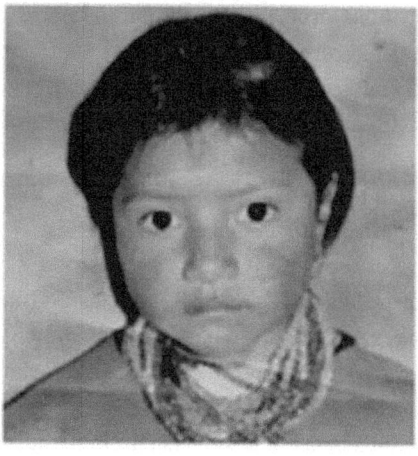

Noemi's case reflects a more generalized migratory phenomenon of youths and minors, with unprecedented dimensions that present a complex challenge for destination countries (United States), transit countries (Mexico), and origin countries (Honduras, Guatemala, and El Salvador) that are more directly involved; 53% of the minors have traveled alone, without being accompanied by a parent, guardian, or a relative of legal age (José Antonio, 2014). The US government declared the existence of a "humanitarian crisis" in the border with Mexico in early June 2014, in response to this exodus, mainly of Central American origin—55% of the youths and minors detained in the period were from Honduras, 27% from Guatemala, and 18% from El Salvador (*id.*). This trend started in October 2013 and has since (July 2014) grown to include over 57,000 unaccompanied minors—most of them aged between 12 and 17 years, but at least 20% of them aged between 0 and 11 years—detained in inhumane conditions near the Mexican border between October 2013 and May 2014 (*id.*).

These trends increased by 97% in 2013-14, compared to the same period the previous year, and it is projected to include over 90,000 minors in these conditions by the end of 2014 (*id.*). A total of 39,000 women were also detained during that same period. Most of these women were traveling with children under the age of 12 years (*id.*). The case of Noemi indicates that the evident increase in the migration of youths and children does not imply a phenomenon that is restricted to Central America; cases like that of Noemi actually reflect the reproduction, in the Andean region, of patterns that are characteristic of those processes in the Mesoamerican region, and which share the same structural causes.

Recently, a significant flow of Ecuadorian underage migrants who seek to reunite with their families in the United States has been identified [Frontera News Service (FNS), 2014]. Many of those minors, either from the Mesoamerican or the Andean region—48% in the case of Guatemala (UNHCR, 2014)—are of indigenous origin.

Children are especially significant because they represent a society's potential and future. In this sense, the policies and initiatives that aim to defend children assume their true essential dimensions as actions "in defense of the future." The material conditions associated with poverty and inequality seriously jeopardize multiple dimensions of the rights of the children and of society as a whole. Each child thus involves a potential utopian horizon, outlined by the limits and scope of their political and cultural contexts and by their socioeconomic status and condition.

This articlewill address issues related to child poverty and indigenous youths, their migration processes in Latin America, and in terms of their complexities and implications from a broader, interdisciplinary conceptual framework centered on the dynamic relationship between human rights, hegemony, and utopia at the continental and global scale. The focus will be on the exploration of the migration of indigenous children and youths—of Mexican, Central American, and Andean origin in transit to the United States across the Mexican territory—and their intercultural dimensions, as a case study of the complex relationship between structural violence, poverty, indigenous peoples, and migration processes in these contexts.

This perspective includes recognizing that the true essence of poverty is in these convergent forms of violence, and in the multiple violations of rights they imply, and it provides a foundation to characterize them as a crime against humanity. In this sense, talking about "poverty" without referring to the inherent condition of violence that constitutes it and characterizes it would be a euphemism.

II. Reference frameworks

Mexican, and Latin American, history is a history of poverty and inequality. It is also a history of governments and ruling elites who have accumulated power and wealth as a result of those historical injustices and who continue to assume themselves as the legitimate enforcers of the processes that reproduce it. These are the same sectors that have been celebrating the twentieth anniversary in 2014 of the enactment of the North American Free Trade Agreement (NAFTA), with events such as the tri-national summit held in Mexico (February 2014) during the same days as the seminar that gave rise to this book.

But the same sectors often forget that the history of this section of the world also involves resistance and rebellion by its peoples, from the ground up, who have configured their most decisive contributions to the emerging global scenario of the contemporary struggles for dignity and justice. These are the sectors whose actions have been permeated by the guiding lines of a vibrant political imagination that is able to conceive liberation of some kind from their own suffering by developing more hopeful alternatives for their children. This article assumes the position of that collective space of action.

1. Human rights, hegemony, and utopia in Latin America

There is a long tradition linking the development of utopian visions in Latin America with the defense of human rights (Dussel, 1998). This tradition is reflected in recurring processes of resistance and rebellion among its indigenous, and Afro-descendant, peoples and other excluded sectors, against colonialism, slavery, racism, imperialism, and other forms of domination during the past 500 years, including their contemporary equivalents in the context of the neoliberal capitalist globalization and "free trade." This legacy of rebellion and resistance and its cultural and intellectual expressions had a special relevance in the convening of the seminar that gave rise to this book during the same week in February 2014 of the tri-national summit to commemorate and celebrate the twentieth anniversary of the enactment of the NAFTA.

All this provides the groundwork to emphasize in this articlethe core nature of the struggles for the recognition of the rights of the indigenous peoples in the contexts of poverty and of migration processes, which imply an implicit or explicit challenge to the hegemonic constructs with respect to the nation-state, citizenship, democracy, participation, and human rights, and the need to revise them. This is heightened when addressing these concepts in a critical manner from the perspective of the migrating children and teenagers of indigenous origin, in very diverse contexts, such as the Cañar regions in Ecuador, Guerrero in Mexico, or the Mayan highlands in Guatemala, and their growing presence in the streets of New York.

Latin American social policies that focus on fighting poverty recognize in various ways that the indigenous identity has been associated with the production and reproduction of poverty and inequality, and that the initiatives against poverty as such in the region must consider factors related to this identity in terms of their design, content, and scope. This also reflects the fact that the indigenous identity in Latin America has a very significant correlation with the spatial dimensions in terms of the concentration of poverty among certain sectors of the population, for example, the countryside and in certain regions (e.g., the La Montaña region of Guerrero, the Chiapas highlands and the Mayan regions of Guatemala, the North of the Cauca in Colombia, the Andean highlands in Ecuador, Peru, and Bolivia, the original land of the Mapuche in Chile and Argentina, the Atlantic coast of Nicaragua, etc.). All this is evident in the disaggregated variant analyses of the UNDP's Human Development Index (HDI).

But there are important variants in the region in terms of the extent and the manner in which programs against poverty and other social programs specifically recognize the indigenous dimensions of national poverty and also in terms of the extent to which they recognize the rights of the indigenous groups consecrated in international law (in the 2007 United Nations Declaration on the Rights of Indigenous Peoples and its yet-to-be-approved draft, equivalent in the context of the Inter-American system, to ILO's Convention No. 169, and, in light of the jurisprudence of the Inter-American Human Rights Court, as key sources, in addition to the significant variants in the relevant national legal frameworks).

2. Indigenous children and youth, poverty, and migration

Indigenous children have been repeatedly identified as a group that is particularly vulnerable to poverty and death as a result of starvation, preventable diseases, and other conditions attributable to structural inequalities and racial and ethnic discrimination patterns, in the context of Mexico and Latin America (and the rest of the world). This has prompted the prioritization of diagnostic and substantial measures focused on indigenous children as part of larger efforts aimed at the prevention, reduction, and eradication of poverty.

The emphasis here is on poverty and inequality as structural factors that trigger the decision to migrate, commonly assumed in liberal mythology as a "rational," individual, and "voluntary" choice, and understood herein more as the result of a "forced migration" process (Castles, 2003; Pérez-Bustillo and Hernández, 2012). It is in light of reflections of this kind that the human rights center Centro de Derechos Humanos de la Montaña (CDHM) "Tlachinollan" in Tlapa, Guerrero, has developed the "Migrate or Die" project aimed at the defense of the rights of indigenous migrants of the region, one of the poorest in the country (CDHM Tlachinollan, 2005, 2011). These migration processes are characterized not only by an internal, massive, "traditional" migration of entire families of agricultural laborers to the agroindustry fields in northern states such as Sinaloa and Baja California but also by a growing migration toward the United States, and to the city of New York in particular.

Other important sources of the critical perspective on migration issues reflected herein include the current demands of migrant movements and their advocates in key destination countries or regions of the major contemporary world, such as the United States, Western Europe, and Australia (Pérez-Bustillo, 2009), related theoretical reflections (Benhabib, 2004), and vital contributions such as those of the Binational Front of Indigenous Organizations (FIOB; see Fox and Rivera-Salgado, 2004), the Civil Association of Las Abejas de Acteal (an organization of Maya-Tzotzil victims of the Acteal Massacre in Chiapas), and the Assembly of Indigenous Migrants of the Federal District (Mexico). It also includes the arguments that have characterized the presentation of cases related to these issues before the International Tribunal of Conscience of Peoples in Movement (TICPM, 2011), and the Permanent Peoples' Tribunal (TPP), in its consideration of the Mexican case (2011-14), and other related cases submitted or to be submitted before the Inter-American Human Rights Court and the European Court of Human Rights.

This article understands migration and displacement as "forced" processes, when they are the result of the convergence between structures, policies, and processes that reflect three types of violence: (1) state violence, (2) structural violence, and/or (3) systemic violence. State violence is the most visible one, which is directly or indirectly attributable to state actors, policies, or practices. This includes, for example, both state actions that contribute to poverty and inequality and the inefficacy of its policies that are allegedly aimed at fighting them. Structural violence includes starvation, preventable diseases, all the various kinds of discrimination, and all serious violations of economic, social, and cultural rights—to health, housing, work, education, and so on—and also any violations to the right to autonomy and self-determination of indigenous peoples, ecological devastation, and so on. Systemic violence is, in turn, inherent to the capitalist way of production and neoliberal policies and to the mechanisms and effects of "free trade" and "free market."

Issues related to poverty among indigenous children and youth in Mexico and Latin America cannot be addressed and understood without referring to the persistent inequalities in the entire region in terms of the status and rights of indigenous peoples. These conditions reflect the general trend, inherent to neoliberal policies, of producing, reproducing, and intensifying the underlying structures and patterns of discrimination and racial, ethnic, and cultural stratification that are deeply rooted in their history. The progress and setbacks in terms of the recognition of the rights of indigenous peoples are core issues in contemporary reflections on the protagonist role of various expressions of the human rights demands, narratives, policies, and practices both at the state level and in the counter-hegemonic social movements.

It has often been argued that the status of children and youths in a society and the related dimensions of their vulnerabilities—for example, in terms of child mortality, starvation, vaccination level and health trends, school attendance and graduation rates, the persistence of child labor, and so on—constitute indicators that are specially significant to the ranking of a country in terms of its compliance with internationally accepted standards on the levels of development, the implementation of desirable social policies, and with international human rights standards.

This childhood- and youth-oriented perspective also has epistemological and methodological implications, which include an insistence on evaluating the levels of compliance of a society with international standards from the perspective of actual welfare among those sectors, and in measuring its progress or setbacks with respect to that starting point. This childhood- and/or youth-oriented approach has at least partial convergences with other approaches derived from tenets with roots in philosophy, ethics, theology, and liberation theology and/or the "epistemologies of the south, such as the influence of thinkers such as Enrique Dussel or Boaventura de Sousa Santos, who highlight the importance of addressing the critique of any social, economic or political system, or of any policy, 'from the perspective of its victims'" (Dussel, 1998).

3. Migration, poverty, and human rights

For indigenous migrants, the condition of vulnerability is also constructed in terms of their recognition as a racial and/or ethnic group differentiated by cultural and/or linguistic identity. The fact that migrants may be identified as a national or social group due to their migratory condition, their gender, age, disability, social status, or other characteristics that may be subject to protection measures, and in the case of indigenous migrants as belonging to a racial and/or ethnic group differentiated by its cultural and/or linguistic identity, has been pointed out in several instances by the universal human rights system, by the regional systems, and by the national systems as basis to recognize their vulnerability, as a "suspicious category," for the discriminatory purposes of public policies and the actions by government authorities of every level, and to provide them with special protection measures.

III. Context of migratory flows in the Mexican territory

The Mexican context, in terms of migration processes, includes its prominent role at the global and regional level, both as a source and a transit country. There are data on a minimum of 30 million people of Mexican origin (seven million of them with Mexican citizenship) that reside in the United States, with approximately 400,000 trying to migrate every year (over 1,000 a day). This yields estimates that suggest that one in every two Mexican families has relatives living "on the other side" of the longest border between the "first" world (or the "Global North") and the "third" world (the "Global South") in the entire planet. But its additional key role as a transit country is evidently derived from its geographical location en route to the United States from the rest of Latin America, and it is reflected in the fact that the figures on the number of migrants in transit (mainly Central Americans of Honduran, Salvadoran, and Guatemalan origin) have also been between 250,000 and 400,000 a year since 2007 (TICPM, 2010).

Massive migration and the transit through Mexico of persons of Central American origin reflect the continuation, by other means, of state terrorism and the regional wars that took place in the 1970s and the 1980s in Guatemala, El Salvador, Nicaragua, and Honduras as part of the military interventions of the United States in that period. The havoc wreaked by armed conflicts in Central America has subsequently increased as a result of the neoliberal "free trade" policies (Central American Free Trade Agreement, CAFTA) that have systematically devastated and undermined the material conditions required to make a dignified living possible and sustainable in the source communities and countries of these migrations. Central American migration and the crimes committed against its protagonists thus constitute the continuation of these wars by other means, which today involve a regional war against migrants, stirred by the extraterritorial imposition and enforcement of the migratory policies of the United States based on the criminalization of migrants. The current conditions and vulnerabilities of the Central American migrants of those countries are therefore the result of the ongoing criminality of the said interventions and impositions, and they represent an attempt to illegitimately transfer the responsibility of the state, and its costs, to the source countries and towns and to the Mexican people.

All this is reflected in the fact that in recent years Mexico has experienced a massive forced movement of around 800,000 persons or more per year, including both people of Mexican origin and people from other countries in transit to the north through its territory. The criminalization of these movements turns it into a captive market for the worst acts of predation by the state and private actors who conspire to exploit and abuse these migrants. This feeds into state terror against those groups, and it produces a growing humanitarian catastrophe characterized by the recurring violation of the dignity and human rights that are the fundamental protagonists of the said processes, and that constitute the contemporary equivalent of slavery and the slave trade.

The prevailing trend in this context is the attempt to reduce the migrants to overexploited sources of cheap labor, "with no papers" and "with no rights," through the hegemonic paradigms of migration policies. In this way, migrant workers are simultaneously *structurally essential but conjuncturally disposable*: essential in structural terms for the generation of the wealth and remittances that are appreciated by destination and source countries, but disposable in certain junctures because they belong to a sector that is easily reproduced. Their allegedly "disposable" nature is reflected both in the crimes against humanity that constitute the tens of thousands of unpunished deaths of migrants in transit in the deserts and the seas toward the United States and Europe, and as a result of dangerous and unhealthy job conditions, and of emerging modalities of state and parastatal terror, which stimulate and manipulate the conditions that produce forced migration and displacement as part of its domination and plundering strategies. All of this is heightened in terms of a true multiplication of the vulnerabilities of underage minors, given the fatal attraction they constitute for transnational smuggling and human trafficking networks.

1. NAFTA and its complements as context

The origin of the shared responsibility and complicity we address here, among other factors, is the economic and legal framework of the North American Free Trade Agreement (NAFTA, enacted on January 1, 1994) and its effects. This includes intensified forced migration and forced displacement patterns starting in 1994, as a result of the convergence between state and structural and systemic violence processes, including poverty, inequality, discrimination, and the despoliation of land, territory, and resources, propitiated by neoliberal "free trade" policies, megaprojects, and ecological devastation and climate change. These processes generate conditions that make a dignified living impossible in the source communities.

A complement of NAFTA and its neoliberal policies includes "cooperation" policies in "national security" (and "antiterrorism") issues between the United States of America, Mexico, and Canada reflected in the Security and Prosperity Partnership of North America (SPP) and the Merida Initiative (as part of "antidrug" strategies that have been combined with migration policies). This has included the "securitization" (the subordination to the alleged priorities of "national security") of policies and the militarization of borders (for Mexico, it specifically refers to its northern and southern borders).

This focus in the "securitization" and militarization of migration policy has been extended to source and transit countries by way of their "externalization" (extraterritorial enforcement and implications) and "regionalization" (their generalization and implementation through related legal frameworks and public policy in key countries of the American continent, but also on a global scale in contexts such as Europe, Africa, and the Middle East, and in Australia and eastern Asia). The deepening and intensification of these trends is underway, as a result of the so-called migratory reform that is taking place in the United States. The deaths in the desert and en route to the United States that are the result of those policies (over 6,000 since the start of the militarization of the border as an invisible counterpart to the enactment of NAFTA in 1994) and the growing number of murders of migrants and others by the US Border Patrol belong to the same criminal machinery of regional and transnational destruction as the San Fernando massacre, mass graves, the migrant victims of related crimes, such as the Cadereyta massacre, and the tens of thousands of migrants kidnapped, disappeared, and raped in Mexican territory since 2007.

This in turn reflects the deep interrelationship between NAFTA, SPP, the Merida Initiative, and their various expressions and implications for migration policies and the equivalent frameworks in the context of the countries and peoples of Central America, the Caribbean, and South America, such as CAFTA, CARICOM, the Pacific Alliance, the Plan Colombia, and the Free Trade Agreement Between Colombia and the United States. These same trends were imposed in Ecuador and El Salvador with the formal "dollarization" of their economies, which intensified migration patterns of expulsion already deeply rooted in both contexts; the "dollarization" in turn is derived from the protagonist role of remittances as a basis (Larrea/Clacso, 2007; Gaborit *et al.*/BID, 2012).

2. Empirical dimensions

A. Childhood, youth, and indigenous migration

The number of migrants like these in the Mexican, Mesoamerican, and Latin American context who are women, indigenous, or minors continues to grow. The office of the United Nations High Commissioner for Refugees (UNHCR) recently published (March 2014) a report documenting the dimensions and characteristics of the migration of children and underage youth, many of them unaccompanied or separated from their families, of Mexican, Guatemalan, Salvadoran, and Honduran origin toward the United States, approximately 60,000 minors a year (*id.*). The figure that corresponds to Mexican minor migrants has doubled in the same period (*New York Times*, 2014), and it includes a significant increase in the number of migrant minors detained at the US border, from 13,000 in 2011 to 15,709 in 2012 and 18,754 in 2013 (UNHCR, 2014).

The dimensions of these migrations across the Mexican territory from Central America and the Andean region are reflected in the evident increase in the number of migrant minors detained and deported by Mexican authorities, from 4,160 in 2011 to 6,107 in 2012 and 9,813 in 2013, a 137% increase between 2011 and 2013; the most recent figures indicate the current persistence of these flows, with 855 people detained and deported in just one month, in January 2014 (*id.*, UNHCR). The intensification of the flows was reflected, for example, in the detention of 370 minor migrants (163 of them unaccompanied, mainly of Guatemalan, Salvadoran, and Honduran origin) in a single week (March 17–24, 2014) who were abandoned by smugglers.

These trends are also reflected in the growth in the number of unaccompanied minors or minors who are separated from their families of Guatemalan, Salvadoran, and Honduran origin who have been detained by US authorities, from 4,059 in the fiscal year 2011 to 10,443 in 2012 and 21,537 in 2013, which represents a 432% increase between 2011 and 2013; and the figures doubled from 2011 to 2012 and again between 2012 and 2013 (UNHCR, 2014).

The 2010 data from the National Migration Institute indicated that around 40,000 Mexican children were deported or repatriated "voluntarily" each year from the United States and that almost half of them arrived without family accompaniment; in addition to this figure, another 12,000 children are intercepted each year before they cross the border, approximately 142 a day (*Migración infantil y catástrofe*, editorial in *La Jornada*, November 12, 2010: 2). In 2009, one out of every 12 migrants in transit through Mexico was below 18 years, and US migration authorities deported 16,000 Mexican minors, of whom 79% traveled unaccompanied (*id.*).

The UNHCR report also underscores the correlation between the multidimensional forms of violence associated with poverty (both violence of state origin and violence from mafias and crime), the impact of material deprivation, and the origins of the migration flows. The study was based on a representative sample of over 400 interviews with minor migrants of Mexican, Guatemalan, Salvadoran, and Honduran origin. One of the most pertinent conclusions for this article is that the material deprivation factor has significance throughout the sample, but its most forceful impact was among indigenous interviewees, mainly of Guatemalan origin (48% of the sample of the interviewees from that country) (UNHCR); 55% of Guatemalan interviewees indicated "deprivation" as the main precipitating factor of their decision to migrate (*id.*).

B. Poverty, indigenous peoples, and migration in Mexico and Ecuador

In general, poverty-related data in Mexico indicate worrying trends in terms of its increase and concentration, starting in 2010. This reflects global crisis' impact, which intensified between 2008 and 2009 and persisted through 2013 and 2014. This includes an increase in the levels of household poverty from 42.7 to 51.3% between 2006 and 2010 (a higher level than that reported in 2004, e.g., covering 52 million people) and from 13.8 to 18.8% in food safety levels (which in Mexico is considered an indicator equivalent to that of "extreme poverty") [2012, 2013; World Bank (WDR), 2013]. Meanwhile, according to the indicator defined in terms of the lack of access to an adequate diet, a broader category configured by the basic necessities package, combined with other indicators, also worsened between 2008 and 2010 from 21.7 to 24.9% (*Mexico Social*, October 2012: 6), along with an increase from 16.7 to 19.4% between 2008 and 2010 in the percentage of the population with income under the line established by the threshold of the basic necessities package (Mexico Social, October 2012: 7). At the same time, 128 of the 2,456 municipalities in the country had 50% of their population with nutritional deficits (*Mexico Social*, October 2012: 8). This included 28 million people living in hunger (*La Jornada*, October 2012), of whom five million are minors, and a million people who were malnourished (*id.*: 52).

Meanwhile, in 2006 Mexico was (and continues to be) the Latin American country with the highest number of malnourished minors (despite the fact that Brazil has a much higher population in absolute numbers) (*Mexico Social*, October 2012: 47), whereas another study (quoted by Enciso in *La Jornada*, October 2012) performed by the Salvador Zubirán National Nutrition Institute in Mexico projects a figure of at least *10,000 preventable deaths of Mexican minors a year* (which involves an increase from the 8,450 deaths registered in 2010, see *Mexico Social*, October 2012: 4) for reasons attributable to chronic malnutrition.

This comes to approximately *25 dead minors per day* (*Mexico Social*, October 2012: 52), which includes one in every three deaths related to malnutrition, birth processes, or contagious diseases, registered in the 100 municipalities with the highest levels of marginalization (*Mexico Social*, October 2012: 24). This same study estimates that the *accumulated amount of these preventable diseases in the past 30 years adds up to around 1.3 million preventable deaths of children under 5*. During that entire period, and to the present.the child mortality rate among indigenous children has exceeded by far the equivalent rate among nonindigenous children, especially among those aged under 5 years.

World Bank data (*id.*) underscore additional dimensions of the situation, which include a generalized reduction in income among a majority of Mexican homes starting with the 2008–09 crisis, and during the same period, a 30% loss in access to employment (concentrated among persons who are decidedly excluded from the labor market), and a 20% reduction in the levels of access to health services.

The RIMISP/IDRC/IFAD (2011) study also indicates how the targeted programs of conditional transfers associated with the process of the so-called Second Agrarian Reform in Mexico (started in 1992) such as *Oportunidades*, *Progresa*, and *Procampo* have contributed to generalized increases in poverty and inequality in the country precisely because their targeted design does not consider the preexisting inequalities that are rooted in the territorial and regional configurations in Mexico, which mainly affect indigenous peoples (RIMISP/IDRC/IFAD: 9–11, 13). The result is that rural poverty in general and its most extreme expressions are highly concentrated among the indigenous peoples of the country, in regions such as Chiapas, Oaxaca, and Guerrero, where the concentration of that population is high.

According to a 2010 report by the UNDP, this means in practice that all the 257 municipalities with an indigenous population above 55% were classified as municipalities where concentrated poverty rates affect the majority of the population, and that in general, 85% of the indigenous population of the country lives in poverty (*id.*). This includes several municipalities in the region of La Montaña in Guerrero that not only are the municipalities with the highest poverty and lowest HDI levels in the country but also are the poorest in all of Latin America (PNUD, 2010). The highest rate of extreme poverty—32.8%—characterizes the state of Chiapas, followed by Guerrero, with a rate of 28%, and Oaxaca with 26.6%; these three states, combined, have the highest concentration of the indigenous population of the country (*Mexico Social*, October 2012: 4).

Indicators of this kind also make it possible to gain insight into implicit correlations at deeper levels, reflected, for example, in the fact that the municipalities with the lowest HDI levels and the highest poverty levels in the Mexican state of Guerrero, and, correspondingly, with the highest rates of child and maternal mortality, low birth weight, limited physical growth, hunger, and fatal but preventable childhood diseases are precisely the municipalities with the highest concentration of indigenous population (80 or 90%)—located in the region of La Montaña.

This region includes eight of the 50 municipalities with the lowest HDI levels in the country, with (1) HDI levels more or less equivalent to some of the poorest countries in Africa, such as Gambia or Rwanda (which, with HDI of 0.390 and 0.385 respectively, rank 154 and 155 out of 172 in the 2012 report by UNDP, among the 18 countries with the lowest levels, slightly higher than Sudan and Afghanistan), and (2) they are also the same source communities that expel the highest number and proportion of its inhabitants to interlinked internal (national) and international migration circuits, toward more prosperous regions of Mexico in the north of the country and toward the United States, for example, New York.

C. Implications of the Central American exodus

The exodus of Central American minors in 2013-14 has brought up the need to extend humanitarian treatment to each of these minors and families, which should include special transitory protection measures and/or the recognition to their right of refuge or asylum, for the "higher interest" of the minors involved, and their right to the reunification of their families, which have been divided largely as a consequence of the toughening of US migration policies. All this exceeds the traditional limits of the definition of "refuge" or "asylum" under international law, which also were not adjusted to the massive migrations from Central America as a result of the regional wars between 1979 and 1996. Meanwhile, both the US government and the Mexican government insist on applying a very restricted interpretation of the concept of "refugee," which excludes these minors; for example, in 2013 only 50 migrant minors were granted that status in Mexico, out of a total of 9,893 who were intercepted—84% of them were deported to their countries of origin (Castellanos,2014).

The US government obstinately insists on taking punitive measures, combining transitory detention, and processing measures of migrants, with the intention of accelerating the mechanisms required for mass deportation. This occurs in the face of passivity and fragmented action by the governments from which the migrants originate. This crisis has generated a broad convergence between migrant organizations, their advocates, and other nongovernmental sectors throughout the region, which demand integral measures for the protection of the rights of migrants in transit by the immediate establishment of a "humanitarian corridor."

A series of regional summits on the subject were held in June and July 2014, involving chiefs of states and officials from the key source countries and Mexico, including a visit by the vice-president of the United States, Joseph Biden to Guatemala and a visit by the Central American chiefs of state to Washington to meet with President Obama. These meetings failed to produce forceful integral measures for the protection of migrant minors. The response from the Obama administration to the crisis has included opening makeshift shelters with high levels of overcrowding, poor sanitary conditions, and limited psychosocial attention services in the border region and in US military bases in Texas, Oklahoma, and California, and the converging insistence from the US and the Mexican government on activating the relevant mechanisms to deport thousands of these youths. These measures reproduce similar responses in the United States to the massive flows of Haitians and Cubans in the Caribbean in the 1980s and the 1990s, which included the first use of the US military base of Guantánamo as a detention center.

IV. Origin and characteristics of indigenous ecuadorian migration

El Cañar is one of the source regions that is most frequently involved in the massive flows of indigenous Ecuadorian migrants to the United States and Spain (UNICEF, 2008), triggered by the economic crisis of 1999-2000 in that country, which ended in its "dollarization." The social worker of the regional high school of the district of El Tambo estimates that at least 60% of the students have migrant parents and are being looked after by their grandparents, uncles, or older siblings (*id.*), while they wait for the eventual reunification of the families. This family uprooting and fragmentation process due to migration-related reasons includes 48% of the indigenous households in the region of El Cañar (UNICEF, 2008: 10).

Hundreds of thousands of minor migrants, such as Noemi, have embarked on the eventful journey to be reunited with their parents in the United States, which necessarily involves crossing Mexican territory and which many times includes a maritime segment between Ecuadorian and Guatemalan shores (*NYTimes, Denver Post*, 2004). It is there, when they arrive to Guatemala, that the migrations from Ecuador converge on their way to Mexico with those from Honduras and El Salvador. These migrants are subsequently transported—or mutilated—by the freight train known as "The Beast," which crosses Mexico from south to north (Martínez, 2010).

The region of El Cañar in Ecuador, the place of origin of Noemi Álvarez Quillay, shares many of the elements described herein for La Montaña in Guerrero. According to a UNICEF study (2008), it is one of the regions of Ecuador where the effects of the historical "social exclusion processes" (UNICEF, 2008: 11) of that country persist, and where this legacy is reflected in the prevalence of "conditions that are more unfavorable than most of Ecuadorian households" (*id.*). This includes lower education, health, and nutrition levels: "Cañarense children are in high risk of malnutrition" (33% exposed in El Cañar *vs.* 18% in the rest of the country); "for indigenous and farmer children, the risk is even higher (42 and 37%, respectively). These figures place El Cañar among the five *cantones* (municipalities) with the highest level of childhood malnutrition in the country" (*id.*).

V. Conclusion

The region of El Cañar in Ecuador, the place of origin of Noemi Álvarez Quillay, shares many elements described herein for La Montaña in Guerrero and the Mesoamerican region that are within a framework centered on child and youth vulnerability in contexts of poverty among indigenous people and in their susceptibility to forced migration processes. The regions of La Montaña in Guerrero, Mexico, and El Cañar in Ecuador reflect a broad scenario that is converging across the continent, characterized by frequent violations of the migrants' rights. The more concentrated effects of that generalized pattern of structural violence are particularly evident in contexts of poverty among indigenous people, and especially among children and youth. These processes reflect the combined effects of the intensification of ancestral injustices (poverty, inequality, racism, and discrimination) as a result of the neoliberal policies associated with NAFTA, CAFTA, and their equivalents. All this is exacerbated by forced migration and forced displacement process attributable to the militarization promoted under both the so-called antidrug war and counterinsurgency policies, and due to the effects of the development of megaprojects, ecological devastation, and climate change. The systemic character of the resulting violations of rights requires a systemic answer in social and antipoverty policies, one that adequately takes into consideration the social and cultural specificity of the victims and the representative demands of their permanent resistance. These migrant children and youths, and their hopes and challenges, are the realization today of the spirit of the "sweeping utopia of life" invoked by Gabriel García Marquez in his Nobel Prize acceptance lecture in December 1982 (García Márquez, 1982) as a synthesis of the emancipation aspirations of our peoples:

> In spite of this, to oppression, plundering and abandonment we respond with life. Neither floods nor plagues, famines nor cataclysms, nor even the eternal wars of century upon century have been able to subdue the persistent advantage of life over death. An advantage that grows and quickens: every year, there are seventy-four million more births than deaths, a sufficient number of new lives to multiply, each year, the population of New York sevenfold. Most of these births occur in the countries of least resources-—including, of course, those of Latin America.
>
> Faced with this awesome reality that must have seemed a mere utopia through all of human time, we, the inventors of tales, who will believe anything, feel entitled to believe that it is not yet too late to engage in the creation of the opposite utopia.A new and sweeping utopia of life, where no one will be able to decide for others how they die, where love will prove true and happiness be possible, and where the races condemned to one hundred years of solitude will have, at last and forever, a second opportunity on earth.

This is the second chance that Noemi, and all the migrant minors who have shared her journey, deserves.

VI. Bibliography

UNHCR, 2014, *http://www.unhcr.org/53206a3d9.html*, *http://www.unhcrwashington.org/sites/default/files/UAC_UNHCR_Children%20on%20the%20Run_Full%20Report.pdf*.

Amnesty International, 2010, *Invisible Victims*, London, Amnesty International.

World Bank (WDR), 2013, World Development Report.

Benhabib, Seyla, 2004, *Los derechos de los otros: extranjeros, residentes, y ciudadanos*,Madrid, Gedisa.

Castellanos, Laura, 2014, "Mexico niega asilo a niños migrantes,"*El Universal*, *http://www.eluniversal.com.mx/nacion-mexico/2014/mexico-niega-asilo-a-ninios-migrantes-1026219.html*.

Castles, Stephen, 2003, "Towards a Sociology of Forced Migration and Social Transformation," *Sociology*, No. 37.

CDHM Tlachinollan, 2005, 2011, *http://www.tlachinollan.org/Archivos/Migrar %20o%2 0morir.pdf, http://www.tlachinollan.org/Descargas/Migrantes_somos_web.pdf.*

Centro Pro/WOLA, 2011, *http://www.wola.org/es/informes/un_trayecto_peligroso_por _mexico_violaciones_a_derechos_humanos_en_contra_de_los_migrantes_.*

Dussel, Enrique, 1998, *La ética de la liberación en la edad de la globalización y la exclusión*,Barcelona, Trotta.

Enciso, Angélica, 2012, "Este año morirán 10 mil niños por enfermedades de la desnutrición,"*La Jornada, http://www.jornada.unam.mx/2012/10/16/sociedad /040n1soc.*

Excelsior, 2014, *http://sipse.com/mexico/fosas-clandestinas-mexico-guerra-narcotrafico-7 8892.html.*

Frontera News Service (FNS), 2014, *http://fnsnews.nmsu.edu/a-little-girl-named-nohe mimartyr-of-migration/.*

Gaborit *et al.*/BID, 2012, *http://www10.iadb.org/intal/intalcdi/PE/2013/11 480.pdf.*

García Márquez, Gabriel, 1982, "La soledad de América Latina, "*http://www.nobelprize.org/ nobel_prizes/literature/laureates/1982/marquez-lecture-sp.html, http://www.ciudadseva.com/textos/otros/la_soledad_de_america_latina.htm.*

Grosfoguel, Ramon, Entrevista, *http://www.analectica.org/entrevista-a-ramon-grosfoguel/* .José Antonio, Gurrea Colin, 2014, "Viaja sólo 53% de los menores migrantes,"*El Universal, http://www.eluniversal.com.mx/estados/2014/impreso/viaja-solo-53- de-los-menores-migrantes-95295.html.*

La Jornada, 2010, "Migración infantil catástrofe" (editorial), *La Jornada, http://www.jor na.da.unam.mx/2010/11/12/edito.*Ciro, Pérez Silva, 2014, "Desacató Mexico trámites esenciales en caso de niña muerta en albergue,"*La Jornada, http://www.jornada.unam.mx/2014 /07/10/politica/016n1pol.*

Larrea, Miren/Clacso, 2007, *http://www.biblioteca.clacso.edu.ar/ar/libros/grupos/barba/ 13la rrea.pdf.*

Martínez, Óscar, 2010, *Los migrantes que no importan*, Oaxaca, Sur + Ediciones.

Mexico Social, octubre de 2012.

Mignolo, Walter, 2001, "La colonialidad: la cara oculta de la modernidad, "*http://iberoamer icanaliteratura.files.wordpress.com/2012/07/walter_mignolo_modernologies_ca s.pdf.*

New York Times, 2014, Spanish version published in *El Diario de El Paso, http://diario.mx/ El_Paso/2014-04-19_708296f5/solo-queremos-recuperarnos-y-seguir-adelante/,* and in English: *http://www.nytimes.com/2014/04/20/nyregion /a-12-year-olds- trek-of-despair-ends-in-a-noose-at-the-border.html.*

UN, 2013, http://www.hchr.org.mx/index.php?option=com_content&view=article& id=925: examen-periodico-universal-mexico-segundo-ciclo&catid=100:historias-destacad as&Itemid=94.

Pérez-Bustillo, 2009, "Ningún ser humano es ilegal," in *Balance de los derechos humanos en el sexenio de Fox*, Mexico, UACM/PRD.

Pérez-Bustillo, Camilo, and Hernández,Mares (comps.), 2012, *Los pueblos en movimiento: selección de documentos de trabajo de la primera etapa del eje sobre migración y desplazamiento forzado del proceso mexicano del Tribunal Permanente de los Pueblos (TPP), 2010–2012*, Mexico, Regional Office of the Rosa Luxemburg Foundation.

PNUD, 2010, *Los municipios de Mexico en el contexto internacional de IDH*, http://www.und p.org.mx/spip.php?page=area_interior&id_rubrique=123&id_pa rent=119.

Quijano, Aníbal, 2000, "Colonialidad del poder, eurocentrismo y América Latina," in Lander, Edgardo (comp.), *La colonialidad del saber: eurocentrismo y ciencias sociales, pers pectivas latinoamericanas*, Buenos Aires, CLACSO, http://biblioteca virtual.cla cso.org.ar/ar/libros/lander/lander.html.

RIMISP/IDRC/IFAD, 2011, *El Informe Latinoamericano sobre Pobreza y Desigualdad*, http://www.idrc.ca/EN/Programs/Agriculture_and_the_Environment/Agriculture _and_Food_Security/Pages/ResultDetails.Aspx?ResultID=103, http://www.in for melatinoamericano.org/.

Rajagopal, Balakrishnan, 2005, *El derecho internacional desde abajo: el desarrollo, los movimientos sociales, y la resistencia del tercer mundo*, Bogotá, ILSA, http://ilsa.org.co:81/biblioteca/dwnlds/eclvs/eclvs08/Eclvs08-00.pdf.

de Sousa Santos, Boaventura and Rodríguez, César (comps.), 2005, "Introduction," in *El derecho y la globalización desde abajo: Hacia una legalidad cosmopolita*, Mexico, Antropos-UAM Iztapalapa, http://ilsa.org.co:81/biblioteca/dwnlds/eclvs/eclvs 08/Eclvs08-00.pdf.

TICPM, 2011, *Ningún ser humano es ilegal: Conclusiones iniciales del Tribunal Internacional de Conciencia de los Pueblos en Movimiento*, Mexico, Oficina Regional de la Fundación Rosa Luxemburg.

UNICEF, 2008, http://www.unicef.org/socialpolicy/files/Childhood_and_Migration_in_Canar.pdf.

CHILDREN RIGHTS: A FRAMEWORK FOR THE CONSTRUCTION OF SOCIAL POLICY AND FOR THE ERADICATION OF POVERTY IN LATIN AMERICA AND THE CARIBBEAN

Yedith Guillén Fernández[1]

> I. The focus of children's rights and the need to develop social protection for the children. II. TMC *vs.* universal protection schemes to eliminate poverty and deprivation among children in Latin America. III. An analysis of the socioeconomic factors that impact deprivation among children in the case of Mexico. IV. Compared social policy model and children's rights for the elimination of child poverty in Latin America. V. Conclusions. VI. Bibliography. VII. Appendix.

I. The focus of children's rights and the need to develop social protection for the children

The international treaty on the "Rights of the Child" emerged from a universal consensus among the international community in the 1989 United Nations Convention (Convention on the Rights of the Child, UNCRC), which considers children as persons subject to protection and, therefore, promotes compliance with these rights [United Nations General Assembly (UNGA), 1989]. This framework is derived from the Universal Declaration of Human Rights (UDHR), approved in 1948, which includes the universal acknowledgment that all human beings are entitled to the rights and freedoms that have been universally agreed, including the right to a standard of living adequate for themselves and their families, through access to food, clothing, housing, and medical care, and necessary social services, social

---

[1] Doctoral candidate in social policy from the University of Bristol; graduate studies researcher for the "Child Poverty and Quality of Government-A global analysis" project from the Swedish Research Council, which includes the participation of the University of Gothenburg and the "The Townsend Centre for International Poverty Research" of the University of Bristol.
We appreciate the comments received for the final version of this paper from the participants of the international "Child Poverty, Public Policy and Democracy" seminar and its Committee. We also thank David Gordon, PhD, director of the Townsend Centre for International Poverty Research of the University of Bristol and Professor Ricardo Mora Téllez, doctoral candidate in Population Studies from Colegio de México.

security, and *social protection for all children*[United Nations General Assembly (UNGA), 1948; articles 25 and 26]. Under the specific framework of children rights (1989), the United Nations Convention has established obligations for the state, society, and families to guarantee the protection and safeguarding of the welfare of the child. For example, article 26 of the UNCRC assigns states parties the responsibility of recognizing for every child the right to benefit from social security and indicates that the necessary measures shall be taken to achieve the full realization of this right in accordance with their national law.

In this way, the United Nations recognizes that *child poverty and deprivation involve the violation of the rights of the child* and for that purpose define the set of basic needs and services children must have access to so that their rights are guaranteed:

> Children living in poverty are deprived of nutrition, water, and sanitation facilities, access to basic health-care services, shelter, education, participation and protection, and that while a severe lack of goods and services hurts every human being, it is most threatening and harmful to children, leaving them unable to enjoy their rights, to reach their full potential and to participate as full members of the society. [United Nations General Assembly (UNGA), 2006: 46]

Gordon *et al.* (2003) state that severe deprivation of basic rights has serious adverse consequences that may be irreparable in the short- or long term for the health, well-being, or the development of the children. Therefore, the ratification of the international human rights treaties and declarations makes nation-states into parties and makes them assume obligations under international law to guarantee their compliance with human rights; therefore, governments must cooperate for that purpose, providing procedures to implement international treaties in their internal legal system. This implies that if the national legal protection cannot solve human rights abuses, then there is a regional and international mechanism for the application of international human rights regulations at the local level [United Nations General Assembly (UNGA, 1948)]. Therefore, since legal structures are available, adequate mechanisms for the judicialization of human, social, and children's rights are implemented through cooperation between local and national governments. Approximately 191 nation-states defined mechanisms for compliance with children rights. The states determined sanctions in the 1989 UNCRC to protect children from malnourishment, maltreatment, neglect, abuse, and exploitation to prevent them from being deprived of public services they are entitled to, including education and information. In addition, they agreed that adequate institutions must be created to give their citizens the right to social security [United Nations General Assembly (UNGA, 1989)].

Pemberton et al. (2012) have described the value of the human rights approach for the reduction of child poverty, and they support their arguments on Robinson (former UN High Commissioner for Human Rights), who in 2002, during the World Summit for Sustainable Growth, highlighted the importance of human rights conventions, because they impose transcendental duties on nations-states. She mentions in her speech that " a human rights approach adds value because it provides a normative framework of obligations that has the legal power to render governments accountable" (Robinson, 2002: 1). Given that the framework of human rights establishes universally agreed standards, which are violated by the existence of child poverty, then, this framework suggests comprehensive social protection models and evaluation mechanisms for the social policy formulation and implementation process [Committee on Economic, Social and Cultural Rights (CESCR), 2001; United Nations, 2004; Townsend, 2009; Pemberton et al., 2012; Donald and Mottershaw, 2009; Gordon and Nandy, 2012].

1. Social policy and mechanisms for the protection of children rights

The human rights principles that have been established in the UDHR are universality, interdependence, indivisibility, equality, and nondiscrimination (1948). Based on this perspective, Despouy (1996) argues that poverty is not considered as a denial of a right or of a category of rights in particular, but as a denial of human rights as a whole; therefore, social protection systems must be developed from this perspective. Townsend (2009) recognizes that the policies offered to protect the welfare of children in the developing world have not been enough to achieve the 2000 Millennium Development Goal of eradicating extreme poverty, hunger, and child mortality by 2015; likewise, the author identifies the problem that the approach of social security for children is based on the family unit, that is to say, derived from the social benefits the household may or may not be entitled to have access to as a whole; therefore, the child is not recognized as a subject of rights on its own.

In this sense, the International Labour Organization (ILO) (2001) indicates that there is a major problem with respect to social security coverage, particularly in the developing world, where a large portion of the population is engaged in informal activities. If this is true, then many children are not entitled to social security and health care, as they depend on their parents; in this sense, the right to access these public services, and particularly health care, must be seen as a right of each individual, from birth. These issues lead us to address the problem of access to social security for all citizens, as stipulated in the UDHR. It is thus that Cichon and Scholz (2009) have analyzed the correlation between economic growth and the increase of the investment in social protection in OECD (Organization for Economic Cooperation and Development) countries. The authors showed that a *redistributive mechanism, such as social security transfers*,[2] is necessary to find an incentive for the reduction of poverty and, thus, have an effect on social development; therefore, economic growth is not a direct or automatic mechanism to alleviate poverty. Rather, it is necessary to invest in social protection to boost the economy and to prevent and eradicate poverty.

The following figures (chart 1) show a change in the incidence of poverty as a measure of income,[3] before and after the transfers (it includes social benefits and cash transfers), for OECD countries, including Chile and Mexico. In this way, we can see that these two Latin American countries show that the social and public spending percentage, as a percentage of GDP, is low, and therefore, they reduce income-based poverty in a small proportion, before and after the transfers in 2011, with respect to European countries, which spend a greater percentage, as can be seen. This is an example of how social transfers may impact the reduction of poverty, as a measure of income, if there is a greater investment in social spending; however, the rest of the study argues that poverty is multidimensional, and it shows that the social protection system is broader, and that social programs such as the TMC in LatAm have not substantially reduced poverty and deprivation among children.

---

2   Social transfers, according to the definition by the Organization for Economic Cooperation and Development (OECD) (2003), include social security benefits, other social security benefits in kind, social assistance benefits in kind, individual transfers of goods and services produced as nonmarket output.
3   The poverty threshold is set at 50% the average income of the population.

Chart 1. Income-based poverty among OECD countries, before and after social transfers, 2011

Country	Net total social spending as a percentage of GDP*	Public spending in families as a percentage of GDP**	Public spending in health as a percentage of GDP	Rate of poverty in the total population***	
				Before the transfers	After the transfers
Chile	13.2	1.5	3.7	0.23	0.18
Mexico	9.2	1.1	3.1	0.27	0.21
United Kingdom	27.6	3.8	8.1	0.30	0.10
Sweden	26.3	3.7	7.3	0.27	0.10
Norway	20.5	3.2	6.2	0.26	0.08

Source: Prepared internally with information from Organization for Economic Cooperation and Development (OECD) (2014).
Note: The information on the spending categories is from 2009.
*The information includes cash transfers and benefits.
**The information includes benefits in kind and in cash.
***The poverty line is set at 50% of the average income of the population before/after transfers and taxes. The information for Mexico is from 2012.

Townsend proposes the development of mechanisms to comply with the principle of progressivity, as a strategy to deal with affordability in the coverage of social security and public health services. For example, Thailand is characterized by starting a fragmentary approach that started serving the poor with a low-income scheme implemented in 1975 and it also involved a progressive initiative that subsequently allowed for universal coverage in 2002. Since its democratic transition in 1990, South Africa has set in motion strategies for progressive compliance with human rights and social security, and economic growth has not been hindered (Townsend, 2009). In Latin America, Costa Rica has the most comprehensive social security health coverage, and it is compulsory for the entire population (van Ginneken, 2003). In Norway, two general types of social plans have been considered: the universal scheme, which is particularly important to provide free education and health care and for the development of infrastructure, and the focalization involved in providing social security only to those that are classified as poor based on a certain poverty threshold (Villanger, 2008). Thus, it is proposed that policies must be progressive to respect the social rights of the citizens; the issue of the affordability of social protection plans may be overcome through various economic strategies, specially linked to tax collection and redistribution, but this issue is also linked to other social factors, such as solidarity (Lister, 2007; Townsend, 2008).

2. Rights in childhood and citizenship

This section shows that the recognition of child citizenship facilitates progress toward compliance with children's rights. One of the aspects of the recognition of child citizenship is exercising justice for the children who live in poverty, which implies social commitment, political participation, decision-making, among other aspects, so that children may have access to economic, social, and public resources. For this purpose, the accessibility of services, the availability of information, and advice are crucial in the reduction of the gap between formal rights and the actual enjoyment of rights in practice, especially for groups that live in poverty (Lister, 2008). The link between citizenship and rights allows us to find new avenues to apply democracy. Thus, the recognition of citizenship contributes to the fight against poverty, social exclusion, discrimination, and social inequalities (Gibbons, 2006). Several researchers have argued for the need to consider children as full-fledged citizens, so that they may have access to the public services provided by the state, and therefore, participate in the social benefits provided by their societies. Child poverty implies the violation of children rights and the denial of the minimum guarantees and freedoms that have been established in the UNCRC. Children who endure poverty and social deprivation do not participate as full members of society, and therefore, the state and society do not provide the means for their personal and social development (Townsend, 1979, 2008; Gordon et al., 2003; Minujin et al., 2006).

Minujin (2009) states that the most pressing poverty is the one that emerges from the denial of citizen rights, and citizenship integrates social, cultural, economic, civil, and political rights. Likewise, citizenship includes the enjoyment of social rights, in addition to the form of guaranteeing them for them to become effective. The author resorts to Marshall (1998) to argue that it is the condition of citizenship that allows everyone to have equal rights and duties in society; in particular, participation, which is one of the principles defined in the UNCRC, captures the essence of the meaning of citizenship; the concept refers to "the ability to express the decisions that are recognized by the social environment, and which affect the lives of everyone and the life of the community where one lives." Therefore, we can deduct from this statement that children are part of the community as a whole and, therefore, they are citizens in their own right (Minujin, 2009, quoting Hart, 1993:23–4). This would allow the possibility of implementing a mechanism for the judicialization of children rights. Bustelo (2001) indicates that the way to extend citizenship in Latin America, where enormous differences in the distribution of income and wealth prevail, is through the respect of the social and economic rights, because it is in their domain that citizenship may converge toward equality. Thus, the social policy agenda in Latin America must be oriented toward the advancement of social citizenship, with the aim of preventing poverty, social exclusion, and inequalities. In addition, the author holds that this implies a concept of governance that includes respecting social rights, and it depends on a global commitment for its expansion and for the strengthening of participative democracy. But citizenship may also be oriented through Universalist schemes as a social protection system that may contribute to the development of stable democratic nations where social, civil, and political rights are respected, as has been seen in historical processes in most developed countries (Neubourg, 2009).

A democratization process that started in the 1990s can be seen in Latin America, where the UNCRC, enacted in 1990, influenced the creation of national laws for the realization of human rights in those countries. The UNCRC represents a transcendental effort in the contribution of social change in LatAm countries on behalf of children, given that poverty has been criminalized for children who lack sufficient means for an adequate standard of living. In Brazil, for instance, children rights were incorporated in article 227 of the 1988 Constitution, and in Chile, after 20 years of reducing social spending during the dictatorship, the state started a process of educational reform, established in their constitution since 2003, which guarantees the right to complete 12 years of free education for all children. From that moment on, UNICEF started the commitment to participate in the development of social policies to meet the minimum standards established in the convention (UNCRC). In consequence, Chile benefited from the consolidation of these processes and from the creation of democratic institutions; therefore, it started to correct various social inequalities (Gibbons, 2006). The importance of considering children as full-fledged citizens leads to the possibility that children, or someone acting on their behalf, may claim their social rights, and the possibility that society and the state may develop legal and social policy mechanisms to guarantee that the rights of children are respected, and that children may participate in society.

II. TMC vs. universal protection schemes to eliminate poverty and deprivation among children in Latin America

The social protection system is defined by the United Nations (2000) as a set of public policies and programs approved for different contingencies to compensate the absence or reduction of income, as well as to assist families with children and to provide access to health and housing services. Cecchini and Martínez (2011) explain that the lack of social security is a problem, and it may be a cause of poverty: The authors mention that, based on data from Comisión Económica para Latin America y el Caribe (CEPAL) (2010), there were 183 million people living in poverty in LatAm in 2009, that is to say, a third of the total population of the region. Of them, 74 million people lived in extreme poverty or destitution, and between 2008 and 2009, three million people fell in extreme poverty, due to the world economic crisis, the rise of unemployment, informality, and *insufficient social protection mechanisms*.

In addition, less than half of those employed are included in the formal labor market and have some kind of contributive social protection to face contingencies and structural risks; however, this does not apply to those who are excluded from the formal labor market, and therefore have no access to mechanisms of this kind. Likewise, there are other groups that are not included in the contributive regime; therefore, if they do not belong to another kind of social protection, they face a significant risk of falling into poverty, for example, in adverse economic circumstances. These groups are *elderly citizens, children*, and *people with disabilities*. Noncontributive social protection systems, such as social transfers programs, were designed to cover this population. Based on the above, the social protection system in Latin America may be classified into two main types: noncontributive regimes, known as *social assistance programs*, which may include universalist or focalized measures, and the contributive social protection system, known as the *socialsecurity regime* (Román, 2012). However, the different countries in the region have a particular history in the execution of their social protection system as a whole, as well as in the design of policies against poverty.

Evidence shows that conditional cash transfer programs (TMC) have some positive impacts on only some of the fields of human capital, such as education and nutrition, as in Nicaragua, with the implementation of the "Social Protection Network" (RPS) program.[4] However, these programs do not reduce or alleviate poverty; their impact is more in the reduction of the poverty gap in some countries of Latin America, as happened with the *Oportunidades* program in Mexico, which tends to have an important effect on the severity of poverty, but the impact on the proportion of poor homes is minimum (Skoufias and Parker, 2001; Godoy, 2004; Maluccio and Flores, 2004). Other assessments of the impact, for Brazil, in the application of the *Bolsa Escola* program, show that grants in Brazil have had a low impact on the reduction of poverty due to the small amount of transfers that have been made. Also, the program has had no positive effects for families to generate autonomous income (Godoy, 2004). Also Rawlings (2002) posits that, for Colombia, the *Familias en Acción* program shows an inability to cover rural and isolated areas, because the areas selected must meet basic eligibility criteria, such as the existence of a bank and the presence of an adequate supply in terms of education and health, which results in a significant likelihood of exclusion, or, for Nicaragua, in the application of the RPS program, where geographic distance is a determining factor for children to attend school (Villatoro, 2005). The viability of TMC programs to guarantee that their beneficiaries may cross the line of poverty is not clear: in the short term, it depends on the amount of transfers received; and in the focalization of the program, the more poor the households are, the more complex it will be for them to overcome the poverty threshold, and it also depends on economic crises not taking place. In the medium term, it will depend on the ability of families to generate income independently, which in turn depends on the quality of education, employment rates, general rates of return of the education, and so on (Villatoro, 2004; Britto, 2006). From all of this, we may deduct that TMC programs are aimed at the poor, and their purpose is to mitigate the effect of the economic crisis, whereas universalism has a different logic, as it implies respecting the social rights of the people.

---

4   According to the impact assessment study of the "Social Protection Network" (RPS) in Nicaragua, a double difference was estimated in enrollment changes between the group of the intervention and the control group, 22% between 2000 and 2001 and 18% between 2002 and 2000 (Maluccio and Flores, 2004).

However, the panorama is more promising in terms of the eradication of child poverty for Chile, Costa Rica, and Uruguay. Child poverty and deprivation figures may be analyzed in light of their social protection system. CEPAL and UNICEF (2010) estimate that child poverty, as measured by household income, shows the lowest rates in Costa Rica, with 21% of the children; in Chile, with 23% of the children; and in Uruguay, with 24%. In addition, when moderate and severe deprivations are calculated jointly, Chile, Costa Rica, and Uruguay show lower rates than the Latin American average; the average for the three countries is considered to be 5% for deprivation to the access to education, 6% for sanitation, 5% for drinking water, 12% for housing quality, and 3% for information. The social security system of Costa Rica, compared to other Latin American systems, shows a series of significant achievements; although social security is very low in two-thirds of Latin America, Costa Rica is the country in the region with the largest social security coverage in terms of health, with 87% of the total population (Mesa-Lago, 2008). According to Robles (2009), universal social assistance programs in LatAm have been initiatives by the governments of Chile, Argentina, Uruguay, and Costa Rica.[5]

III. An analysis of the socioeconomic factors that impact deprivation among children in the case of Mexico

Several pioneers of poverty studies, such as Townsend (1979), Altimir (1979), Sen (1982), and others, argue that poverty and deprivations have a multidimensional nature; therefore, it is necessary to develop pertinent measurements, aimed at the development of social policies that seek the enforcement of the rights to alleviate child poverty. The design of the current social policy against poverty in Latin America in general has not considered specific measures of child deprivation; that is to say, children are not identified directly when they present violations to their rights; child poverty is estimated indirectly, considering the children as part of their households; for example, the *Oportunidades* program in Mexico selects its target population based on the poverty threshold measured as per their monthly

---

5   For example, Chile implements the "Chile Crece Contigo" program, therefore it provides children under 5 years universal access to public services in the fields of healthcare, early childhood education, among others. This program is based on the Law No. 20.379, which establishes that every child must be treated as an individual with his own rights (Ministry of Planning, 2009).

per capita income, not based on specific childhood indicators that speak of their social deprivations [Gordon, 2008; Minujin *et al.*, 2006; Diario Oficial de la Federación (DOF), 2013]. Not all resources can be expressed in terms of money; there are public goods and services distributed in areas other than the market, which are also part of social welfare (Ringen, 1988; Boltvinik, 2000).

Consejo Nacional de Evaluación de la Política de Desarrollo Social (Coneval) (2010)[6] has developed a multidimensional childhood poverty measurement index that involves economic welfare and social rights. The results appear in UNICEF and Coneval (2013), and it is estimated that as of 2012, 76.2% of children in Mexico showed at least one social deprivation, thus indicating that social policies have not sufficed to eradicate child poverty. Likewise, it has been proposed that the population of children in poverty and deprivation is a heterogeneous set that presents different characteristics, which are related to multiple aspects of inequality, such as the status of income, the gender, ethnic origin, or geographic location [United Nations Research Institute for Social Development (UNRISD), 2011]. Therefore, this study proposes exploring the factors that are associated with social deprivations in childhood; for example, a determining factor is the size of the site in which children in poverty and deprivation live, because the incidence of poverty shows a 26% difference between rural and urban locations, but this difference grows to 35% when related to deprivations due to access to social security. In the same way, indigenous childrenpresent greater disadvantages with respect to the total of the children population; that is to say, 94% of indigenous children present one or more social deprivations. On the contrary, the number of wage earners in the household tends to reduce poverty; particularly noteworthy is the case of homes with at least of two wage earners, since this is associated with the possibility of the members of the home having social security. Likewise, the higher educational level of the head of the family keeps an inverse relationship with respect to the incidence of childhood poverty; that is to say, the figure of childhood poverty is reduced from 65 to 37% when the head of the home has secondary or higher studies (UNICEF and Coneval, 2013).

---

6 The National Council for the Evaluation of Social Development Policy in Mexico was created under the General Law for Social Development (LGDS) for the implementation of institutional mechanisms to evaluate and monitor social development policies [Consejo Nacional de Evaluación de la Política de Desarrollo Social (Coneval), 2010].

In consequence, it is imperative to explore the factors associated with deprivation among children, to find out not only the social deprivations of the children but also the conditions in which they live. In this way, we can provide adequate public services and implement policies that are consistent with the enforcement of children's rights. In this analysis, we consider the case of Mexico using data provided by the Socioeconomic Conditions Module of the 2012 ENIGH (the National Household Income and Spending Survey), and we estimate a logistic regression model. As a dependent variable, we use the index of social deprivation among children based on the poverty measurement methodology developed by Coneval[7] for children aged between 3 and 17. This measurement indicates if the child is deprived of at least one of the social rights from this set; in this case, the dependent variable assumes the values of 1 and 0 when the child has no social deprivation. The explanatory variables or factors associated with deprivation among children that were significant in the logistic regression model are as follows:

- The gender of the head of the home, which controls whether the woman supports the home.
- The type of location: urban or rural.
- The rate of dependency, which shows the ability of the homes to generate income.
- The benefits (cash transfers) from government programs, including the *Oportunidades* program.
- The educational level of the head of the home.
- The number of wage earners in the home.

(Chart A1 in the Appendix shows the operational construction of the variables.)

---

7   For the construction of the dependent variable, we considered specific childhood indicators, such as access to food and educational level; however, access to health, social security, housing quality, and quantity are defined with respect to household income.

Chart 2. Logistic model: beta coefficients, significance, and the odds ratios of presenting deprivation among children

Variables	β_i	Odds ratios	P>|z|
Constant	2.733	15.385	0.000
Gender of the head of the home	0.082	1.085	0.001
Type of location	1.033	2.810	0.000
Dependency rate	0.215	1.240	0.000
Government benefits	0.000	1.000	0.000
Educational level of the head of the home	−0.318	0.728	0.000
Number of wage earners in the home	−0.138	0.871	0.000

Source: Model estimated with data from the 2012 ENIGH survey.
Note: The significance level of regressors is *P*<0.05.

In chart 2, we can see that coefficients β_i of the regression are significant, and their sign shows the direct or inverse relationship between the different factors associated and the dependent variable (deprivation among children). Likewise, the odd ratios estimated show the probability ratio of experiencing deprivation *versus* not experiencing it, given a certain risk factor, and maintaining everything else constant. See graph 1, which allows us to identify that when the confidence interval for the odd ratios falls in 1, it means that there is no difference in the occurrence of deprivation among children *versus* the nonoccurrence, given a risk factor; but when the interval exceeds 1, it means that the occurrence increases; on the other hand, a value of less than 1 means that the occurrence is reduced (Morris and Gardner, 1988) (chart A2 in the appendix shows the values of the intervals). Therefore, odd ratios reflect a higher likelihood of occurrence of deprivation among children under 18 years when they live in *rural areas* compared to their counterparts who live in urban areas. Likewise, the occurrence of the event increases, but to a lesser degree, for each additional person at home who is considered as *not economically active*, and when children live in homes where there are *female heads of family* than when men are the heads of the family.

Graph 1. Confidence intervals for odds ratios of the occurrence of deprivation among children

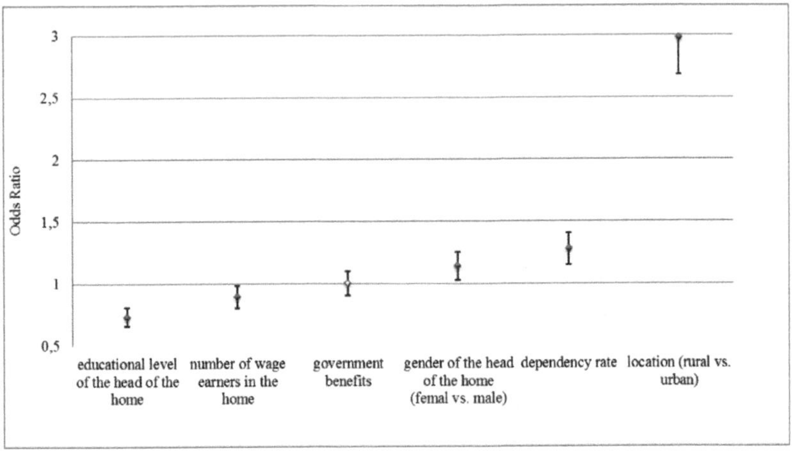

Source: Prepared internally from the results of the logistical model estimated to obtain the odds ratios of the occurrence of deprivation among children and with data from the 2012 ENIGH.

On the contrary, the number of wage earners and the *level of additional education of the head of the home* are factors that influence the reduction of deprivation among children in Mexico. However, the governmental benefits, measured as economic transfers, do not influence the increase or decrease of social deprivation in childhood. This confirms that, to eradicate deprivation among children, it is necessary that the state complies with the provision of public services associated with the rights of the children, with a universal policy, which shall be implemented considering not only the deprivation that children experience but also their environment, that is to say, considering the factors of greater risk.

IV. Compared social policy model and children's rights for the elimination of child poverty in Latin America

The comparative model presented in this section is the result of a review of the social protection systems and some questions related to the legal framework for the enforcement of children's rights in Latin American countries. Theorizing the design and implementation processes related to social policies against poverty in Latin America involves deep reflections on the relationship between children's rights, the policy mechanisms required for their enforcement, their relationship with poverty and social deprivation, and the evaluation of the empirical studies with respect to the social protection and social assistance regimes that have been implemented in LatAm. Tag (2013) indicates the importance of the development of analysis strategies; therefore, this paper proposes several guidelines for Latin American countries to assist them in finding viable mechanisms for the application of policies against child poverty and to guarantee children's rights.[8]

The strategies to implement social protection schemes for the enforcement of children's rights may follow different paths in each country. Several scholars have classified Latin American countries based on their social protection schemes and on the role of the state in the implementation of the policies against child poverty, known as "welfare regime typologies." Filgueira and Filgueira (2002) identify the capacity of the Chilean and Uruguayan states to assume commitments to benefit their citizens, based on rights-based content; their social protection system is identified as a *universalsocial security system* and as an *incremental welfare system*, respectively. Chile started a neoliberal system in the 1990s, and it implemented a social scheme based on groups of people who live in extreme poverty; their system is incremental, because currently it is expanding its social protection scheme based on citizenship, and it implements social assistance programs for the most vulnerable groups, and a universal system based on early childhood in the areas of health, education, disability, community welfare, among others, through its national legal system (Ministry of Planning, 2009).[9] Robles (2009) identifies three major components in these two countries: social assistance, social security, and regulation of job markets; with this perspective, the state is able to coordinate the supply of public services with the incorporation of *regulatory and legal*

---

8   Tag (2013) is based on the idea of the theorization for dissemination and quotes Strang and Meyer (1993), who argue that social entities, individuals, organizations and states are constructed in world politics as modern actors in theoretically complex, standardized and comparable forms, therefore, these theorized forms earn legitimacy (Tag, 2013: 32). Theorizing social policy processes to implement more adequate policies allows society and the State to influence the different institutions to enforce the rights of the child.

9   The program is Chile Crece Contigo, which is a program targeted at early childhood, created under Law No. 20.379, which guarantees children's rights (Ministry of Planning, 2009).

frameworks that support the social rights established in the UNCRC. In general, Latin American countries have incorporated the framework of children's rights into their internal legal system; however, in the Caribbean region, there are restrictions because international human rights treaties are not fully applicable in the internal law of the countries, despite their ratification by Caribbean nation-states. Haiti is an exception, because its constitution recognizes that the international treaties ratified by the state must be incorporated into the law (Morlachetti, 2010, 2013).

On the other hand, Filgueira (1998) also identifies two types of social security systems and welfare regimes that are not universal: dual and exclusionary regimes. Mexico and Brazil may be classified as dual regimes, because they are heterogeneous in the distribution of resources, which implies diversity in the implementation of social protection plans, such as stratified forms in urban areas and exclusionary forms in rural areas. Exclusionary regimes are represented by Bolivia, Ecuador, El Salvador, Guatemala, Honduras, Nicaragua, and the Dominican Republic, where specific or elite groups are selected as beneficiaries, according to Martínez (2008). They can be classified as residual states characterized by a nonexistent public redistribution of resources.

Based on the Latin American experience, it is possible to deduce some strategies to make the transition to an integral social protection system, which have been defined since the 1990s by Comisión Económica para Latin America y el Caribe (CEPAL) (2006), such as the creation of a social and fiscal pact, which includes the development of social institutions with equity, solidarity, and efficiency goals, and which may be materialized in the national legal system and public policies. Norton *et al.* (2009) include the supervision of the enforcement of social rights in social policy, which implies informing the citizens of their social rights, benefits, and the mandatory standards, so that, as Robles (2009) mentions, basic rights are explicit, guaranteed, and enforceable, which is compatible with the idea of the judiciability of the rights.

Chart 3 summarizes the elements discussed in this section on the analysis of the social protection schemes of some countries of Latin America and compares them with social spending percentages and their incidence of child poverty; it also lists the national laws that stipulate children's rights and that therefore recognize the provisions of the UNCRC. Some countries were selected based on low, medium, and high levels of child poverty, as a measure of moderate and severe deprivations:

Chart 3. Compared social policy model and children's rights in Latin America

Country	Type of social protection scheme*
	Universal Scheme

Costa Rica		
Social spending as a % of GDP 2011**	Child poverty incidence (%) 2011***	Laws enacted to enforce the social rights of children
23	20	-Law 7739 Code for Childhood and Adolescence (1998)
Chile		
14	16	-Law 20.032 Children and Teenager Care System
Uruguay		
23	19	-Law 17823 Code for Childhood and Adolescence (2004)
Dual Scheme		
Brazil		
26	34	-Law 8.242 (1991) and Decree 5089 (2004) National Council of the Rights of the Child and the Adolescent (CONANDA)
Mexico		
12	38	- Law for the protection of the rights of Children and Adolescents (2000)
Exclusionary Scheme		
Ecuador		
9	41	-Code for Childhood and Adolescence, Law 100 (2003)
Honduras		
11	63	-Code for Childhood and Adolescence (1996)

Source: Prepared internally with data from CEPAL (2013: 101), Comisión Económica para Latin America y el Caribe (CEPAL) (2012: 173), Morlachetti (2013), and Filgueira and Filgueira (2002).
*The classification of social protection regimes based on Filgueira *et al.* considers Costa Rica and Chile in the universal scheme because they implement integral social protection regimes.
**Social spending for Brazil is that of 2010.
***Child poverty is measured with respect to moderate and extreme deprivation among children. The incidence of child poverty for Mexico and Honduras is from 2010.

If we consider social spending as an indispensable component for the realization of the principle of progressivity established in the UNCRC (article 44), it can be seen that the countries that have implemented universal protection schemes and those that allocated a significant percentage of social spending as a percentage of GDP meet the goal, because they show lower levels of child poverty, as happens with Costa Rica, Chile, and Uruguay, with an average incidence of child poverty of 18% and an average social spending of 20% in 2011. Brazil and Mexico integrate the dual scheme, and in these countries, there is an average child poverty incidence of 36%, but a different level of social spending; it must be noted that Brazil shows higher rates of rural poverty compared to the countries of the region, 82% compared to 61% in Mexico (CEPAL, 2013: 196); however, Mexico presents social spending levels similar to those of Ecuador and Honduras, which have implemented exclusionary social protection schemes and have high levels of child poverty. The provision of public goods and services for the enforcement of basic child rights also depends on transparency and efficiency mechanisms for the implementation of social policy. Therefore, we propose establishing a commitment among the Latin American states that have ratified the convention to implement measures to evaluate the social protection schemes based on the principle of progressivity.

V. Conclusions

Lastly, we will respond to the research questions of this paper. First, poverty in childhood is a violation of the rights of the children. To prevent children from experiencing social deprivation, it is necessary to implement universal social protection systems in Latin America that provide public goods and services for all children, to meet the basic rights to nutrition, water, and sanitation, access to basic health care services, housing, participation, and protection, defined by the United Nations General Assembly (UNGA) and established in the UNCRC. Evidence shows that the implementation of focalized TMC programs in the region has not reduced child poverty and deprivations. In turn, the experiences of countries such as Chile, Uruguay, and Costa Rica show low levels of child poverty and deprivation incidence and stand out for the implementation of universal social protection schemes aimed at the enforcement of rights. Likewise, we propose that the design of child poverty policies is based on specific children indicators that account for their social deprivations and for the presence of risk factors associated with child deprivation, such as the rural environment, a high dependency rate, and a low educational level of the head of the home, because those factors have proven to be related in a significant manner to the lack of public services.

Likewise, we conclude that the eradication of child poverty will not be achieved unless there is work on the social policy and legal mechanisms required for the development of children citizenship, and thus, for the enforcement of their rights. We also recommend that the member states of the UNCRC implement progressive initiatives that may converge on a universal coverage of children's rights, with tax collection and redistribution and solidarity mechanisms, as well as by providing social security and social transfers. The compared policy aspects analyzed in the Latin American region made it possible to distinguish that countries such as Costa Rica, Chile, and Uruguay, which show the lowest poverty levels in LatAm, have implemented universal social protection systems supported by codes for children that recognize the rights of the child; it is necessary that state members of the UNCRC recognize these rights in their internal legal systems for them to be enforced and incorporated into social policy at all levels, so that children, or someone acting on their behalf, may claim the social rights that correspond to them as citizens, and to realize the idea of the judiciability of basic rights.

VI. Bibliography

Altimir, Oscar, 1979, *La dimensión de la pobreza en América Latina*, Santiago de Chile, Cuadernos de la CEPAL.

Boltvinik, Julio, 2000, "Métodos de medición de la pobreza. Una evaluación crítica," in *Socialis. Revista Latinoamericana de Política Social*, No. 2.

Britto, Tatiana, 2006, "Conditional Cash Transfers in Latin America," in *Poverty in Focus: Social PROTECTION, the ROLE of CASH TRANSFERS*," June.

Bustelo, Eduardo S., 2001, "Expansion of Citizenship and Democratic Construction. Contemporary Challenges and New Paradigms," in *The Poverty of Rights. Human Rights and the Eradication of Poverty*, London-New York, Zed Books-CROP International Series on Poverty.

Cecchini, Simone and Martínez, Rodrigo, 2011, *Protección social inclusiva en América Latina. Una mirada integral, un enfoque de derechos*, Santiago de Chile, United Nations-CEPAL.

CEPAL and UNICEF, 2010, *La pobreza infantil en América Latina y el Caribe*, United Nations.

Cichon, Michael and Scholz, Wolfgang, 2009, "Social Security, Social Impact and Economic Performance: A Farewell to Three Famous Myths," in *Building Decent Societies. Rethinking the Role of Social Security in Development*, London, Palgrave Macmillan.

Comisión Económica para Latin America y el Caribe (CEPAL), 2012, *Panorama social de Latin America, 2012*, Santiago de Chile, United Nations-CEPAL.

Comisión Económica para Latin America y el Caribe (CEPAL), 2010, *Panorama social de Latin America, 2009*, Santiago de Chile, United Nations and CEPAL.

Comisión Económica para Latin America y el Caribe (CEPAL), 2006, *La protección social de cara al futuro: acceso, financiamiento y solidaridad*, Santiago de Chile, United Nations.

Committee on Economic, Social and Cultural Rights (CESCR), 2001, "Substantive Issues Arising in the Implementation of the International Covenant on Economic, Social and Cultural Rights: Poverty and the International Covenant on Economic, Social and Cultural Rights," in Statement No. E/C.12/2001/10, May 10, 2001, Geneva, UN, *http://www.cetim.ch/es/documents/escr-pauvrete-esp.pdf* (retrieved in July 2012).

Consejo Nacional de Evaluación de la Política de Desarrollo Social (Coneval), 2010, *Metodología para la medición multidimensional de la pobreza en Mexico*, Mexico, Coneval.

Despouy, Léandro, 1996, "Rapport final sur les droits de l'Homme et l'extrême pauvreté, Rappourteur de la sous commission de la lutte contre les mesures discriminatoires et de la protection des minorités du Conseil *Économique* et Social de l'ONU, Quarantehuitième sesión," in *UNDocument ONU*, E/EC.4/Sub.2/1996/13, June 28, 1996, UN.

Diario Oficial de la Federación (DOF), 2013, "Acuerdo por el que se emiten las Reglas de Operación del Programa de Desarrollo Humano Oportunidades, para el ejercicio fiscal 2014,"*Diario Oficial de la Federación*, December 30, 2013, *http://www.oportunidades.gob.mx/Portal/work/sites/Web/resources/ArchivoCo ntent/2479/DOF%20-%20PDHO%20301213.pdf* (retrieved on July 2014).

Donald, Alice and Mottershaw, Elizabeth, 2009, *Poverty, Inequality and Human Rights: Do Rights Make a difference?*, York, Joseph Rowntree Foundation.

Filgueira, Fernando, 1998, "El nuevo modelo de prestaciones sociales en América Latina: residualismo y ciudadanía estratificada," in Roberts, Brian (ed.), *Ciudadanía y política social*, San José, Costa Rica, Flacso-SSRC.

Filgueira, Carlos H. and Filgueira, Fernando, 2002, "Models of Welfare and Models of Capitalism: The Limits of Transferability," in *Models of Capitalism. Lessons for Latin America*, Pennsylvania, The Pennsylvania State University Press.

Gibbons, Elizabeth D., 2006, "La Convención sobre los Derechos del Niño y la implementación de los derechos económicos, sociales y culturales en América Latina," in *Derechos económicos, sociales y culturales en América Latina. Del invento a la herramienta*, Canadá-Mexico, Centro Internacional de Investigaciones para el Desarrollo-Plaza y Valdés.

Godoy, Lorena, 2004, "Programas de renta mínima vinculada a la educación: las becas escolares en Brasil," in *Políticas Sociales*,División de Desarrollo Social, United Nations and CEPAL,Series No. 99, November.

Gordon, David and Nandy, Shailen, 2012, "Measuring Child Poverty and Deprivation," in *Global Child Poverty and Wellbeing. Measurement, Concepts, Policy and Action*, Bristol, The Policy Press.

Gordon, David *et al.*, 2003, *Child Poverty in the Developing World*, Bristol, The Policy Press.

Gordon, David, 2008, "Children, Policy and Social Justice," in *Social Justice and Public Policy. Seeking Fairness in Diverse Societies*, Bristol, The Policy Press.

Hart, Roger A., 1993, "La participación de los niños, de la participación simbólica a la participación auténtica," in *Ensayos Inocenti*, No. 4, UNICEF.

International Labour Organization (ILO), 2001, *Social Security: A New Consensus*, Geneva, ILO.

Lister, Ruth, 2007, "Social Protection: Principles and Dilemmas," in *Social Protection Initiatives for Children, Women and Families*, New York, The New School.

Lister, Ruth, 2008, "Inclusive Citizenship, Gender and Poverty: Some Implications for Education for Citizenship," *Citizenship Teaching and Learning*, vol. 4, No. July (1). Citized.

Maluccio, John A. and Flores, Rafael, 2004, "Impact Evaluation of a Conditional Cash Transfer Program: The Nicaraguan Red de Protección Social," *International Food Policy Research Institute (IFPRI). FCND Discussion Paper, No. 184*, July.

Marshall, Thomas H., 1998, *Ciudadanía y clase social*, Madrid, Editorial Alianza.

Martínez, Juliana, 2008, "Welfare Regimes in Latin America: Capturing Constellations of Markets, Families, and Policies," *Latin American Policies and Society*, vol. 50, No. 2.

Mesa-Lago, Carmelo, 2008, "Un reto de Iberoamérica en el siglo XXI: La extensión de la cobertura de la seguridad social,"*América Latina Hoy*, vol. 48, No. April.

Ministry of Planning, 2009, "Ley 20.379. Crea el Sistema Intersectorial de Protección Social e institucionaliza el sistema de protección integral a la infancia Chile Crece Contigo," in *Library of the National Congress of Chile, Enacted 09-12-2009*, http://www.crececontigo.gob.cl/wp-content/uploads/2010/03/Ley-20.379.pdf (retrieved in July 2014).

Minujin, Alberto *et al.*, (2006). "The definition of child poverty: A discussion of concepts and measurements," *Environment & Urbanization*, vol. 18, No. 2, October.

Minujin, Alberto, 2009, *Evaluación de las políticas de infancia en Mexico, Distrito Federal*, Mexico, Consejo de Evaluación de Desarrollo Social del Distrito Federal.

Morlachetti, Alejandro, 2010, *Legislaciones nacionales y derechos sociales en América Latina. Análisis comparado hacia la superación de la pobreza infantil*, Serie Políticas Sociales, No. 164, July.

Morlachetti, Alejandro, 2013, *Sistemas nacionales de protección integral de la infancia. Fundamentos jurídicos y estado de aplicación en América Latina y el Caribe*, Santiago de Chile, United Nations-CEPAL-UNICEF.

Morris, Julie A. and Gardner, Martin J., 1988, "Calculating Confidence Intervals for Relative Risk (Odds Ratios) and Standardised Ratios and Rates," *British Medical Journal*, No. 296.

Neubourg, Chris de, 2009, "Social Protection and Nation-Building: An Essay on Why and How Universalist Social Policy Contributes to Stable Nations-States," in *Building Decent Societies. Rethinking the Role of Social Security in Development*, London, Palgrave Macmillan.

Norton, Andrew *et al.*, 2009, "Introduction: Social Policy, Citizenship, and the Realization of Rights," in *Building Equality and Opportunity Through Social Guarantees*, Washington, D.C., The International Bank for Reconstruction and Development-The World Bank.

Organization for Economic Cooperation and Development (OECD), 2003, "Social Transfers in Kind," in *Glossary of Statistical Terms*, http://stats.oecd.org/glossary/detail.asp?ID=2498 (retrieved on July 2014).

Organization for Economic Cooperation and Development (OECD), 2014, "Social Expenditure. Aggregated data," in *OECD. StatExtracts*, http://stats.oecd.org/# (retrieved on July 2014).

Pemberton, Simon *et al.*, 2012, "Child Rights, Child Survival and Child Poverty: The Debate," in *Global Child Poverty and Wellbeing. Measurement, Concepts, Policy and Action*, Bristol, The Policy Press.

Rawlings, Laura, 2002, "Colombia Social Safety Net Assessment," in *Report No. 22255-CO, in Human Development Department*, World Bank, http://www.ifpri.org/sites/default/files/pubs/events/conferences/2002/092302/colombia.pdf (retrieved on July 2014).

Ringen, Stein, 1988, "Direct and Indirect Measures of Poverty," *Journal of Social Policy*, vol. 17, No. 3.

Robinson, Mary, 2002, *United Nations High Commissioner for Human Rights at the World Summit on Sustainable Development Plenary Session*, Johannesburg, South Africa, August 29, 2002, http://www.un.org/events/wssd/statements/unhchrE.htm (retrieved on July 2014).

Robles, Claudia, 2009, "América Latina y la protección social: avances y desafíos para su consolidación," in *Taller de expertos: Protección social, pobreza y enfoque de derechos: vínculos y tensiones*, United Nations-CEPAL-GTZ, draft, October.

Román, Isabel, 2012, *Social Protection Systems in Latin America and the Caribbean. Costa Rica*, Santiago de Chile, United Nations-ECLAC.

Sen, Amartya, 1982, *Poverty and Famines. An Essay on Entitlement and Deprivation*, Oxford, Clarendon Press.

Skoufias, Emmanuel and Parker, Susan W., 2001, "Conditional Cash Transfers and Their Impacts on Child Work and Schooling: Evidence from the Progresa Program in Mexico", *International Food Policy Research Institute (IFPRI). FCND Discussion Paper, No. 123*, October.

Strang, David and Meyer, John W., 1993, "Institutional Conditions for Diffusion," *Theory and Society*, vol. 22, No. 4.

Tag, Miriam, 2013, "The Cultural Construction of Global Social Policy. Theorizing Formations and Transformations," *Global Social Policy*, vol. 13, No. April (1).

Townsend, Peter, 2008, *The Abolition of Child Poverty and the Right to Social Security: A Possible UN Model for Child Benefit?*, Bristol–London, LSE-University of Bristol.

Townsend, Peter, 2009, *Building Decent Societies. Rethinking the Role of Social Security in Development*, London, Palgrave Macmillan.

Townsend, Peter, 1979, *Poverty in the United Kingdom: A Survey of Household Resources and Standards of Living*, Harmondsworth, Penguin Books.

UNICEF and Coneval, 2013, *Pobreza y derechos sociales de niñas, niños y adolescentes de Mexico, 2008-2010*, Mexico, UNICEF Mexico-Coneval.

United Nations General Assembly (UNGA), 1948, *Universal Declaration of Human Rights, Resolution 217 A (III) from December 10, 1948*, Paris, United Nations.

United Nations General Assembly (UNGA), 1989, *Convention on the Rights of the Child, Resolution 44/25 from November 20, 1989*, New York, United Nations.

United Nations General Assembly (UNGA), 2006, *Promotion and Protection of the Rights of Children: Report of the Third Committee*, New York, United Nations.

United Nations Research Institute for Social Development (UNRISD), 2011, *Combating Poverty and Inequality. Structural Change, Social Policy and Politics*, Geneva, UNRISD.

United Nations, 2000, "Enhancing Social Protection and Reducing Vulnerability in a Globalizing World," in *Report of the Secretary-General to the Thirty-Ninth Session E/cn.5/2001/2*, Washington, D.C., Economic and Social Council, http://www.icsw.org/un-news/pdfs/csdsocprotect.PDF (retrieved in July 2014).

United Nations, 2004, *Human Rights and Poverty Reduction. A Conceptual Framework*, Nueva York-Ginebra, UN.van Ginneken, Wouter, 2003, "Extending Social Security. Policies for Developing Countries," in *Social Security Policy and Development Branch, ESS Paper No. 13*, Ginebra, International Labour Organization (ILO).

Villanger, Espen, 2008, "Cash Transfers Contributing to Social Protection: A Synthesis of Evaluation Findings," in *Synthesis Report 2/2008*, Oslo, Norad (Norwegian Agency for Development Cooperation).

Villatoro, 2004, "Programas de reducción de la pobreza en América Latina. Un análisis de cinco experiencias," *Serie Políticas Sociales*, No. May (87).

Villatoro, Pablo, 2005, "Conditional Cash Transfer Programmes: Experiences from Latin America," *CEPAL Review*, No. 86, August.

VII. Appendix

Chart A1. Logistic regression model. Operational definition of the variables

Dependent variable	Operationalization of the variables
Probability of presenting deprivation in childhood	Dummy 1 = child deprivation (the child presents at least one social deprivation) 0 = another case
Independent variables*	
Gender of the head of the home	1= female head of the home 0 = male head of the home
Type of location	0 = urban 1 = rural
Dependency rate	Number of persons between 0 and 14 and persons 65 and older, the number of persons between 15 and 64
Government benefits	Benefits from government programs (cash transfers)
Educational level of the head of the home	1 = no education 2 = preschool 3 = incomplete primary school 4 = complete primary 5 = incomplete secondary school 6 = complete secondary school 7 = incomplete high school 8 = complete high school 9 = incomplete professional studies 10 = complete professional studies 11 = graduate studies
Number of wage earners in the home	Discrete variable

Source: Prepared internally with information from the Socioeconomic Conditions Module of the 2012 ENIGH.

*Other independent variables were adjusted to the model: the gender of the children, the family income from agricultural and nonagricultural sectors. These variables were not statistically significant; therefore, they were removed from the model to prevent the loss of degrees of freedom and to preserve parsimony in the model.

Chart A2. Confidence intervals for odds ratios of the occurrence of child deprivation

Associated factors	Exp (β)	Confidence interval for Exp (β)	
		Inferior	Superior
Educational level of the head of the home	0.728	0.722	0.734
Number of wage earners in the home	0.871	0.849	0.893
Government benefits	1.000	1.000	1.000
Gender of the head of the home (female vs. male)	1.085	1.033	1.140
Dependency rate	1.240	1.203	1.278
Location (rural vs. urban)	2.810	2.651	2.980

Source: Prepared internally from the results of the logistical model estimated to obtain the odds ratios of the occurrence of deprivation among children and with data from the 2012 ENIGH.

Note: Confidence intervals were estimated at 95%.

POVERTY AND CHILD POVERTY: ELEMENTS FOR THE DEBATE IN THE PREPARATION OF A SOCIAL PROTECTION POLICY IN HAITI

Jorge I. VÁSQUEZ[1]

> I. Brief overviewof the economic, social, and political situation of Haiti before and after the 2010 earthquake. II. Poverty, the poor, and impoverishment; proposal of an analytical framework for reflection. III. Poverty in Haiti: Key concepts and measurement. IV. Child poverty in Haiti. V. Summarizing political aspects and exploring conditions that reproduce impoverishment. VI. Haiti after the 2010 earthquake: Questions in relation to the possibility of a social protection policy for childhood. VII. Final questions. VIII. Bibliography.

I. Brief overview of the economic, social, and political situation of Haiti before and after the 2010 earthquake

The economic situation of Haiti has been strongly affected in recent decades, both by political junctures and by humanitarian disasters such as the January 2010 earthquake. According to the 2012 Human Development Index, prepared by United Nations Development Program, Haiti is ranked 161 among 180 countries, the lowest spot for a country from Latin America and the Caribbean (UNDP, 2013). Understanding and adding dimension to this indicator involves understanding its evolution in historic-economic terms and, therefore, contextualizing how its current status of poverty is structured.

According to Enel Vil:

> After the 1981-1982 recession period, the GDP followed a phase of stagnation leading to a chronic reduction of 8 per cent between 1991 and 1994, a period in which the international community imposed trade sanctions on Haiti for the 1991 coup. Starting in 1995, there was a

---

[1] Universidad de Chile Sociologist, Master in Social Research Methodologies, Bristol University, England; volunteer professional in the América Solidaria Foundation and coordinator of the Planning and Development Office of Foi et Joie Haiti. I wish to thank Felipe Lagos Rojas for his comments, criticism, and contributions for the preparation of the final document.

> favorable deviation of GDP, but between 2000 and 2004 particularly, its behavior is more like stagnation with an average growth rate of −0.8 per cent, which provoked a reduction of per capita GDP by 529 dollars in 2000 to 449 dollars in 2004; a fact that reveals a significant setback in the living standard of the population. (2009: 42)

This way, based on the annual analysis of the economic numbers by the Institut Haïtien de Statistique et d'Informatique (IHSI), a lower net growth can be noted between 2007 (3.4%) and 2008 (1.2%), as a result of the excessive increase of the prices of basic necessities in an economy that is highly dependent on the global prices of the food and oil; this is in combination with the impact of Hurricane Dean in the country, where the primary production sector suffered the consequences of the displacement of people, the devastation of large farming fields, infrastructure, and vegetal and animal production materials.

After a brief recovery in 2008–09, for the fiscal year of 2010—after the devastating earthquake—the Haitian economy again suffers a drop of −5% in GDP growth, the highest contraction in the past 15 years, only comparable to the effect of the 1993 embargo. Although in 2011 there is a significant recovery of growth (5.6%), it was below the 10% goal established by Haitian authorities in March 2010, due to delays in the reconstruction, political unrest due to the electoral processes (2010–11), and the uncertainty derived from economic-political instability. Although all the areas of the economy showed improvements, there are two growth factors worth noting: namely, a 20.7% increase in direct foreign investment—possibly explainable for the massive humanitarian aid to earthquake victims—and the fact that exports saw an 18% growth in real terms. However, the adverse effect of that process has been a significant increase of inflation, which, in the midterm, impacts the quality of life for low-income earners. As the Institut Haïtien de Statistique et d'Informatique indicates:

> The Haitian economy in 2011 was also marked by the return of inflation, which reached an inter-annual 10.7% and an annual average of 7.5%, compared to 4.1% and 4.7%, respectively, in 2010. Inflationary pressure may be attributed, among other things, to the increase of global prices — after the (however precarious) recovery of the economies of the world

after the 2009/2010 recession — and a deceleration in the supply of local products in the market. (2011: IHSI, free translation)[2]

In short, it is possible to say that after the 2010 earthquake, the level of dependency of the Haitian economy on fluctuations in the global market economy *hasincreased*, which reinforces the previous trend noticed since the radical liberalization of the economy during the 1980s. This is a major factor of vulnerability for the general population, and in relation to it, Lamaute-Brisson indicates that:

> The weakening of productive capacities due to trade liberalization policies initiated in 1987—which were not accompanied by a strengthening in supply—(Couharde, 2005) has led to a restructuring of economic activity. The agricultural sector has lost much in value added, while outsourcing has been accentuated in an economy that is unable to satisfy domestic demand. Imports represented more than 50% of global supply at constant prices in 2000 and almost 60% in 2011. After labour income, the second pillar of household income is remittances, which have increased since 1994 and account for double the country's exports and more than 30% of GDP at 2011 prices. (2013: 9)

With regard to employment, we can analyze some numbers to get an idea of the job situation of the country. According to the results of the 2007 employment survey (IHSI, 2010), there is high unemployment among the young; above 30% ofpeople aged between 20 and 24 years old are unemployed. According to Lamaute-Brisson, "Considering idle people who are available to work, we have calculated that the extended unemployment rate was particularly high among women (48.7% *v.* against 32.3% men) and young people (almost 60% of people between 20 and 24 years old)" (2013: 10). Thus, today also the informalization of economic activity is broadly extended, especially in urban areas.

In this general overview, a third and last point to consider is the low level of confidence in public institutions. This is relevant for an analysis of poverty in the country, if we consider that its political dimension (that is to

---

2   In *http://www.ihsi.ht/pdf/comptes_economiques_en_2011.pdf* (retrieved on April 19, 2014). Attention must be drawn to the analysis of the effect of inflation on poverty performed by Vil in an analysis of the variation of PCI and its impact on actual wages between 1995 and 2005.

say, the capacity of a state in directing welfare and quality of life toward its citizens, and, therefore, the determination of the thresholds of a good life under the right of law) is an integral part of the fight against poverty. The studies conducted show that the situation of Haiti is very complex in this respect.[3] Governance, understood as "the set of traditions and institutions that determine how authority is exercised in a country" (Vil, 2009: 53), has been historically questioned. It is possible to pinpoint at least three historical moments in the conformation of the structure of Haitian society during the twentieth century, in which major aspects of its governance have been undermined: first, the U.S. intervention and invasion from 1915 to 1934 and the push for a modernization (exploitation) of the country that was derived from it;[4] second, the striking succession of *coups d'état* leading to the authoritarian governments of the François Duvalier dynasty in 1956, and the rise to power of his son Jean-Claude Duvalier in 1971; and third, the emergence and subsequent disenchantment of the social movements led by the "Lavalas" movement, and funneled by the government of Jean Bertrand Aristide, which would last until the coup by General Cedras in 1991. All these moments have polarized the different segments of Haitian society and led to the derogatory labeling of the *Failed State* to describe the structural lack of governance of the state, as well as the disrepute of and mistrust in its institutions.[5]

After the 2010 earthquake and its striking consequences,[6] which led to a new decrease in the confidence in the capacity of the state (not only

---

3   Based on the study by Kaufmann*et al.* (1999), Haiti is one of the five countries, along with Colombia, Cuba, Paraguay, and Uruguay, that present the lowest governability indicators (Vil, 2009: 55). Based on the results of that study, the perception of the population of corruption, crime, and instability is very serious (Vil, 2009: 53).
4   To use Haitian labor in the production of rubber.
5   As Bourjolly points out, expressions such as "*Gens de la ville et gens des mornes, analphabètes et gens instruits, gens de bien et 'vagabonds', peaux foncées et peaux claires, français et créole, vaudou et christianisme, Haïtiens vivant en Haïti et Haïtiens vivant à l'étranger, 'roches dans l'eau' et 'roches au soleil'...*" (City people and rural people, analphabets and "learned people," good people and vagabonds, dark skinned people and fair skinned people, French and Creole, voodoo and Christianism, Haitians living in Haiti and Haitians living abroad, "rocks in the water" and "rocks under the sun") (2010: 26) become commonplace.
6   According to Brutus and Chalmers, "Within the three geographic departments affected, the number of persons affected is estimated at 3million, and the loss of human lives around 220,000, the number of injured persons is above 300,000, mutilated persons in excess of 45,000 while those with a psychological trauma are impossible to assess. A sudden and massive movement of people ... The breadth of

internally, but also from a large section of the international community), many authors have posited that, more than a reconstruction process, what is needed today is an actual *refounding* of the state, of its organization capacities, and of its vision and development model, one that encompasses in a holistic manner the refounding of public affairs and public welfare (Saint-Éloi, Trouillot *et al.*, 2010; Rainhorn *et al.*, 2012). This would then be a refounding that facilitates a transition from a "logic of emergency" to "long-term development plans and policies"; otherwise, it would perpetuate *ad-hoc* aid to cover subsistence needs, which, important as it may be, does not allow the development of public policies based on a debate and consensus around *socially accepted standards of living*.

In this way, the factors that make up the current situation of the country are diverse and complex. Without a doubt, it is possible to find a number of other factors that complement the diagnosis of the situation faced by contemporary Haitian society, such as the harsh living conditions in displaced people settlements, the mass exodus of qualified professionals, the difficulties of rural life, the presence of foreign military troops (MINUSTAH), the tense political–economic relationships with the Dominican Republic, among others. However, an attempt has been made to outline some structural points for the context after the 2010 earthquake, allowing an overview of the difficulty of executing proposals for the development of universal protection and childhood protection systems—and, as we will see below, of the outlining of overall poverty, child poverty, and of the government proposals developed so far in relation to children welfare.

II. Poverty, the poor, and impoverishment; proposal of an analytical framework for reflection

The unequal development of the world system has led us to rethink what we consider poverty today. *What is poverty* is an ontological question about its condition as a reality, and on the different elements that are included in that reality, from those of a material and tangible nature—such as not having

---

the damage is estimated at 56% of the GDP: destruction of the public service networks of Ed'H, Teleco, SNEP; destruction of infrastructure and companies that intensifies the fragility of the country; drastic weakening of the institutions, state structures and an accelerated growth of economic (CCI, DSNCRP, debt), financial (transfers from the diaspora, external public debt) food and political dependence (MINUSTAH) (2010: 34, free translation).

drinking water, a home, or food—to suffering physical, sexual, symbolic violence, or the failure to develop sufficient abilities to exercise active citizenship. Another question is whether poverty speaks of individuals or of collectives, depending on the historic-social context, the focus on one of the two shall be privilege.

The development of theories on poverty is deeply rooted in the birth of modern nation-states; thus, it takes into consideration the different notions of development and welfare of these states. Therefore, the definitions of poverty have been developed as a result of the attempt to outline development and welfare thresholds, and a certain notion of *social justice*. In other words, poverty is conceived as a *social problem* each time certain core, generally shared principles of social justice are questioned with systems that reproduce poverty, inequality, and vulnerability. If the said questioning does not exist, poverty will not be seen as a priority issue, and overcoming it will not involve a collective effort; rather it will be assumed as a functional aspect of the current production system, or naturalized with *ad-hoc* arguments. In the specific case of Haiti, the analysis of poverty presents a broad history, and the study by Vil (2009) is a central reference. According to Vil:

> Poverty, especially in contexts of social injustice and lack of channels for political participation, may lead to social unrest, including ongoing violence that affects growth in a negative manner. In this sense, people must not be allowed to be so poor that it offends or hurts society. (2009: 13)

As can be inferred from the text of Vil, the analysis of poverty involves taking a political stance in relation to a set of social justice, participation, and/or responsibility ideas assumed by a state structure related to the issue.[7]

In relation to the conception of the importance of the political dimension of poverty, a common point of reference in the contemporary debate is the statement that *fair human development* should be the goal of a

---

7 In this way, for instance, from a neoliberal perspective, there is no such thing as *social justice*, because any exercise in redistribution by a state in order to guarantee welfare thresholds for citizens is understood as an act of interventionism that infringes on the freedom of individual self-determination. If no principle of justice is violated (according to a particular ideological mind frame), poverty is not a problem; it is a matter of individual responsibility.

society founded upon democratic principles.[8] From a perspective such as this, poverty is reinterpreted today in a broader and more relative sense, not only as a lack of income to cover basic needs but rather under a holistic and broad understanding of human development. Therefore, it is becoming more common to hear discussions, within the scientific community, regarding agreements or consensus in at least two cornerstones of the issue: Poverty would be a multidimensional and dynamic phenomenon, and its existence would seem to threaten collective human development (Thorbecke, 2005; Alcock, 2006; Byrne, 2008; Addison et al., 2009).

In relation to the case of Haiti, according to Vil, "the effectiveness of anti-poverty policies not only needs a subtle and profound identification of the poor, but also of the factors that condition the degradation of the standard of living" (2009: 14). This is the line of analysis of this article, not only using the quantifiable aspects of the phenomenon but also adding historical factors and the set of social relationships that structure the material and symbolic conditions for its reproduction.

III. Poverty in Haiti: Key concepts and measurement

In relation to a contemporary definition of poverty, David Gordon has said that the debate between Amartya Sen and Peter Townsend in the 1980s between relative and absolute poverty "may be considered as resolved by the [Copenhagen] World Summit agreements in 1995."[9] These agreements define the "'absolute' poor as those who suffer worse or deeper conditions of poverty than the 'relative' poor. In effect, the definition of 'overall poverty' and 'absolute poverty'... clarifies this distinction" (Gordon, 2006: 35).

It is thus that the United Nations started using two definitions of poverty in 1995: "overall poverty" and "absolute poverty." The latter is understood as the condition characterized by a severe deprivation of basic human needs, such as food, drinking water, excreta-disposal systems, health,

---

8   And not assuming an exclusive and linear relationship between the overcoming of poverty and economic growth, as in recent decades. It would seem that broader notions of social justice have come into play, which leads us to conceive poverty as something that needs to be redefined not only on an economic dimension (Ranis et al.,2001, Grusky and Kanbur, 2006; Alkire, 2002, 2008; UN, 2000–11). For a critical perspective of this assumption, see McGillivray, 1991.

9   For greater references on the said debate in relation to one of the main discussions on the subject in the twentieth century, see Sen, 1983; 1985; 2003; and Townsend, 1979a,b, 1985, 2006, 2007.

roof, education, and information. It depends not only on income but also on access to basic services. In turn, overall poverty refers to a relative definition of poverty that includes a series of minimum standards of living in a society. This is characterized by the lack of income and production resources to guarantee a sustainable quality of life, the lack of access to education and other services, an unsafe environment, discrimination, and social exclusion, along with the lack of participation in public decisions and in the social and cultural life. Therefore, these are relative deprivations, which are close to the logic offered in the 1980s by Townsend.[10]

In the case of Haiti, the sociohistorical context has led us to pay more attention to absolute poverty indicators. The current indicators can be summarized, according to Vil, in "the international lines of one dollar and two dollars per capita exchanged into local currency (gourde) using the exchange factors of the World Bank for 2000." Due to these considerations, the incidence of overall and extreme poverty, in both cases from an indirect monetary approach, is 76.1 and 55.7%, respectively (Vil, 2009: 71).[11] Although these figures predate the 2010 earthquake, the economic trends presented allow us to assume that, given the existence of inflationary processes, a large portion of the population (more than half, according to conservative estimates) would live in conditions of extreme poverty.[12]

Complementing the monetary poverty approach, it is possible to also consider the basic needs approach[13] as a reflection of structural poverty conditions, that is to say, material poverty independent of the fluctuations in the market value of the income. As Vil writes:

---

10   These definitions are addressed in greater detail in *http://www.poverty.ac.uk/ definitions-poverty/absolute-and-overall-poverty* (retrieved on January 2, 2014).

11   Based on World Bank figures, the incidence of poverty in Haiti for 2001 was estimated at 77% for a population of 10.17 million for 2012 and a life expectancy at birth of 63 years, in *http://datos.bancomundial.org/pais/haiti*(retrieved on April 20, 2014).

12   Which is worrying if we additionally consider a consumer structure in Haitian society where food is the main expenditure (45%) and where several studies have identified signs of nutritional deficiency facing episodes of food safety since 1950 (Vil, 2009: 67).

13   Basic needs are defined as the "set of physical, psychic or cultural requirements, whose satisfaction is the necessary condition for the functioning of human beings in a certain society." The index of unmet basic needs (INB) is built from five indicators, namely: "i) physically inadequate housing, ii) overcrowded housing, iii) homes with inadequate hygienic service, iv) homes with children that do not attend school, and v) homes with a high economic dependence" (Vil, 2009: 74).

> Based on the National Survey on Living Conditions in Haiti, 96.2 per cent of Haitian homes have at least one unsatisfied basic need, and 70.1 per cent, at least two, which means that those who are extremely poor as a result of unsatisfied basic needs account for 70.1 per cent of the population. (Vil, 2009: 74)

These figures offer a general idea of the conditions of poverty before the 2010 earthquake. In turn, the enormous impact of this event on the quality of life means that the figures show, using an absolute poverty approach and an approach addressing unsatisfied basic needs, the potential negative effect of infrastructure damages, lost access to services, and overcrowding in the settlements as an addition to those figures.

In addition to establishing the pertinence of an absolute poverty approach, we propose considering some form of approximation to an idea of overall poverty, that is to say, of those aspects of citizen participation, development of capacities, and access to the structure of opportunities, as this is a social fabric in which economic and cultural resources are concentrated in a small segment of the population.[14] From a critical perspective, it is important to note that "The choice of a certain definition [of poverty] is often driven by pragmatic arguments related to information [data] availability, a political decision or historical arguments" (Hagenaards and Vos, 1987: 212). The good practices may then be followed and reproduced in countries where there is a systematization of reliable information, being precisely this, which is a major problem in countries with harsher conditions of poverty. For the particular case of Haiti, it is very difficult to have figures on poverty after the 2010 earthquake, which is even more serious for the measurement of overall poverty. However, here we argue that it is fundamental to consider overall poverty to understand the historical reproduction of poverty.

Aligned with this search for the expansion of the concept of poverty, Gordon rejects the idea of the existence of a *paradigmatic incommensurability* between both perspectives; on the contrary, he argues that they can be used simultaneously, as different *research programs* applicable to different aspects (anomalies) in the ongoing reformulation of what should be understood as poverty. Furthermore, as noted before, he

---

14   A reflection of that is the Gini index for the country, which reaches "66 per cent in 2001, according to the National Survey on Living Conditions; and 61 per cent, according to the 2000 National Poll on Income and Spending" (Vil, 2009: 80).

presents the issue as finalized and resolved by the scientific and political community, since both perspectives, however different, are complementary for the development of public policy. Hereinafter, the problem would then be how to best define the outline between the aspects of absolute and overall poverty.

IV. Child poverty in Haiti

We said above that the scientific community has reached a certain consensus in, at least, two key areas of research about poverty: (i) conceiving it as a multidimensional and dynamic phenomenon, and also (ii) in relation to an idea of collective human development.

Thus, in relation to the determination of child poverty—and echoing the definitions obtained in Copenhagen—UNICEF, without necessarily formulating a definition, refers to the particularity of child poverty in the following terms:

> Children experience poverty as an environment that is damaging to their mental, physical, emotional and spiritual development. Therefore, expanding the definition of child poverty beyond traditional conceptualizations, such as low household income or low levels of consumption, is particularly important. And yet, child poverty is rarely differentiated from poverty in general and its special dimensions are seldom recognized. By discriminating against their participation in society and inhibiting their potential, poverty is a measure not only of children's suffering but also of their disempowerment. (UNICEF, 2005)[15]

In relation to the preceding paragraph, we must highlight the work of UNICEF to determine multidimensional conditions of child poverty from a rights-based approach. The *Child Poverty in the Developing World* (Gordon *et al.*, 2003) study is one of the studies that points to a development of the research on childhood in this direction.

For the particular case of Haiti, Gordon and Shailen make a child poverty measuring exercise (2007). Using information from the Demography and Health Survey (2005) and the methodology of multiple deprivations, they highlight that "4 out of every 10 children in Haiti (1.62 million) live in

---

15 In http://www.unicef.org/sowc05/english/povertyissue.html (retrieved on January 2, 2014)

absolute poverty (2 or more deprivations), while 7 out of every 10 children (2.66 million) experience at least one of the forms of deprivation considered in the study" (Gordon *et al.*, 2007: 11).[16]

According to the results of the study by Gordon and Shailen:

- Over half of the children (2.1 million) are severely impaired in terms of housing. This means that they live in dirt or mud floor dwellings, or in severe overcrowding conditions, with more than five persons per room.
- Four out of every ten children (1.7 million) are severely deprived of excreta disposal systems, living in houses where there is none.
- A third of the children (1.2 million) are in conditions of severe deprivation in terms of health. They have not received immunization for any diseases, or health care in the event of an illness.
- Almost one of every five children (861,000) is severely deprived of access to drinking water.
- Over 100,000 children under five are so severely deprived of food and adequate nutrition that, if they survive, their health will be affected for the rest of their lives.
- One quarter million children between 7 and 18 have never attended school.
- 5% of the children between 3 and 18 are severely deprived of information and have no access to media in their homes (for example, radio, television, newspapers). (Gordon and Shailen, 2007: 12)

V. Summarizing political aspects and exploring conditions that reproduce impoverishment

For the purposes of this article, the meaningful aspect to be considered in terms of the authors reviewed (particularly those that are based on the tenets of Amartya Sen and Peter Townsend) is that, generally, these proposals are critical of the dogmatic reductionism of the observable aspects of poverty and the pretensions of scientific neutrality on the matter. However, in my consideration, they are within what Habermas calls

---

16   The deprivations considered are: (i) housing, (ii) hygiene, (iii) health, (iv) access to water, (v) access to food, (vi) education, and (vii) information.

"nomothetic-positivist" knowledge, that is to say, the type of reasoning that allows the technical control of the operationalization of a set of causal relationships (cit. in Giddens, 1997: 81). In light of the above, a holistic definition of poverty (with its correlative in terms of measurement) would be adequate for a given state to design plans to overcome it, in the context of governance that the state presents. However, this implies at least one prior discussion on the standards of living expected, an ethos of development, and a debate on which are the principles of justice at stake; otherwise, the methodological proposals, at best, will continue to reproduce assistance, mitigation, and short-term-oriented practices. Definitely, what we want to propose is that *there is no universal or optimal way of measuring poverty*: This would not be an exclusively technical debate, and it ultimately depends on which issues are defined as relevant by a given political community.Although poverty (and, thus, child poverty) may be expressed in the indicators presented by Gordon and Shailen, I consider that it is important to keep in mind their current reformulation, as an ideological construct in the general framework of a production system that justifies the accumulation of wealth. Precariousness and vulnerability before natural disasters, social and state violence, the forced displacement of people, food insecurity, illiteracy, stigmatization, and racism are simultaneously causes and consequences of a highly unequal distribution of resources and opportunities, which shows the importance of considering *the issue of poverty* beyond the outlines that isolate it and alienate it from the set of social relationships. These are the relationships that finally structure the material and symbolic conditions that allow its reproduction.

In other words, it is necessary to have interpretations that allow opening the debate to the reasons of its reproduction, rather than the determination of how many resources are needed to mitigate this indicator or the other. Having analyzed the conditions involved in the reproduction of impoverishment in the case of Haiti, I propose understanding poverty and social exclusion as a result of conflicting interests of multiple and diverse social groups that do not necessarily reach consensus.

VI. Haiti after the 2010 earthquake: Questions in relation to the possibility of a social protection policy for childhood

This section presents the case study of Haiti in the current context, which, as we mentioned, shows the need for a transition in the search of social policies aimed at overcoming the phase of contingent responses to emergency situations to give way to long-term development approaches. For that purpose, we analyze the complex situation of the country in terms of governance, as well as the role of international cooperation in it.

1. Difficulties for the development of a child development policy in Haiti

On the subject of the development of a social protection policy in Haiti, the research of Lamaute-Brisson (2013) must be highlighted, as it shows the main characteristics of the programs of the state that are aimed at social protection and promotion. According to Lamaute-Brisson:

> Created in the late sixties, the public social security bodies (social security and social assistance) have seen little development to date. After the dictatorial regime (1986), new institutions and programs were created. This includes the creation in 1990 of the social investment fund known as the Economic and Social Assistance Fund (FAES, as per the acronym in French). This brought about an expansion and diversification of the social protection mechanisms. Likewise, social promotion policies for education, health, food safety, housing and employment have been developed. (Lamaute-Brisson, 2013:8)

Without describing the entire social protection and promotion system of the Haitian state, it is necessary to highlight, with respect to childhood, the development of the Social Welfare and Research Institute (IBESR), whose main functions are protecting minors, offering social services, and controlling prostitution; the Free and Compulsory Universal Schooling Program (PSUGO), which subsidizes schooling in public and private schools; and the National Program of School Canteens (PNCS), which distributes and regulates the delivery of meals at public schools. Another highlight is:

> The recent creation (May 2012) of the position of Minister for Human Rights and the Fight against Extreme Poverty, under the authority of the

> Prime Minister. His mission consists in overseeing the organization of social protection programs and to guarantee in this field, and in the fight against poverty, consistency between government actions and the inter-institutional support required. (Lamaute-Brisson, 2013: 17)

Although the commissioning of these initiatives encourages future development—at least in institutional terms—of an integrated protection system, it must be noted that "social spending fell between 2002 and 2011, from 2.7% to 1.5% of the GDP ... This volatility is associated with the fragile political junctures and the volatility of GDP growth" (Lamaute-Brisson, 2013: 18).

However, it is possible to find some points of inflection that jeopardize the sustainability of the system, raising questions to be considered in the future development of an integral child protection policy. Lamaute-Brisson highlights the following points:

- The financial and operational backing of bilateral and multilateral donors is decisive, although accurate evaluations are still needed. This support allows the Haitian State to assume social protection and promotion functions that, otherwise, would be non-existent or extremely restricted, particularly after the 2010 earthquake.
- Likewise, delegating functions to the private sector has been one of the strategies of the State to evade its own inefficiency or inertia. This is illustrated with the contracting of a private company to provide health insurance to public officials while, under the law, this mission pertains to OFATMA.
- While non-governmental organizations (NGOs) have made a base here since the sixties to fill the voids left by the State with the support of external donors, several of them currently act as foremen of the State in the fields of social assistance and promotion. (Lamaute-Brisson, 2013: 17)

Thus, a major development of the rights-based approach for the protection for the children is required. One case that requires attention is domestic child labor in Haiti, where there are cultural practices that jeopardize the physical and mental integrity of children. In relation to this, "the domestic work of girls sometimes is culturally justified when the employers send them to school, give them clothes and a roof, maintaining a relationship of servitude and exploitation that is outside the law, but socially tolerated" (Montaño and Milosavjlevic, 2009: 8). This practice, known in Haiti as *restavék* ("living with someone else" in Creole), involves a condition of subservience in which girls from the rural world perform domestic tasks in homes that are supposedly better off in urban sectors. As Montaño and Milosavjlevic point out, social tolerance of the practices has its origin in the justification that girls are being sent to school and are given a home and food; however, they are the first to suffer the consequences of any crisis that the home may go through, especially in those cases where the alleged better status of the receiving family is not real.[17] This is a clear example of a practice that generates impoverishment, because, as we have argued before, it involves a reproduction of social relations that in turn reproduce clear gender disadvantages, social stratification, and a series of infringements of rights: estrangement from the family nucleus, exposure to physical, sexual, and symbolic violence, and mistreatment and exploitation. Without a doubt, it should be an important element to consider in the development of a childhood development policy in Haiti, as a cultural aspect to be identified, described, and analyzed with greater accuracy.

2. The role of international cooperation

In addition to the above, the role of international cooperation in Haiti is a subject of frequent debate, with positions that point to the existence of postcolonial practices and its importance to the situation of emergency (Grünewald, 2012; Salignon, 2012; Ramachandran and Walz, 2012).

As for the context, following Andrews *et al.* (2012), we can agree that one of the biggest challenges lies in the construction of capacity when the capacity is that of a state. As the authors indicate:

> Much of the literature on [the development of] capacities and corruption centers on the role of the agents in that situation. It is common to hear statements such as: "The country will only progress if it has leaders that are less corrupt and has public officials with awareness and training". In

---

17 According to Myriam Merlet, "in May 2003, the Parliament passed a law to derogate chapter IX of the labor code of Haiti, which authorized domestic work for *restavék* children. While the draft law explicitly prohibits child labor, it encourages Haitian families to continue with the tradition of informal adoption of disadvantaged children to offer them education and healthcare equal to that of their own children, as established in title X of the Constitution" (Merlet, 2009: 10) The following case studies can be consulted: *"Les enfants restavek"* by Miguel (2007) and *"The Uses of Children: A Study of Trafficking in Haitian Children"* by Smucker and Murray (2004).

this way, blaming the *agents*, the problem is personalized, instead of assuming a systemic approach to why countries stay poor. (Andrews *et al.*, 2012: 9, free translation)

An undermining that certainly has concrete effects, as Ramachandran and Walz indicate:

[F]rom the figures available, it would seem that NGOs and private contractors are the middleman in the assistance and reconstruction funds, and very little money goes to the Haitian government...Humanitarian agencies, NGOs, private contractors and other services outsourced by the State received 99 per cent of humanitarian aid, less than 1 per cent went to the Haitian government. (2012: 10, free translation)[18]

The question is then, whether international cooperation allows for the development of greater degrees of governance or not, considering governance as a key aspect for the reduction of impoverishment conditions, and, in particular, for the elaboration of a strategy that is articulated from the state for the mitigation of child poverty in the long term.

VII. Final questions

Based on the main arguments presented in this article, we submit some questions to be addressed in the horizon of an institutional-state concern on the future of the child poverty conditions in Haiti.

Assuming the assert of Gordon on the existence of a general consensus on the debate on absolute and relative poverty, along with the fact that the problem today would be finding the best definition of its outlines, *education* should be one of the dimensions to be considered in both cases. In this respect, it is relevant to consider at least a discussion on the standards of living expected for education, both in terms of access and in terms of quality. Lastly, the consequences of the earthquake urge us to pay special attention to the educational system as a key aspect to be considered in terms of child poverty, even more if we consider the importance of the development of the

---

18   These authors carry out an exhaustive study on the destination of international aid money in Haiti in recent years. They argue that the current flow of money, eluding state administration, undermines the leadership of the state to make investments in public policies in the long term.

educational system as a relevant factor both for the future development of welfare and for social integration. As Lamaute-Brisson indicates, after the earthquake "over four thousand schools (4,268) were destroyed or damaged, that is to say, 77% of the public school infrastructure and 79% of nonpublic schools" (GTEF, 2011) (2013: 34).

With a view to an integral childhood protection system, the reinforcement of the educational system, at the preschool, fundamental, secondary, or technical level, is a task to be boosted and financed with universal state programs that have a rights-based approach, such as PSUGO, with support from the international community in alliance with the state, and this prevents the replication of the private initiatives (outside the action of the state) that are not sustainable in the long term.

In relation to the measurement of child poverty in the country, the proposal of degrees of deprivation developed by Gordon seems like a good alternative to account for a condition of absolute poverty based on degrees of access or severe deprivation and infringement of the basic rights of children. However, in relation to the operationalization of overall poverty, progress may be made in indicators that help to manifest the particularity of child poverty, for example, the type of education received, gender differences in relation to school abandonment, the exposure to child labor, and some degree of exposure to physical or symbolical violence, as factors that are present in the reproduction of child poverty in particular.

To develop public policies, it is important both to consider the recommendations of experts in terms of *good practices* as well as to promote intersectoral participation, and public and private roundtables that foster debate on the pertinence and enforceability of the proposals and that consider a rights-based approach as the basis for dialogue to determine the generally shared standards of living.

In this way, one transitions from emergency practices to long-term development policies. This is a key element in facing the structural rationales at play in the reproduction of impoverishment. We must ask how to boost cooperation today and into the future, so that Haitian society's governance and sovereignty will enable its own decision-making. This constitutes a task that requires deeper analysis.

Finally, the deployment of research related to child poverty in Haiti requires a joint effort from various actors, such as technicians, politicians, and social groups, to allow contextualizing the problem in the current juncture of the country, and the capacity of the state and its apparatus to gradually develop a structural child protection policy with a rights-based approach. The task is not easy, considering the governance, economic deficiencies, and cultural characteristics described that make consensus and debates on the conditions of welfare so difficult to achieve. However, this endeavor is defended as a proposed roadmap for gradually achieving a solution to strengthen sovereignty and self-determination in Haitian society in the transition from emergency action to long-term policies.

VIII. Bibliography

Addison, Tony; HUME, Dave y KANBUR, Ravi (eds.) (2009) *Poverty Dynamics, Oxford.*
Alcock, Pete, 2006, *Understanding Poverty*, 3rd ed., Palgrave Macmillan.

Alkire, Sabina, 2002, "Dimensions of Human Development," *World Development*, vol. 30.

Alkire, Sabina, 2008, "Choosing Dimensions: The Capability Approach and Multidimensional Poverty," *MPRA Paper No. 8862, Posted 26*, May 2008, Online at http://mpra.ub.uni-muenchen.de/8862/.

Alkire, Sabina and Foster, James, 2011, "Understandings and Misunderstandings of Multidimensional Poverty Measurement," *OPHI Working Paper No. 43*.

Andrews, Matt *et al.*, 2012, "Escaping Capability Traps Through Problem-Driven Iterative Adaptation (PDIA)," *CGD Working Paper 299*.

Bourdieu, Pierre, 2007, *La miseria del mundo*, 3rd ed., Fondo de Cultura Económica.

Bourjolly, Jean-Marie, 2010, "Haïti: quelle reconstruction?" in Buteau, Pierre *et al.* (eds.), *Refonder Haiti?*, Mémoire d'encrier.

Brutus, Émile and Camille, Chalmers, 2010, "Construire ou reconstruire Haïti? Acteurs, enjeux et représentations," in Buteau, Pierre *et al.* (eds.), *Refonder Haiti?*, Mémoire d'encrier.

Buteau, Pierre *et al.* (eds.), 2010, *Refonder Haiti?*, Mémoire d'encrier.

Byrne, David, 2008, *Social Exclusion*, 2nd ed., Open University Press.

CEPAL-UNICEF, 2009, "Trabajo infantil en America Latina y el Caribe: su cara invisible,"*Boletín Desafíos, No. 8*.

Gordon, David *et al.*, 2003, *Child Poverty in the Developing World*, The Policy Press.

Gordon, David, 2006, "The Concept and Measurement of Poverty," in Pantazis, Christina *et al.* (eds.), *Poverty and Social Exclusion in Britain: The Millennium Survey*.

Gordon, David and Shailen, Nandy, 2007, *Absolute Child Poverty in Haiti in the 21st Century Report for UNICEF Haiti*, University of Bristol.

Grünewald, François, 2012, "L'aide humanitaire: quel bilan deux ans après le séisme," in Rainhorn, Jean-Daniel (ed.), *Haïti réinventer l'avenir*, Editions de la maison des sciences de l'homme, Editions de l'Université d'État d'Haïti.

Grusky, Dabid. B. and Kanbur, Ravi, 2006, *Poverty and Inequality*, Stanford University Press.

Hagenaards, Aldi and Vos, Klaas de, 1987, "The Definition and Measurement of Poverty," *The Journal of Human Resources*, vol. 23.

Lamaute-Brisson, Nathalie, 2013, *Sistemas de protección social en América Latina y el Caribe-Haiti*, Santiago de Chile, CEPAL, United Nations.

Rainhorn, Jean-Daniel (ed.) (2012), *Haiti réinventer L'avenir*, Editions de la maison des sciences de L'homme, Editions de l'Université d'État d'Haiti.

Ramachandran, Vijaya and Walz, Julie, 2012, "Haiti: Where Has All the Money Gone?," *CGD Policy Paper 004*.

Ranis, Gustav *et al.*, 2000, "Economic Growth and Human Development," *World Development*, vol. 28.

Salignon, Pierre, 2012, "Haïti: républiques des ONG: 'l'empire humanitaire' en question," in Rainhorn, Jean-Daniel (ed.), *Haïti réinventer l'avenir*, Editions de la maison des sciences de l'homme, Editions de l'Université d'État d'Haïti.

Sen, Amartya, 1983, "Poor, Relatively Speaking," *Oxford Economics Papers*, vol. 35.

Sen, Amartya, 1985, "A Sociological Approach to the Measurement of Poverty: A Reply to Professor Peter Townsend," *Oxford Economics Papers*, vol. 37.

Sen, Amartya, 2003 [1983], *Poverty and Famines, An Essay on Entitlement and Deprivation*, Published to Oxford Scholarship Online.

Thorbecke, Erik, 2005, "The Many Dimensions of Poverty," *International Conference, UNDP International Poverty Centre*, Brasilia, August 29–31.

Townsend, Peter, 1979a, "The Development of Research on Poverty," in *Department of Health and Social Security, Social Security Research: The definition and Measurement of Poverty*, Londres, HSMO.

Townsend, Peter, 1979b, *Poverty in the United Kingdom*, Harmondsworth, Middlesex, Penguin Books.

Townsend, Peter, 1985, "A Sociological Approach to the Measurement of Poverty—A Rejoinder to Professor Amartya Sen," *Oxford Economics Papers*, vol. 37.

Townsend, Peter *et al.*, 2006, "The International Measurement of 'Absolute' and 'Overall' Poverty: Applying the 1995 Copenhagen Definitions to Britain," in Pantazis, Christina *et al.* (eds.), *Poverty and Social Exclusion in Britain: the Millennium Survey*.

Townsend, Peter, 2007, "Poverty-An Historical Perspective," in *Compendium of Best Practices in Poverty Measurement*, Río de Janeiro, Rio Group, 2006.

UNDP, 2013, "The Rise of the South: Human Progress in a Diverse World," *Human Development Report 2013*, UN.

United Nations, 1995, *The Copenhagen Declaration and Programme of Action, World Summit for Social Development*, United Nations, Nueva York, March 6-12, 1995.

United Nations, 2000, "United Nations Millennium Declaration, United Nations, Nueva York, September 6-8, 2000", *http://www.un.org/millennium/declaration/ares55 2e.htm* (retrieved on August 23, 2011).

United Nations, 2011, *The Millennium Development Goals Report 2011*, New York, United Nations.

Vil, Enel, 2009, *Pobreza y desigualdad en Haiti: un análisis de sus determinantes*, Mexico, Flacso.

VULNERABLE CHILDHOODS AND SOCIAL PROTECTION SYSTEMS: CHILD ALLOWANCE IN ARGENTINA

Ianina TUÑÓN[1]
Agustín SALVIA

> I. Introduction. II. Social security systems in Argentina: coverage, evolution, and focus. III. Background of the mixed impacts of transfer systems. IV. Effects of the AUH on economic welfare and human development indicators. V. Final reflections. VI. Bibliography. VII. Methodological annex.

I. Introduction

In the mid-1990s, countries such as Brazil and Mexico started implementing the income transfer programs, which in their current versions we know as "Bolsa Familia" and "Oportunidades," respectively. The main short-term goal of these initiatives, and of many others developed in the countries of the region, was to reduce poverty. Their medium- and long-term purposes were to develop human capital through the nutrition, health, and education triad.

In the case of Argentina, the equivalent of the Latin American experiences mentioned above was the 2004 "Families for social inclusion" program, which came about as an offshoot of the first mass income transfer program, known as the "Unemployed Heads of Household Plan.""Families for social inclusion" was a focused program, with a geographic reach and limited coverage compared to the regional experiences mentioned.

During the 2009 international crisis, while undergoing a progressive stagnation of full employment creation, the Argentinean state extended the social protection regime targeted at the vulnerable population through the

---

[1] Doctor in social science (UBA); researcher in charge of the "Barometer of Social Debt for Children" project and the 2010-2195 FONCYT PICT project, in the framework of the Observatory of Argentinean Social Debt Program, Universidad Católica Argentina. Associate professor, UNLaM, graduate studies professor, UTREF, and undergraduate studies professor, UCA. E-mail: ianina_tunon@uca.edu.ar.
Doctor in social science (Colmex); associate professor at the Faculty of Social Science (UBA); researcher with Instituto Gino Germani (UBA), CONICET; chief researcher officer with the Observatory of Argentinean Social Debt Program, Universidad Católica Argentina. E-mail: agustin_salvia@uca.edu.ar.

"Universal Allowance per Child for Social Protection" (AUH). This allowance was established by a Necessity and Urgency Decree [Argentina (Decree 1602/2009), 2009],[2] and it constitutes a turning point in the social protection system.

With the AUH, the Argentinean state acknowledges social inequality in the access to social protection, which is reflected in the duality between the population that belongs to the formal sector (with access to health coverage, retirement contributions, and work-related accidents insurance) and the population that has restricted access as a result of being part of the informal market, unemployed, or idle. In average, informal employment in Argentina between 2010 and 2012 affected 35% of the economically active population (PEA). Without a doubt, here lies one of the main differences from other previous and current programs in the region. The eligibility criteria for the population are defined by the relationship of the parents with the job market.

This transformation of the social security system was accompanied by the restructuring of the preexisting economic assistance programs to the extent that the creation of the AUH was accompanied by the immediate incorporation of children under 18 years from homes that up to that moment received income from social programs. It is estimated that, with the restructuring of the system, over 2.2 million children immediately became direct beneficiaries of the new scheme. In 2012, there were 3.5 million of children with AUH (1.9 million of participant households). The cash transfers of this allowance, along with the family pensions and the contributions from other municipally managed income transfer programs, represent between 0.6 and 0.8% of the GDP.

---

[2] To obtain AUH benefits, the responsible adult (father, mother, or guardian) and the child must have a National Identity Document and a minimum three years of residence in the country if they are foreigners. Likewise, they must not receive other noncontributive assistance programs or contributive family allowances, and be unemployed, seasonal workers, social small taxpayers, nonregistered workers, or domestic workers with income under the minimum vital and mobile wage. The payment modality of the AUH is conditioning to the parents meeting certain requirements that act as incentives for investment in the human capital of their children (fundamentally, education and health). About 80% of the economic contribution is paid on a monthly basis and the remaining 20% is accrued and paid on an annual basis when it is certified that the child attended school during the school cycle and complied with the sanitary controls and the vaccination plan.

With this background, one may ask these questions: What is the coverage of each of the social security subsystems and what type of children are still excluded from them? How is the fragmentation of the protection system expressed in the infringement of basic children rights? In addition, and considering the fact that this is a program that has conditional requirements, it becomes necessary to question its impact. It is to be expected that, as a result of the "conditional requirements" of the allowance system, some positive effects are noticed in educational inclusion, and, particularly, among teenagers, where there is a greater deficit in schooling.[3] Now, it is relevant to ask to what extent was the increased educational inclusion associated to the "conditional requirements" of the AUH or if it instead was independent from the benefits offered by the allowance system.[4]

Also to be expected is a positive impact on the per capita income as an effect of the direct transfer of income, and, therefore, in indicators such as destitution, and in aspects that are related to the material resources, but not exclusively, such as food insecurity. In addition, we also wonder about the effect on the propensity to child labor.[5] In this aspect, the AUH system has no

---

3 According to the last Population Census in Argentina (2010), only 1% of children in primary school age at the country level didn't attend a formal educational center. Likewise, school absenteeism in secondary school was 10.9%. In the first cycle of secondary school it was 3.5%, and it increased in the second to 18%. The evolution of absenteeism in the second cycle of secondary school in the 1981–10 period shows that in 1980, 48.2% of the teenagers didn't attend secondary school; this figure decreased almost 11 percentage points toward the end of the decade, with values around 37.4%. This trend continued and grew stronger in the 1990s, whereas absenteeism decreased to 20.6% in 2001. Last, in the 2001–10 period, while school absenteeism was reduced, it did only by 2 percentage points.

4 In the particular case of the educational policies, there are different initiatives directly or indirectly aimed at achieving a greater inclusion and at improving quality. In effect, the 26206 National Education Law of 2005 establishes the mandatory nature of secondary school. At the same time, the Educational Funding Law established an increase of the investment in education from 4 to 6% of the 2005 and 2010 GDP, a goal that was met, and has been kept in recent years. Also the *Conectar Igualdad* program must be considered as an incentive for the schooling of teenagers. This is a program of the national government that seeks to deliver one laptop to each secondary school student in the public system, as well as to the students in the systems of grants and programs aimed at inclusion and at the completion of middle school.

5 The Law 26390 prohibits child labor in Argentina and it increases the minimum age for employment to 16. Work is regulated for teenagers above 15 in terms of time and conditions, because it is acknowledged that work complicates educational inclusion and the mandatory school path in Argentina since 2005.

conditions; however, due to its link with schooling and its potential capacity to offset income, it may have had a positive impact.

Answering these questions seems relevant in itself; however, we offer a reflection on the extent of the expected impacts from a rights-based approach, and in terms of the human and social development of children. Thus, we also ask, "what is the potential of income transfer programs in fostering economic autonomy for the families, distributive equity, and social inclusion for children?"

II. Social security systems in Argentina: Coverage, evolution, and focus

As described, in Argentina there are different public economic assistance subsystems for children. However, the national system with the largest coverage and economic impact is the Family Allowances Regime. It is based on a contribution-based system grounded in the principles of distribution (targeted at children whose parents are dependent workers, who receive a salary under the minimum nontaxable threshold, beneficiaries of the Work-Related Risks System, and beneficiaries of the Integrated Unemployment Benefits System), and a noncontribution-based system (targeted at children from poor families or disabled children, which includes the AUH regime). On the other hand, there is a system targeted at homes with children whose parents receive income as dependent workers and/or higher autonomous workers at a minimum scale with the right to deduct from the annual income tax a fixed sum as tax credit per child.

Table 1a shows the coverage attained by each of the aforementioned subsystems, social programs, and the population that still has not been covered by any of the regimes.

Data show, on the one hand, that the wage increase of the 2011–12 interannual period among formal workers was not accompanied by the corresponding increase of the minimum non-taxable scale of the income tax regime, which had an increase of 7.7 percentage points in coverage. On the other hand, the children receiving economic assistance through the AUH and other social plans in urban Argentina between 2010 and 2012 were, in average, 36%. In this sense, there would seem to be no changes in state coverage in the period, the coverage of the AUH grew moderately, and the assistance through other social programs decreased. Despite the growing coverage, of the new social plans, and due to the changes occurred in social security in general, it is estimated that almost 20% of the children—in average, in the 2010–12 period—does not receive economic assistance from the state.

Table 1a. Evolution of the different public economic assistance systems for children in urban Argentina. Years: 2010, 2011, and 2012.
Percentage of children aged between 0 and 17 years

	2010	2011	2012
Tax credit per child	6.9	9.5	17.2
Family Allowances Regime	38.0	35.9	26.0
Universal Allowance per Child (AUH)	29.0	30.3	30.8
Other social programs	7.8	5.9	5.6
No coverage	18.3	18.4	20.4

Source: EDSA-Bicentenario 2010–12. Argentinean Social Debt Observatory.

Now we may ask what is the incidence of vulnerable childhoods in terms of economic family welfare, access to food, schooling, and child labor, in each of the economic protection subsystems. It is easy to notice that over 45% of the most vulnerable childhoods in terms of per capita family income—under one and two basic food baskets (CBA)—and in a situation of food insecurity as a direct measure of poverty are under the AUH system. Without a doubt, that indicates an adequate focus on child poverty, but it also shows the inclusion challenge represented by the 16% of homes that do not receive income equivalent to a CBA or the 19% in situation of food insecurity.

Children who suffer educational deficits, and/or exposure to economic labor, present a clear fragmentation within the allowances systems (see table 1b). Based on the acknowledgment of this heterogeneity, there is a valid question to be asked about the impact of the AUH on economic poverty and on the human capital indicators analyzed.

Table 1b. Segmentation of the allowances system for economic poverty in the household and human development indicators of childhood.
Percentage of children aged between 0 and 17 years*

	1 CBA 0–17 years **	2 CBA 0–17 years ***	Food insecurity 0–17 years	Does not attend school 5–17 years	Economic labor 5–17 years
Tax credit per child	–	0.4	2.7	5.5	7.0
Family Allowances Regime	14.5	19.8	19.9	24.5	28.2
Universal Allowance per Child (AUH)	49.9	46.1	47.2	28.0	29.6
Other social programs	19.6	12.3	11.1	15.1	12.7
No coverage	16.0	21.5	19.1	27.0	22.6

Source: EDSA-Bicentenario 2010–12. Argentinean Social Debt Observatory.
*Base average stacked EDSA 2010-11-12.
**Population under one Basic Food Basket per capita with a value of US$77.6.
***Population under two Basic Food Baskets per capita with a value of US$155.

III. Background of the mixed impacts of transfer systems

The noncontributive pension programs and the conditional income transfers in Latin America were expanded in the past decade in terms of coverage and investment (Cecchini and Madariaga, 2011). The literature reports mixed results in terms of their impact. There are consensuses around the positive effects on schooling, on the amount and nutritional composition of what is consumed in the households (Fiszbein and Schady, 2009; González de la Rocha, 2010; Bastagli, 2008), as well as in the reduction of income-related poverty and destitution (Fiszbein and Schady, 2009). With respect to health, there have been improvements in the use of primary attention centers and in preventive care such as vaccination (Veras Soares, 2009). While the reduction of child labor is often not an explicit goal of these programs, the evaluations that have been performed indicate an impact that is somewhat bigger among the little children than the teenagers, it has occurred both in urban and rural areas, and in some cases there has been a greater impact on domestic labor than in economic labor (Cecchini and Madariaga, 2011).

At the local level, and little after the implementation of the AUH, a series of simulation exercises were carried out, based on the Permanent Households Survey (EPH-INDEC), which showed the potential of the transfer policy over different social indicators (Gasparini and Cruces, 2010; Basualdo *et al.*, 2010; Maurizio and Perrot, 2011). The study by Bustos (2011) recognizes a positive impact of the AUH in the income of beneficiary households *versus* non-beneficiary households.

Our own studies show that the positive distributive impacts of the AUH (Salvia *et al.*, 2013) produced a significant increase in household income, which implied a reduction of destitution and poverty rates. Likewise, the AUH would have tended to reduce the risk of suffering events of food insecurity, whereas it would have had an eventual positive effect over secondary schooling.

With respect to the first of the findings, a greater reduction of food insecurity in the households that received AUH income compared to those that did not receive them was noticed during the peaks of the 2010–12 period. In addition, participation of households with food security that received income from these social programs increased. Generally speaking, this positive impact of the allowance would have been great at a time of economic growth (2010–11), whereas in the recessive and more inflationary phase of the period (2011–12), there was a drop in the effect. With respect to the second finding, it was seen that educational inclusion through schooling among teenager would not have had an immediate response before the expansion of the protection system until the 2011–12 interannual period, where there is a more noticeable effect in terms of teenage school inclusion. The main source of this partial positive effect would have been the "return" and/of "retention" of non-attending beneficiaries. Likewise, a portion of the non-schooled beneficiary teenagers and of the non-schooled non-beneficiary teenagers would have migrated to the situation of double exclusion associated with not being participants of the AUH regime and not attending secondary school (Salvia *et al.*, 2013; Tuñón and González, 2012).

However, the truth is that these multiple approaches to the estimation of the effects of the AUH have been able to recognize modest effects in the reversion of structural childhood exclusion conditions. A time effect has been recognized in part in the implementation processes of the system, but it is also necessary to recognize a non-negligible problem in terms of the reliability of the results, related to the fact that, in addition to the fact that the studies are not quasi-experimental or panel studies, the differences observed are generally statistically significant; therefore, these results must be, in general, interpreted as indicators of plausible effects, and not as robust statistical relations.

Based on these preliminary approaches, we decided to make a quasi-experimental study that would allow us to homogenize the characteristics of the comparison (control) group with those of the group receiving the AUH, and in that sense gaining more reliability in the comparisons and in the evaluation of potential impacts.[6]

IV. Effects of the AUH on economic welfare and human development indicators

1. Estimation of the impact on destitution and food safety

Although the benefit provided by the AUH transfers to the average per capita income of the family (IPCF) of participant households was US$22.2, the real impact on the IPCF, controlled/controlling the counterfactual action of nonparticipant households, is estimated at US$8.9 (see table 2a). However, this effect does not control the indirect aggregated impact of the AUH/7H[7] over the capacity of (nonparticipant) households to generate additional incomes through the labor market and/or by receiving interfamily transfers.

Table 2a. Impact of the AUH over the average per capita income of the family (IPCF) by study group

IPCF of participants with AUH/7H (1) (US$)	IPCF of participants without AUH/7H (2) (US$)	IPCF of the comparison group (counter factual) (3) (US$)	Benefit of the AUH/7H to the IPCF of participant households (1)-(2) (US$)	Net impact of the AUH/7H on the IPCF of participant households (1)-(3) (US$)
116.5	94.3	107.5	22.2	8.9

Source: EDSA-Bicentenario 2010-12. Argentinean Social Debt Observatory.
Note: The exchange rate used was US$1 = AR$5.8.

The positive effect observed of the average per capita income of the family allows one to infer a positive impact on the situation of destitution and food insecurity of the children. Given a CBA per capita of US$77.6, the rate of children and teenagers with AUH—for the 2010-2011-2012 period—with

---

6 See the methodological specifications of the study in the annex of this paper.
7 The treatment group includes children under the noncontributory regimes of AUH and the pension for seven children because both are conditional transfers for similar amounts.

IPCF under that value is 13%, whereas for the comparison group, it is 19.9%. That is to say, participating in the AUH program reduced the risk of extreme poverty by 34.9% (6.9 p.p.) for the beneficiaries.

But, considering the value of two CBA per capita (US$155) as the parameter, the rate of participant children and teenagers with IPCF under that value is 62.5%, whereas for the comparison group, it is 65.6%. That is to say, in that case the AUH program reduced the risk of extreme poverty by less than 5% (3.1 p.p.) for the beneficiaries (see table 2b).

Table 2b. Reduction of the risk of being under the value of one/two CBA per capita and/or of suffering food insecurity by study group. Percentage of children aged between 0 and 17 years

	AUH/7H participants group	Comparison group (contrafactual)	Impact of the AUH/7H	
			In p.p.	In %
One CBA	13.0	19.9	-6.9	-34.9
Two CBAs	62.5	65.6	-3.1	-4.8
Food insecurity	10.9	13.5	-2.6	-19.2

Source: EDSA-Bicentenario 2010-16. Argentinean Social Debt Observatory (ODSA-UCA). Year 2010-12.

2. Estimation of the impact on school attendance and economic labor

The AUH imposes the conditional requirement that children and teenagers aged between 5 and 17 years should attend the compulsory formal education publicly managed system. As mentioned, schooling between 5 and 12 years of age in urban Argentina has almost reached a full coverage, whereas the inclusion challenge lies with the teenagers in age of attending secondary education.

The analysis of table 3a allows us to estimate a positive impact of the AUH/7H on the schooling of 61.6% of those aged between 5 and 17 years in the participant group compared to the comparison group. In effect, although absenteeism was 3.6% in the participant group, in the comparison group it was 9.5% (a difference of 5.9 p.p. in favor of the former). Although the impact in relative terms was similar on children in age of attending primary education (5-12) and on teenagers in age of attending secondary school (13-

17) (59.4 and 61.2%, respectively), the absolute impact was significantly higher in the reduction of absenteeism among teenagers.

Although the reduction of child labor was not an explicit goal of the allowances system, it is inferred that there may have been a positive effect as a consequence of the schooling requirement that involves a tension with child labor and of the improvement of family income. The truth is that this study identifies a positive effect in the reduction of economic labor between 5 and 17 years. The difference between the rates yields a positive effect of 2.4 p.p. for the participant group, or a 14.3% reduction (table 3a). The effect in percentage terms was higher between 5 and 12 years than between 13 and 17 years (15 and 12%, respectively), whereas in terms of absolute impact, the reduction was greater among the teenagers.

The impact of the AUH in the reduction of school absenteeism in relative terms was four times the relative impact on in the reduction of economic labor. This difference is not surprising to the extent that educational inclusion is a "conditional requirement" of the system, and no restriction associated with child labor was included. Although the relative differences show a greater impact among children than among teenagers, both for schooling and for child labor, the absolute impact was clearly higher among teenagers, which are the most vulnerable demographic group in terms of educational exclusion and economic exploitation.

Table 3a. Not attending school and performing economic labor by study group. Percentage of children aged between 0 and 17 years.

	Age group	AUH/7H Participants group	Comparison group (contrafactual)	Impact of the AUH/7H	
				In p.p.	In %
Does not attend school	5–17	3.6	9.5	−5.9	−61.6
	5–12	1.3	3.2	−1.9	−59.4
	13–17	7.7	20	−12.2	−61.2
Performs economic labor	5–17	14.3	16.7	−2.4	−14.3
	5–12	8.3	9.8	−1.5	−15.1
	13–17	25.1	28.5	−3.4	−12.0

Source: EDSA-Bicentenario 2010–16. Argentinean Social Debt Observatory (ODSA-UCA). Year 2010–12.

V. Final reflections

The AUH confirms a trend toward broader base income transfer policies. Its distributive impact, however insufficient to overcome income-related destitution in childhood, has been firmly progressive. Now, the important role of economic protection performed by the allowance also reflects the persistence and reproduction of an excluded population without access to full employment with all rights and to a more integral protection system; therefore, receiving the said income transfer programs is also an indicator of the deficit in terms of economic autonomy, distributive equality, and social inclusion that is a burden to broad sectors of the population, and which particularly affect children.

The AUH has attained a broad coverage in the target population; however, we estimate that 20% (approximately 2,600,000) of the children were excluded from the allowances regimes in 2012. In that sense, there is a pending challenge of providing social protection to children and of reviewing the current eligibility and universality criteria.

In the framework of a fragmented social protection system, the AUH reaffirms the condition of employment informality of a large portion of the Argentinean population, and which is not reverted in the period under review by the percentage of coverage of the allowance, which has not changed. The employment paths of the vulnerable sectors are changing and unstable, but the state must promote their full inclusion. In that sense, the employment status should not be an eligibility criterion, but rather the status of children whose basic rights are being infringed.

The impact of the AUH on per capita family income has been modest, but positive. However, it is necessary to ask about the purchase power of the said income, in the framework of the high levels of inflation registered in recent years, which have a liquefying effect over the amount of the benefit. Somehow, the partial impact of the allowance over the income can be noticed in the percentage of the reduction of the rate of destitution and food insecurity among socially vulnerable children, which was 34.9 and 19.2%, respectively. The analysis of the differentiated effects made it possible to notice the paradox of the higher relative effects over destitution, which has no correlation with the decrease of food insecurity. Of course, the increase of household income improves their purchasing power, and particularly, their power to buy food; however, it seems complex that it would certify their nutritional value and guarantee access in terms of quantity and quality.

Schooling in the publicly managed educational system is one of the conditional requirements of the AUH system. This study has estimated a positive effect on the schooling of 61.6% in the population aged between 5 and 17 years that is under social vulnerability conditions. Although the relative effect was similar among age groups, the absolute effect was significantly higher in the reduction of absenteeism among teenagers, which are the demographic group that is most affected by educational backwardness and exclusion. However, it is necessary to ask about the effect of income transfer systems on human capital to the extent that they are not accompanied by more substantial transformations of the integrative capacity of the educational system for the new generations. In the framework of a fragmented educational system, how could we expect allowances regimes to guarantee the investment in human capital if schooling is not synonymous to valuable learning, or to equivalent educational results?

In the framework of homes with unstable and precarious forms of integration to the job market, the secondary workforce is often an important resource, and this workforce includes children and, particularly, teenagers. Although the AUH does not establish an explicit conditional requirement related to child labor, this study has estimated a positive effect on its reduction. Probably, the economic contribution of the children to the home with the allowance along with the restriction of time that is available to work as a consequence of the requirement to attend school have jointly influenced the 14.3% effect, which is clearly insufficient, and shows that the allowance may partially offset the income generated by child labor.

Without a doubt, income transfer programs fulfill a fundamental role in a society where a strong core of poverty persists, one that includes a relevant proportion of children. However, the limits of this system in reducing destitution and food insecurity raise the urgency to define the limits of these programs, including the AUH, to meet the minimum goal, which is eradicating extreme poverty.

In that sense, from the perspective of social rights, attention must be drawn to the fact that the improvements achieved in the living standard and welfare of households with children through this economic assistance, although clearly indispensable, are far from being a platform for social inclusion or an indicator of sustainable and socially integrated human development. The positive achievements of the transfer programs may be maintained and, simultaneously, be expanded, if they were accompanied by more integral human and social development policies.

Mainaxes of debate:

The impact assessment of the AUH for this article was performed considering the first three years of its implementation. This period may be considered as insufficient for an assessment. In effect, the impacts generally are noticed after a longer time. However, in this particular case of the AUH, the purpose was to achieve an immediate impact over the income of the households as well as produce effects over schooling and preventive health care (its conditional requirements). Likewise, it must be mentioned that this transfer of income was not complemented with any other action that may allow the conclusion that the passage of time may be an intervening factor. In any case, it must be noted that controls in the compliance of the conditional requirement demand implementation time, and in that sense, they may exercise an effect in the short term.

Also, it is necessary to ask what should be evaluated as an effect of the AUH. The effects that were expected of the AUH were the increase of family income, the increase of schooling, and increase in preventive health controls. However, in the framework of this study, we also sought to evaluate its effect on child labor. It is clear that this is not an effect or goal that was expected of the program, and, even though in that sense it may not be legitimate to demand the said impact from the state, its positive effect seems plausible to the extent that schooling takes time away from work and, at the same time, the household offsets the income with the transfer.

In the region, there is a debate on the conditional requirements of the income transfer programs. This debate has different angles; on the one hand, the angle related to the discrimination represented by requiring a condition to have access to a right such as the social protection of children, and on the other, the actual effect of requiring the condition over the strategies of the households. In this case, the schooling requirement was useful to the extent that there was a comptroller of the condition, and its effect was seen more clearly in the second year of implementation of the allowance.

It is still necessary to continue to work on nonobservable external factors that may shed some light over the reasons for which a portion of Argentinean children continue to be in social vulnerability conditions and do not participate in the AUH. Precisely, a problem of the quasi-experimental method offered by matching, even after being corrected with a regression, is how to capture nonobservable factors related to the motive, the ability to withstand, among others, that may be associated. Although the matching took into account a considerable set of variables, there are nonobserved features for which we were not able to match the groups. However, it seems unlikely that there are factors not being represented in any of the observable factors introduced, but it cannot be ruled out for sure. In that framework, the factors that cause a proportion of vulnerable children to be still not under an allowance regime are various: migratory origin, family structure, extreme marginality, among others. All of them are factors that were introduced in the matching.

VI. Bibliography

Argentina (Decree 1602/2009), 2009, "Por medio del cual se incorpora el Subsistema no Contributivo de Asignación Universal por hijo para Protección Social,"*Poder Ejecutivo. Decreto 1602 de 2009*.

Bastagli, Francesca, 2008, "From Social Safety Net to Social Policy? The Role of Conditional Cash Transfers in Welfare State Development in Latin America," *Working Paper No. 60*, Brasilia, IPEA-UNDP.

Basualdo, Eduardo *et al.*, 2010, "La asignación universal por hijo a un año de su implementación,"*Documento de Trabajo No. 7*, CIFRAS.

Bustos, Juan Martín, 2011, "Asignación Universal por Hijo. Evaluación del impacto en los ingresos de los hogares y el mercado de trabajo,"*Serie: Trabajo, ocupación y empleo, SSPTyEL-MTEySS, No. 10*.

Cecchini, Simone and Madariaga, Aldo, 2011, "Programas de transferencia condicionada," *Balance de las experiencias recientes en América Latina y el Caribe, Cuadernos de la CEPAL 95*.

Dehejia, Rajeev and Wahba, Sadek, 1998, "Causal Effect in Non-Experimental Studies: Re-Evaluating the Evaluation of Training Programs," *Working Paper Series 6586*. National Bureau of Economic Research.

Fiszbein, Ariel and Schady, Norbert, 2009, "Conditional Cash Transfers. Reducing Present and Future Poverty," *Policy Research Report*, Washington, DC., World Bank.

Gasparini, Leonardo and Cruces, Guillermo, 2010, *Las asignaciones universales por hijo. Impacto, discusión y alternativas*, La Plata, CEDLAS.

González de la Rocha, Mercedes, 2010, "Una perspectiva latinoamericana desde Mexico: evaluaciones a los programas de transferencias condicionadas,"*Quinto Seminario Internacional Programas de transferencias condicionadas en América Latina y el Caribe: Perspectivas de los últimos 10 años*, Santiago de Chile.

Maurizio, Roxana and Perrot, Bárbara, 2011, "Transferencias monetarias a la niñez. Algunas reflexiones a partir de la experiencia de América Latina," in *Distribución del ingreso. Enfoques y políticas públicas desde el sur*, Buenos Aires, PNUD-MTEySS.

Rosenbaum, Paul and Rubin, Donald, 1983, "The Central Role of the Propensity Score in Observational Studies for Causal Effects," *Biometrika*, vol. 70, No. April (1).

Rosenbaum, Paul and Rubin, Donald, 1985, "Constructing a Control Group Using Multivariate Matched Sampling Methods that Incorporate the Propensity Score," *The American Statistician*, vol. 39, No. 1.

Salvia, Agustín *et al.*, 2012,"Informe sobre la Inseguridad Alimentaria en la Argentina. Hogares Urbanos. Año 2011,"*Documento de trabajo del Observatorio de la Deuda Social Argentina*, Buenos Aires, ODSA, UCA.

Salvia, Agustín *et al.*, 2013, "Análisis de impacto de la AUH en materia de inseguridad alimentaria y déficit educativo,"*Documento de trabajo del Observatorio de la Deuda Social Argentina*, Buenos Aires, ODSA, UCA.

Tuñón, Ianina and González, María Sol, 2012, "Efecto de las políticas de transferencias Condicionadas en la inclusión educativa,"*Revista CEE*, vol. 42, No. September (4).

Veras Soares, Fabio, 2009, "El impacto de los PTC y sus desafíos frente la crisis,"*Seminario Internacional: Repensar lo social en tiempos de crisis*, La Antigua, Guatemala, May 28 and 29.

VII. Methodological annex

1. Argentinean Social Debt Survey (EDSA)

The Argentinean Social Debt Survey is a multipurpose survey carried out at the national level since 2004 to date, on an annual basis. The EDSA studies for the 2010–16 Bicentennial started a new era in which the sample extended its reference framework. The annual measurement is carried out every third quarter of the year. The EDSA is based on a probabilistic multistage sampling design with nonproportional stratification and systematic selection of households and homes at each sampling point. The sample covers 18 urban agglomerations with over 80,000 inhabitants: the Metropolitan Area of the Greater Buenos Aires (Buenos Aires City and 24 Districts of the Metropolitan Area), Greater Cordoba, Greater Rosario, Greater Mendoza, Greater Salta, Greater Tucuman and Tafí Viejo, San Rafael, Mar del Plata, Greater Parana, Greater San Juan, Greater Resistencia, Neuquen-Plottier, Zárate, Goya, La Rioja, Comodoro Rivadavia, Ushuaia, and Rio Grande. This is a sample of homes, with a sample size of 5,700 cases. From this survey, we take information on the households, adults over 18 years, and children and teenagers between 0 and 17 years. EDSA forms and technical specifications on sample design can be consulted in *www.uca.edu.ar/observatorio*.

The sample from which the treatment group and the comparison group were formed using the matching procedure was based on the 2010, 2011, and 2012 stacked samples. These three measurements included questions that sought to identify the different types of social protection systems for children and teenagers, and particularly for the population that receives the AUH/7H.

2. Methodology used in the assessment of the impact

In this study, we made an evaluative design based on a quasi-experimental model that consisted of forming a treatment group and a comparison group to allow us to estimate the impact of the AUH, as the difference between the indicator of the result with the reception of the allowance and its counterfactual value for the receivers in the absence of the allowance. The estimation of the counterfactual was based on forming a comparison group with matched nonreceivers.

First, we selected the children between 0 and 17 years, in whose homes the responsible adult (father or mother) had a salary employment without retirement withholdings and non-salary employees who made no contributions, or unemployed and idle persons who did not receive other noncontributive assistance programs. Within this population, that meets the eligibility criteria of the program, we proceeded, on the one hand, to form a treatment group with children between 0 and 17 years who received, as stated by their reference adults, the AUH/7H,[8] and on the other hand, with those that did not receive the AUH/7H we proceeded to form a control or comparison group with the propensity score matching method, which allowed us to identify a group of children statistically similar to the group selected for the treatment group. For the selection of the comparison group

---

[8] This noncontributory pension is targeted at mothers with seven children or more who are socially vulnerable, who are not covered by provisional or noncontributory injunction. In addition, they must not own a property, goods, or receive any income that may allow subsistence. They must also not have any relatives who have a legal obligation to provide food to their children, or if they have them, they shall be unable to do so. Last, beneficiary mothers shall not be under detention or prosecution. See Law No. 23.746 and Decree No. 2360/90.

we considered a broad set of independent variables that were part of the logistic regression that allowed us to estimate the propensity scores for the matching.[9]

This methodology provided an adequate "matching" of the comparison group to the characteristics of the treatment group,[10] which allows us to evaluate the extent to which the AUH/7H has the expected effect on key aspects such as per capita family income, destitution, severe food insecurity, educational inclusion through schooling, and propensity to economic labor.

The analysis of the data built is carried out with tables that present the mean and ratio differences and their significance, as the case may be, between the participant (treatment) group and the group of nonparticipants (comparison), for each of the dependent variables considered, under the matching and by estimation through linear and logistic regression models (impact estimated with a regression adjustment).[11]

---

9   For the purposes of "matching up" the groups, we used a logit model to estimate a ratio of propensity (Rosenbaum and Rubin, 1983,1985) to being an AUH receiver, which would allow us to select in the control group any children between 0 and 17 years of age with characteristics that were "equal" to those of the receivers of the AUH (members of the experimental group). This way, each receiver is compared with the average characteristics of its most similar n individuals in the control group. See tables 1 and 2a in the annex.

10   The nearest neighbor matching was used as matching criterion, that is to say, one (1) control chosen over the nearest basis of the propensity coefficient. In this case, the individual chosen by the matching had to meet the requirement that the quadratic difference between the propensity index of being a receiver of the AUH and the propensity index of the individual of the control group had to be lesser than 0.05. The study groups (experimental and control) made up with this matching criterion were submitted to a mean difference test for each of the independent variables considered in the logit regression model used to estimate the propensity coefficient used in the "matching." Those mean difference tests indicated that the independent variables considered didn't present significant differences between the study groups as per the matching criterion.

11   The matchingonly distributes the observable characteristics equally. In other words, it assumes that there is no other relevant nonobservable variable that systematically differed between the experimental group and the comparison group and that, then, the result of the experimental group, if it had failed to participate, or to benefit from the program (that is to say, the counterfactual), equals the result of the comparison group that, actually, didn't participate. That is to say, that there is nothing that guarantees that the "matching" generated balanced experimental and comparison group samples with respect to these nonobserved factors, the measure of the impact we obtain may suffer an important bias with respect to its authentic value (Dehejia and Wahba, 1998). A regression may potentially improve the accuracy of the estimates.

The method allowed us to match 3,562 participant cases (out of the 5,476 original cases) with an optimal equalization result: None of the observed variables introduced in the model showed significant differences of less than $p = 0.10$ among the population with AUH/7H and the comparison group (see t test of mean differences in table 1a).

3. Regression models: Variables and operational definitions

Below, table 4a, is a summary chart with the dependent and independent variables included in the linear and logistic regression models, as the case may be, from which we performed the adjustments of the impact estimations.

Six regression models were performed, with which we sought to perform the impact estimations of the AUH/7H in economic welfare and human and social development indicators (table 4 b).

Table 4a. Dependent variables considered in the regression models

Dependent variables	Scale	Values and categories
Per capita income of the family (a)	Metric	
One CBA (b)	Metric	
Two CBA (c)	Metric	
Food insecurity (d)	Categorical	0. Rest (c) 1. Severe deficit
Schooling	Categorical	0. Attends school (c) 1. Does not attend school
Child labor (e)	Categorical	0. Does not work (c) 1. Economic labor

Source: EDSA-Bicentenario 2010–12. Argentinean Social Debt Observatory.
(a) The income has been normalized to December 2012 pesos.
(b) Population under 1 Basic Food Basket per capita with a value of US$77.6.
(b) Population under 2 Basic Food Baskets per capita with a value of US$155.
(d) Severe food insecurity: children who stated they felt hunger due to lack of food in the past 12 months due to economic problems (Salvia *et al.*, 2012).
(e) Children between 5 and 17 years that helped a relative or acquaintance in a job, or who performed an activity on their own to earn money serving as employees or apprentices in the past 12 months.

Table 4b. Ratio ttests for differences in the factors considered in the logit model for the estimation of the propensity index between the AUH participant group and the comparison group

	AUH participant group (%)	Comparison group (%)	Dif. (p.p.)	Significance (t test)
Sex of the child (boy/girl)	49.2	49.1	0.1	0.962
Age group of the child				
0–1 year	10.8	10.9	−0.1	0.881
2–4 years	21.9	23.2	−1.3	0.184
5–12 years	43.1	41.4	1.7	0.152
13–17 years	24.3	24.5	−0.2	0.807
Amount of children in the household				
1 child	14.2	14.7	−0.5	0.524
2 or 3 children	25.1	23.5	1.6	0.108
4 or more children	31.1	32.7	−1.6	0.149
Emotional upbringing environment (with deficit/without deficit) (a)	37.7	39.1	−1.5	0.198
Family configuration (complete parental household/incomplete parental household)	68.6	69.8	−1.2	0.244
Family nucleus (extended/non-extended)	34.1	32.9	1.2	0.268
Age group of the mother				
Up to 24 years	14.4	14.1	0.3	0.759
Between 25 and 34 years	41.3	42.8	−1.4	0.227
Between 35 and 44 years	30.9	30.8	0.1	0.936
45 years and older	13.3	12.3	1.1	0.177
Maximum educational level of the mother				
Up to incomplete secondary school	70.7	70.8	−0.1	0.893
Complete secondary school	23.4	23.5	−0.1	0.914
Tertiary or college	5.9	5.6	0.3	0.646
Migratory origin of the father/mother			0.0	
Native	76.5	75.7	0.7	0.472
Neighboring migrants	3.9	4.4	−0.5	0.287
Other non-neighboring migrants	19.6	19.8	−0.2	0.814

Job situation father/mother				
Regular job	66.0	65.5	0.5	0.665
Sub employed	19.2	18.9	0.3	0.761
Unemployed or idle	14.8	15.6	−0.8	0.366
Number of employed persons in the household (up to 1 employed person/more than 1 employed person)	47.9	47.2	0.7	0.549
NBI (with deficit/without deficit) (b)	38.4	38.9	−0.5	0.656
Socio-residential space (informal urbanization/formal urbanization) (c)	9.2	9.2	0.0	0.998
Ownership regime of the home (owners/not owners)	59.6	57.9	1.7	0.140
Urban population center				
City of Buenos Aires	2.4	3.0	−0.6	0.110
Buenos Aires Metropolitan Area	28.1	26.8	1.2	0.247
Other large metropolitan areas of the province	44.8	44.3	0.5	0.699
Rest of the urban areas of the province	24.7	25.8	−1.1	0.302
Year of the sample				
Year 2010	34.2	35.6	−1.4	0.230
Year 2011	32.7	32.7	−0.1	0.963
Year 2012	33.1	31.7	1.4	0.204

Source: EDSA-Bicentenario 2010-12. Argentinean Social Debt Observatory.

(a) Children in households in which the reference adults stated that they use forms of physical and/or verbal violence as a form of discipline for their children (teaching what is wrong).

(b) Informal urbanization: form of urbanization with no state planning and regulation, produced as a result of the occupation of (private or fiscal) land and of the self-construction of the habitat and the dwelling, with a predominance of the irregular modality of home and land ownership. Formal urbanization: form of urbanization with state planning and regulation in the construction and urban infrastructure.

(c) Unsatisfied basic needs (NBI): children in households that present at least one of the following deprivations: 1—three or more persons per habitable room, 2—living in an inadequate dwelling (room in a tenement, precarious dwelling), 3—homes with no kind of WC, 4—homes with a child in school age (6-12) who does not attend school, 5—homes with four or more persons per employed member, and, 6—additionally, whose head of the family has completed primary school as the highest level of education.

INTEGRAL PROTECTION OF CHILDHOOD THROUGH THE "CHILE GROWS WITH YOU" (CHILE CRECE CONTIGO, CHCC) SUBSYSTEM: ANALYSIS OF A POLICY TO BREAK THE INTERGENERATIONAL CYCLE OF POVERTY AND INEQUALITY

Cristian HERRERA[1]
Alejandra VIVES
Camila CARVALLO
Helia MOLINA

> I. Introduction. II. Purpose. III. Methodology. IV. Results. V. Lessons Learned. VI. Bibliography. VII. Annexes.

I. Introduction

1. Situation of poverty and child inequality in Chile

The "Chile Grows With You" (Chile Crece Contigo, ChCC) integral protection of childhood subsystem is created out of the need of generating more equality among children. Inequality is one of the main challenges that our country must face today. To put it in context, child poverty has decreased

---

[1] Pontificia Universidad Católica de Chile physician; Universidad de Chile master in Administration (MBA) and London School of Economics and Political Science (LSE) master in public policies. Currently assistant researcher at the Public Health Department of Pontificia Universidad Católica de Chile, and cabinet advisor of the health minister of the government of Chile.
Universidad de Chile physician, Universidad Católica de Chile specialist in public health, and Universitat Pompeu Fabra, Barcelona PhD in epidemiology and public health. Assistant professor in the Public Health Department of Pontificia Universidad Católica de Chile, and associate researcher with the Centro para el Desarrollo Urbano Sustentable (CEDEUS), "Conicyt/Fondap/15110020."
Pontificia Universidad Católica de Chile psychologist and candidate to a master's in policy and government from Universidad Diego Portales. She has participated in several evaluations of the Biopsychosocial Development Support Program of Chile Crece Contigo.
Universidad de Chile physician, specialist in pediatrics and Universidad de Chile master in public health. Pediatrics and Public Health Professor at Pontificia Universidad Católica de Chile; national executive secretary of Chile Crece Contigo until 2010 Ministry of Health. She is currently the minister of health of the government of Chile.

significantly in Chile since the return of the country to democracy (approximately 60% between 1990 and 2006 for children under 17 years). However, and despite the growth of per capita GDP, since 2009 the decreasing trend in the incidence of poverty in Chile stagnated for all age groups (figure 1).

Chile is a country of contrasts and paradoxes. Although child poverty is present, and its reduction is much slower than that of the general population, health and nutrition indicators are comparable to those of countries with much higher per capita income. The figure of child mortality in 2013 was 7.4 per 1,000 born alive, which makes Chile the country with the lowest child mortality in Latin America. Also the child malnutrition is very low and, in most cases, it is associated with chronic diseases of the child. Conversely, there has been a progressive increase of overweight and obesity, which, like most damages to health, is more prevalent among the population of lower socioeconomic level.

However, in Chile there is major income inequality: Among the countries with high and very high human development (PNUD, 2011), it has one of the highest inequalities in income distribution. In relation to the autonomous per capita income of the households, the households in the richest decile concentrate around 40% of the income, whereas the households in the poorest decile concentrate only 1%.

Likewise, there is a major gap in poverty levels among adults and children and teenagers in the country. According to the data from 2011, 22.8% of the children and teenagers were poor in Chile, practically twice the number found in the population above 17 years, among whom poverty was 11.5%.

Figure 1. Trends of poverty among children (%), teenagers, and adults. Chile 1990-2011

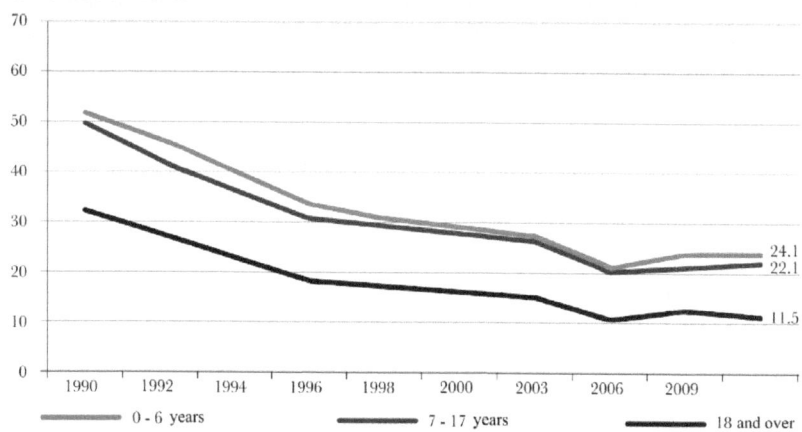

Source: Prepared with data from the Social Development Ministry 2012.

This is explained because the incidence of poverty is 3.3 times higher in the households that have children and teenagers among their members (18.3%), compared to the households where there are none (5.4%) (Ministry of Social Development, 2012). The reasons that may contribute to this increased poverty among families with children or teenagers may possibly include a higher rate of fertility and less female participation in the job market among the households with lower income. In the households of the lower decile, only 24% of the women participate in the job market, compared to 63% in the richest decile (Ministry of Social Development, 2012). Another reason may be the growing proportion of female heads of monoparental households in the lower socioeconomic levels (Ministry of Social Development, 2012).

2. Child development in Chile

Child development not only consists of growing up and maturing but also involves a set of processes through which they gradually form their functions, roles, and capacities. The daily experiences of children in exchange with their different characterizational environments allow the deployment of functions in several domains: physical, social, emotional, linguistic, and cognitive (Bedregal, 2010). Backwardness is the situation in which a child has not attained the functions expected of the child for his or her age (Bedregal, 2010).

Despite the fact that by 2006 poverty had been reduced to 13.7% (Social Development Ministry, 2011), the backwardness and retardation rates in child development were high. The Quality of Life and Health Survey, Encavi 2006, collected a nationally representative sample that evaluated early child development (Vallebuona, 2011). Based on the data collected there, backwardness affected 29.9% of the population between 2 months and 5 years, and it was markedly higher in the poorest quintile than in the richest one (Molina et al., 2008) (figure 2).

Figure 2. Child development backwardness for I and V income quintiles, by age group. Chile 2006

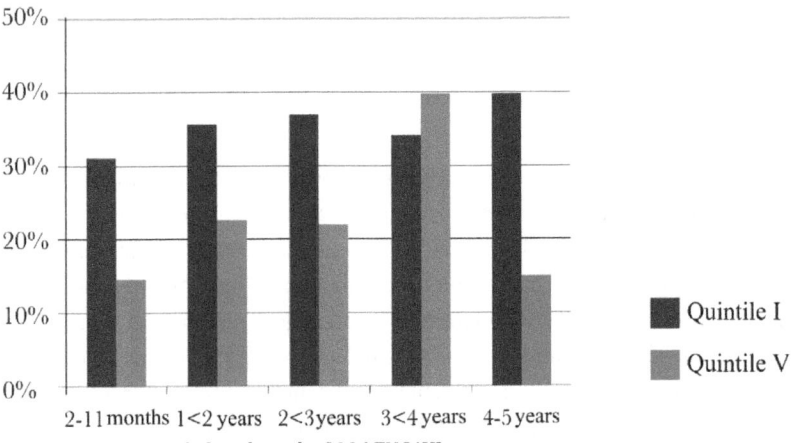

Source: Prepared with data from the 2006 ENCAVI survey.

Considering various criteria that allow measuring the conditions for an adequate child development in Chile, the 2010 Early Childhood Longitudinal Survey (ELPI) verified that 21% of the children did not leave their home for distraction at least four times a week, 19% did not have at least one game that involved muscular activity, 21% did not have literary or musical material at home, 28.5% did not own or share with his siblings three or more books, and 27% did not have learning equipment adequate for their age, as mobiles, table and chair, high chair, baby cage, and others (Behrman et al., 2010). According to the 2010 Early Childhood National Survey, ENPI, around 20% of the children live in neighborhoods where public spaces, the proximity of squares or green areas, and sports courts or centers are considered as poor or very poor by their care providers. Even worse, 40% considers that the recreational spaces or play areas for children under 6 years are poor or very poor (Junta Nacional de Jardines Infantiles (JUNJI), United Nations Children's Fund (UNICEF) and United Nations Organization for Education, Science and Culture (UNESCO), 2010).

3. "Chile Crece Contigo" integral protection of childhood subsystem

The Chile Crece Contigo integral protection of childhood subsystem was created in 2006 as a way of generating more adequate conditions for children to achieve their optimal development potential and of breaking the intergenerational cycle of poverty. The subsystem would be part of the Chilean "Protege" social protection network (figure 3). The Social Protection System is the set of policies of programs aimed at fighting poverty, inequalities, and their structural causes by protecting the most vulnerable groups. Likewise, it is intended to generate a greater independence of the families with respect to the state by promoting the generation of competencies and adequate environments. The social protection system in Chile grants protection throughout the entire life cycle, with various components, which include the "Chile Crece Contigo" integral protection of childhood subsystem. The measures considered by the subsystem have a protective and preventive nature, and they are based on the children's rights approach, understanding the state as the custodian of the enforcement of the rights.

Figure 3. The Chilean social protection system. Main components

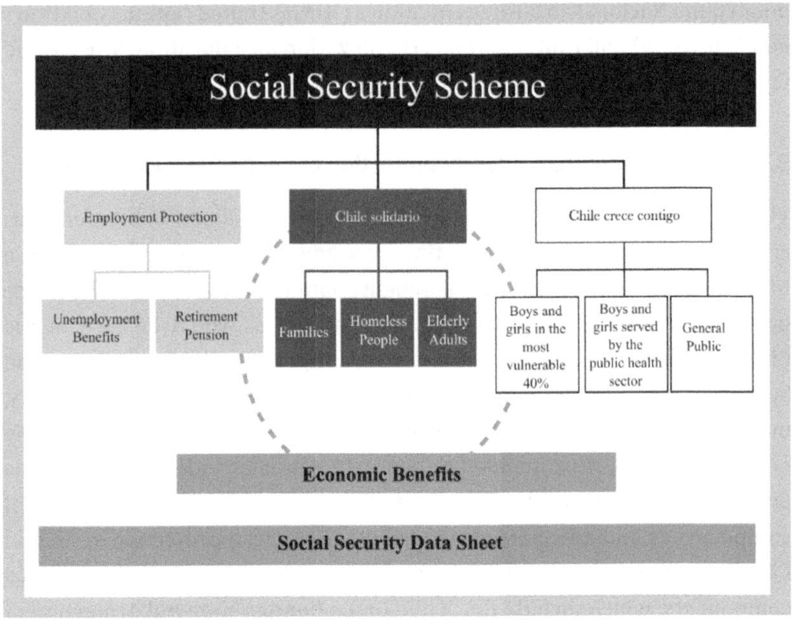

Source: Chile Crece Contigo, government of Chile.

The purpose of ChCC then is to guarantee, from an intersectoral logic, the achievement of the optimum integral (biopsychosocial) development potential of each child, regardless of their socioeconomic conditions, ethnicity, geographical location, or other conditions into which the child may have been born. ChCC seeks to progress toward equal rights and opportunities and to the reduction of equality gaps by standardizing opportunities and supporting the biopsychosocial development from the time of pregnancy until the age of 4, when the school phase starts.

With the creation of the ChCC Subsystem, the benefits and support for children were organized in three levels: those aimed at all the children of the country, those aimed at the children who receive attention in the public healthcare system (approximately 80%), and last, those aimed at children for whom a situation of physical, psychosocial, or economic vulnerability is detected. The benefits provided, in turn, are organized in three components: health, education, and social network. Considering the ecological model of development, the actions are targeted at the child, his or her family, and the community.

Thus, all children in Chile, and the responsible adults, have access to universal benefits, which are consistent of mass education programs (see figure 4 and annex 1), and they benefit from legislative improvement proposals for the protection of children and their families (Silva and Molina, 2010).

The axis program for children who receive attention in the public healthcare network is the Biopsychosocial Development Support program (PADB), which has different components according to the age and condition of the child (see annex 1). PADB constitutes the gateway to the subsystem, and the initial milestone is the first prenatal control, which is performed by the Ministry of Health by way of the Health Services throughout the country.

Finally, for children and families who receive attention in the public healthcare network and who present a situation of vulnerability, ChCC offers differentiated "general" benefits, and for those in extreme vulnerability conditions, preferential access benefits (figure 4 and annex 1) (Chile Crece Contigo, 2014) are given.

Figure 4. Benefits of the Integral protection of childhood subsystem

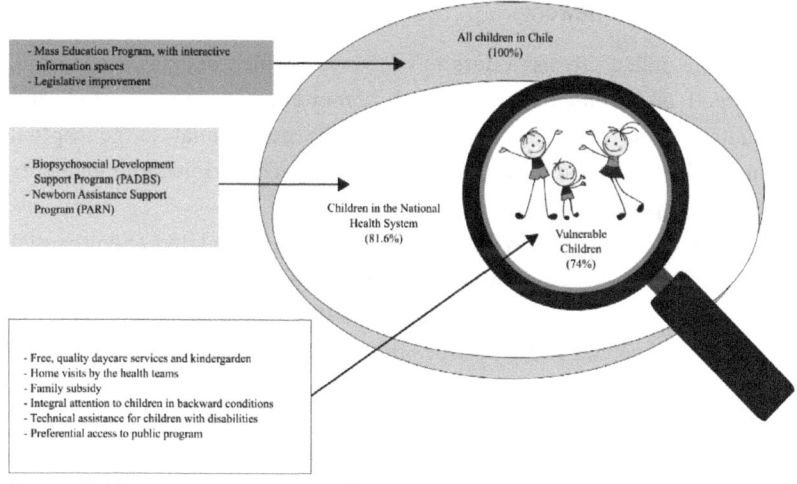

Source: ChCC presentation, year 2012 (http://www.crececontigo.gob.cl/).

In the logic of a longitudinal accompaniment to the development path of the child during the early years, the completion milestone of ChCC is their admission to pre-kinder (pre-kindergarten) at 4 years of age (Silva and Molina, 2010).

II. Purpose

Having described the current situation of the childhood in Chile and the main components of ChCC, we know that many actors and entities were and continue to be involved in the birth and development of the program. The path to earn a space in the public discussion andto have it approved and executed has been complex and informed by various factors. In this context, ChCC has had a public policy process with a structured documentation that may be used for its future review and improvement, and also as an overview that can be used in other countries in the fight against child poverty. This article seeks to explore the development process of ChCC and the factors that influenced its evolution, final content, and its current results.

III. Methodology

1. Conceptual framework

The public policy process refers to the way in which policies are started, developed or formulated, negotiated, communicated, implemented, and evaluated (Buse *et al.*, 2005). Based on the policy analysis conceptual framework of Walt and Gilson (1994), we focus on describing four elements of the development of ChCC:

- The context in which the policy was formulated and executed refers to the systemic—national and international political, economic, and social—factors that may have an impact on it. Leichter (1979) divides them into four factors:
    - *Situational*: transitory, nonpermanent, or idiosyncratic conditions that may have an impact on the policy. For example, wars, natural disasters, the arrival of a certain person to power, and others.
    - *Structural*: relatively non-modifiable elements of society. For example, the political, economic or employment system, technological progress, demographic–epidemiologic characteristics, and others.

- o *Cultural*: the traditions, customs, and social and moral regions that prevail in a country. For example, ethnical or linguistic differences, religions.
  - o *International*: exogenous components that lead to an increased interdependence between states, and that influence policy.
- The actors involved in the formulation of the policy, which may be individuals, groups, or public or private institutions, national or international organizations, and the perceived or real power they may exert.
- The steps associated with the development of the policy, from its inclusion in the agenda, formulation, negotiation and decision, communication, implementation and evaluation.
- The content of the policy, which refers to the different policy alternatives that emerged, were moved and interacted to finally arrive to the final definitions.

There are multiple and varied interactions between these four elements; therefore, although the conceptual framework will serve to systematize the ChCC process, the dynamism associated with any public policy must be taken into consideration.

2. Data collection method

First, we gathered documents, reports, publications, and others, related to the ChCC program, considering anything related to child development, social protection, and public policy in Chile and abroad. This included the review of government websites, general searches in Google Scholar, and expert consultations.

To explore the process of conception and development of ChCC, we performed semistructured interviews with persons who were closely involved in the subject, considering the perspective of three sectors: the Health Ministry, the Social Development Ministry (formerly Ministry of Planning), and academia. The interviews were conducted in person or via videoconference, recording everything the interviewees said, and safeguarding their confidentiality.

IV. Results

1. Policy analysis

A. Context

a. Relevant background

The first relevant precedent for the formulation of ChCC was the creation of a National Policy for Children and Teenagers between 2001 and 2010. This national policy posits that the integrality of the public policy management model is a challenge that demands that the actions aimed at the promotion and protection of the rights overcome the limitations of sectoral perspectives. This national policy presents the need of establishing institutionality and a regulatory framework on early childhood issues.

This national policy was accompanied in 2003 by a Council of Ministers for Children and Teenagers. The council should have informed the president of the Republic on the progress in the field of protection and enforcement of the rights in this age group. However, this Council of Ministers, led by the Ministry of Planning, only issued one report that was presented that year, operated irregularly, and had no political support from the ministries involved. Finally, it was dismissed without materializing a proposal in terms of institutionality (Duarte and Torres, 2010).

A relevant precedent for the subsequent implementation of Chile Crece Contigo is Chile Solidario, which started in 2002 and sought to accompany and provide psychosocial support to Chilean families in extreme poverty, by providing them with tools to overcome this situation. This is the main precedent for the formulation of the Childhood Protection Subsystem, in terms of the interdisciplinary logic and the use of the available benefits.

ChCC is also based on the prior existence of a network of child support services, on top of which it develops a series of services that add integrality and consistency to the existing supply, in addition to delivering tools for detection and early intervention in cases of risk, backwardness, or retardation.

A highlight of the Chilean child services on which the subsystem relies is the several different services destined to maternal-children health. There are long-existing programs for the reduction of problems such as mortality and for the prevention of disease. The country attained, years ago, a wide coverage of professional childbirth attention (99%) and of quality prenatal attention in the public sector (60%).[2] Health care for children in the public health system, articulated around the Program of the Child, is provided at the network of primary attention offices by professional teams (physicians, nurses, midwives, nutritionists, kinesiologists, psychologists, and social assistants) in which some of them act as part of the periodic health controls for the child, and others act when specific needs are detected.

The control of the health of the child used to include the application of an evaluation of psychomotor development and a risk factors survey, but it is estimated that before being installed in ChCC, the coverage of the evaluation of psychomotor development did not reach 20%, and there was no guide or a clear network for referrals if any problem was detected (Bedregal, 2010).

As to cultural factors, before the creation of ChCC children were pretty much invisible for public policy and for the distribution of resources, except for the health system, were the mother–child dyad had a great relevance for primary healthcare (APS), which facilitated the decision of having this start in the health sector.

In terms of structural factors, the country was evaluating that child mortality was to a certain degree "under control"; therefore, new challenges were starting to be explored, where child development gained relevance in the addressing of its social determinants.

As to international influence, for the issue of the social protection of children to start being discussed, the events (e.g., seminars) organized by international bodies such as the World Bank, the Inter-American Development Bank, and UNICEF contributed the first spaces to deal with, discuss, and eventually advocate the subject. In the same vein, they served to disseminate and accumulate scientific evidence on the importance of the early days of life for the future of any person.

b. The first steps toward a protection system

The process of designing the public policy for the protection of chidren started during the government of President Ricardo Lagos. The Ministry of Planning (Mideplan) advanced the initiative of generating a Childhood

---

2   In Bedregal, 2010, with data from Minsal, 2006.

Protection System that would use the same networks used for the installation of Chile Solidario. That ministry gathered a group of technicians to design a proposal. Simultaneously, the Ministry of Finance raised the concern of increasing female participation in the job market, and so there was an interest in financing the process for the creation of a public policy for early childhood, which would also be a participative process that would include gender issues.

The second report on the progress in the field of the protection and enforcement of the rights of children and teenagers was presented in 2004, and it revealed large deficits in complying with the Convention on the Rights of the Child. That is the reason that Mideplan started cost studies in 2005 for the implementation of that public policy. Simultaneously, some scholars presented a project to the UNDP to incorporate a module to measure the situation of Chilean children under 5 years into the National Quality of Life Survey (2006). The survey was carried out in 4,997 homes with national, regional, and urban–rural representativity. This survey revealed the profound inequalities that existed in the country.

As a situational factor, the arrival of Michelle Bachelet to the presidency of the country was very relevant. She, as a pediatrician, was highly aware of child issues and committed a sizable portion of her political capital to see this subsystem through. On the other hand, a Presidential Consultative Commission for the reform of the social security system was formed simultaneously to the development of ChCC, which took most of the media, political, and social attention, which in turn enabled the child protection system to progress more smoothly. In addition, 2006 saw the start of the so-called penguin revolution, in which secondary school students in Chile used public demonstrations and activities to demand the establishment of quality education as a right that was guaranteed by the state, among other things. This, with other factors, including the financial one, led to the reduction of the focus of the social protection system, initially planned until 8 years of age, to 4 years, which is the age in which children join the formal school system, which needed to be reformed before including it in a Child Protection System.

The Presidential Advisory Council for the Reform of Childhood Policy started operations on March 30, 2006, and it worked for a total of three months. Its 14 members and the Technical Secretariat met at (the Presidential Palace of) La Moneda, which show the importance that child issues had for the president. The Commission was led by Jaime Crispi, an economist who had been involved in child and female job participation issues.

B. Actors involved in the ChCC process

As mentioned, President Bachelet had a central role as a political leader in promoting and developing ChCC. Among several other "presidential commissions" formed during her administration, there was the "Presidential Advisory Council for the Reform of Childhood Policy," which in 2006 gathered 14 health, economy, psychology, sociology, and public policy professionals, with different political views and with experience in social policy from different approaches. The mandate was to prepare proposals to generate a system for social protection and for the reduction of childhood inequalities.

This council called other groups to listen to their experiences and opinions, including scientific societies, universities, families, street children, unions, and so on, to receive their proposals. Citizens contributed their opinions through a website that attracted 22,000 contributions from adults and 11,000 from children. In addition, its members were distributed to each of the regions of the country, carrying out workshops on the subject with civil society organizations, and getting informed of the local needs. In the third sector, NGOs such as the Center for Development and Psychosocial Stimulation Studies (CEDEP), the Center for Children and Women Studies and Attention (CEANIM), and the Home of Christ participated, but their influence was more of a consultancy. The "for profit" private sector did not have a significant participation in the work of the commission.

In turn, the creation of a Committee of Ministers for Childhood gave a political and decision-making boost to ChCC. It was integrated by the Ministries of Planning (current Social Development Ministry), of Health, of Education, of Labor, of Justice, of Housing and Urbanism, of Finance, the General Secretariat of the Presidency, and the National Service for Women.

C. Political process of CHCC

The chronological process is shown below:
- 2004–05: isolated pre-investment studies are conducted on some of the alternatives related to a social protection system for childhood. The issue starts to be outlined in the presidential

campaign. In turn, international bodies generate spaces for debate and for the dissemination of information.
- 2006: the Presidential Advisory Council and the Inter-ministerial Council are created.
- 2007: implementation begins in 100 communes throughout Chile, with the intention of making a pilot of the program.
- 2008: ChCC is extended to all the communes in the country. In turn, the draft law for the social protection of childhood is submitted to the Parliament.
- 2009: the law is enacted and the institutional and regulatory framework of ChCC comes into effect.
- 2010-13: a series of process and qualitative evaluations are performed, without carrying out an experimental study to evaluate one of the interventions related to the improvement of the capacities of the parents in terms of the upbringing and development of the children.

The draft law that created the Protection System and the Integral Protection of Childhood Subsystem is submitted to the Chamber of Deputies on December 4, 2008, and it is finally enacted on August 17, 2009, which tells how fast it was discussed in Congress.

2. Political agenda

Its inclusion in the political agenda was largely determined by the boost provided by President Bachelet, who, in addition to giving political priority to the issue, created both the Presidential Advisory Council and the Committee of Ministers for Childhood, which gave a boost to the discussion that would later go to the Parliament. That is to say, it was the political channel that in the end opened a "window of opportunity" (Kingdon, 1995) to which the policy alternatives were submitted, providing a foundation and content to the collaborative discussion that took place in the preparation of ChCC.

3. Negotiations and decision-making

The first negotiations and deliberations occurred in the Committee of Ministers for Childhood, where the proposals of the Presidential Advisory Council were reviewed, and the more transcendental public policy were defined including budget allocations. In the Parliament, the discussion and approval took place without significant setbacks, and the policy was approved unanimously both in the Chamber of Deputies and in the Senate.

A consensus-driven environment was promoted inside the Presidential Advisory Council. One of the points that caused the greatest divergences was precisely education. The selection in the primary and secondary schools was a point of debate, which was finally settled with the limitation of the practice, with the opposition of some of the attendants. Likewise, the cancellation of children enrollment was also a point of debate, and finally it was decided that it would be applied only in extreme cases, with objections from some of the advisors, who said that during the preschool and basic stage, there is no reason that may justify the cancellation of the enrollment. These objections were noted in the final document: "The future of children is always today" (Presidential Advisory Council for the Reform of Childhood Policy, 2006).

Another point of debate in the Presidential Advisory Council was the character of the system, which was proposed as universal, but some of the attendants argued that it should focus on the most vulnerable sectors of the population. The council in the end agreed on a combination of universal and focused policies. Another negotiation that took place was the incorporation and articulation of the National Service for Minors (Sename) with the system. This discussion was complex, as it involved regulating the public–private relationship that exists in this institution in Chile. In it, there was a proposal to make the Sename a part of the Social Development Ministry, dependent on the system, to the opposition of some advisors.

Last, the Presidential Advisory Council also discussed the role of women and their integration into the job market, a discussion where there were differences in terms of value and of the associated public policies, for example, kindergartens and the role of child care. Although this was a central issue in the formulation of the policy, there are no concrete proposals related to the integration of women into the job market, in support of child care or joint responsibility.

The Committee of Ministers made modifications to the proposal advanced by the Presidential Advisory Committee. Although some of the modifications respond to the political context of the time, others may be explained from the economic standpoint. An example of this is the limitation of postnatal to six months, which was approved in Chile some years later, during the Sebastián Piñera administration.

In the Congress, as previously mentioned, the level of consensus was very high. A subject discussed was the need of a new institutionality for public childhood policies, such as the creation of a sub-secretariat. Likewise, some of the members of Parliament questioned the need for the creation of this subsystem, arguing the previous existence of programs that dealt with early childhood issues, primarily from a health perspective. This is because rather than creating new programs, ChCC meant to articulate already existing programs, and from this articulating role, it posited the need of creating this public policy. It was also here where the need emerged to include the six-month postnatal to the project and to make changes to the institutionality of Sename. In the end, the only modifications made to the project at this stage were the increase of the coverage of the benefits, from 40 to 60% for the most vulnerable, and the incorporation of a section requesting the systematic evaluation of the subsystem by an institution that was independent of the government of the day.

4. Implementation

The design of the Integral Protection of Childhood Subsystem was based on the successful installation of Chile Solidario. However, the installation of ChCC experienced greater difficulties than the former.

The interviewees highlighted the difficulties found in this part of the process of the policy, which include the following:

- The human resources lacked the necessary competencies for an integral approach, and for an adequate network effort within the territorial space of the health center. In addition, the primary healthcare model that prevailed (mainly biomedical, assistentialist) clashed with the biopsychosocial model that ChCC sought to implement. The training and online resources were not enough. On the other hand, the staff hired for ChCC is under a contractual regime that offers no job stability or access to a career as an official, which has caused a high turnover.
- For health system workers, ChCC was in many cases seen as an appendix, something extra, new staff conducting new tasks, and therefore, a new problem. Some local teams even rejected it, because they saw it as an imposition.

- The information system for the longitudinal monitoring of the children to evaluate the completion of the actions has seen a progressive impairment, both of the recording and monitoring system as well as of the referrals system. Currently, the information system is out of use at the national level.
- Although there are variations for the different communes throughout the country, a significant portion of the written protocols are not being followed in practice. For example, one recommendation is that house visits should be performed by technical staff, but most of them are performed by professionals.
- The connection of the professionals and the system with the parents and the community is still deficient.
- Despite there being a law approved in 2009, as of August 2014 there is still no rulebook, by the Social Development Ministry, to establish the regulation of the subsystem.
- In recent years, there has been a lack of articulation of the efforts of the health, education, and social development sectors. This has been mainly observed in the practical work of the teams of the different sectors involved.
- The abysmal operational differences of the subsystem from one commune to another, particularly the differences between communes with more human resources *versus* mainly rural communes that have not had sufficient support from the central government.

The factors that have facilitated the implementation of what currently exists include the resource transfer agreements associated with results indicators, which turned out to be a good incentive to harmonize the teams. The Social Development Ministry also has a protected budget to act as an intersectoral coordinator, and it must be highlighted that in recent years the annual percentage increase has been gradually reduced (see annex 2). This sets a difference in the priority given to ChCC between the government that originated it and the following one, in which the policy changed. On the other hand, the Health Ministry in itself is an institution with a culture of processes and protocols, which, along with its presence throughout the country, has contributed to its execution. Finally, the character imposed at the beginning has helped one to maintain the spirit of ChCC, despite the difficulties of recent years.

A very important social communication plan, comprising various strategies, was created to support and promote a better implementation. A website was created for parents, professionals, children, and others, which installed the public policy in the virtual social networks. A national radio program was started, which was coordinated by the Social Development Ministry. In addition, a "Fono infancia" hotline was made available to the public to obtain information and guidance on ChCC. Last, the communication of the policy to the local level was conceived with language as homogeneous as possible, using materials such as diptychs-triptychs, billboards, music CDs, tales, postcards, which sought to position the new ChCC brand. For example, these materials were delivered every time the mother or the child had any contact with the health system, and they also represented sources of information for the staff of the public system.

To support the system, an Executive Secretariat was created for ChCC, which operated between 2007 and 2011 and was in charge of informing the Technical Committee of ChCC and the Committee of Ministers. This model was eliminated in 2011, which undermined the technical support representatives model.

5. Evaluation

The evaluation of ChCC started from the design, including what would be measured and what were the results or outcomes. But the evaluation model was developed as the project progressed. In particular, the path that the evaluation should follow was decided in the political circles. This way, it was decided to evaluate every child, without establishing a control group and to make isolated evaluations with a program evaluation scheme, for example, house visits, parental skills, and others. In addition, there was a monitoring of the coverage attained by the program and its services, which have been lower than expected. The general evaluation model can be seen in figure 5. The interviewees indicated that the results there are today are not reporting the evolution of the policy, and that the execution of some evaluations has not been sufficiently rigorous.

Figure 5. Evaluation model of the Chile Crece Contigo program

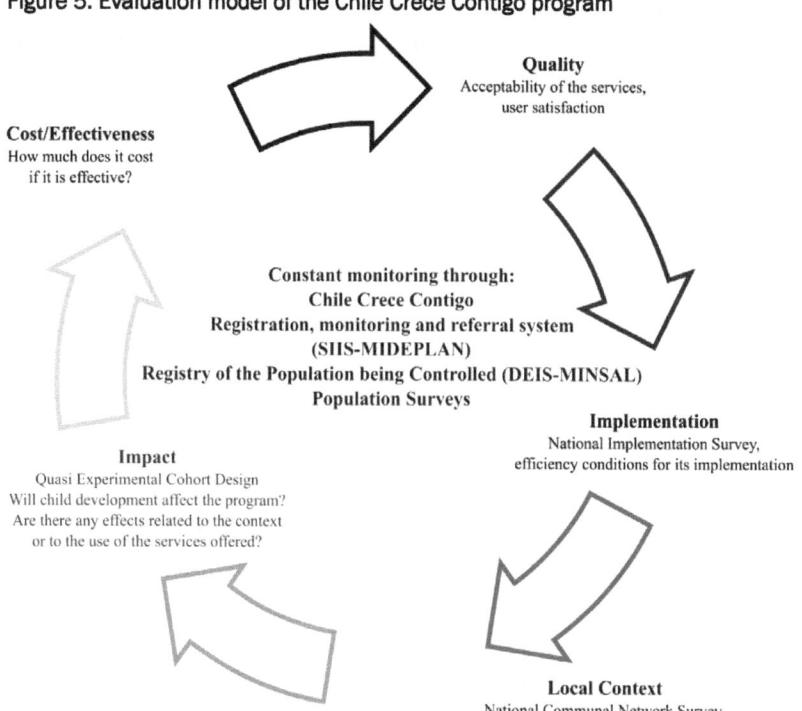

Source: presentation by Dr. Helia Molina, Public Health Department, PUC.

Some of the evaluations performed to date are related to the use and identification of critical bottlenecks and improvements to the Registration, Referral and Monitoring System (EKOS Consultores, 2013), the implementation of the "Nobody is Perfect [Nadie es Perfecto, Centro de Estudios de Desarrollo y Estimulación Psicosocial (CEDEP) 2013]," group workshop of parental competencies, a qualitative analysis of the PADB (Fundación GESTA—Corporación MOVILIZA, 2009), and the monitoring of users cases of the Chile Crece Contigo System (Galerna Consultores, 2012), among others.

A. The content of the policy

The context of the reality of the country was considered within all the potential alternatives of public policies for a national social protection system for childhood. All children and pregnant women approach the health sector, where there is a culture of trust in the medical team, prenatal and postnatal controls, and a public network of primary healthcare attention installed that covers more than 80% of the population, including the most vulnerable families and children. In that sense, it became the executive arm of a large part of the policies of ChCC. It used to be said that the health sector already had the children, and that the only thing that needed to be done was changing the way of doing some things.

With this in mind, all the measures were based on the best evidence available in international and Latin American literature (very little) in terms of what would be the best interventions. It must be noted that there was no formal technical assistance from international agencies.

a. Discussion

This is the first policy analysis of ChCC, the social protection system for children in Chile, of which we are aware. The main findings include that the main actor in the political promotion of ChCC was President Michelle Bachelet during her first administration (2006–11), who as early as her campaign made this a priority. The policy design mechanism is also interesting, with a technical component in the "Presidential Advisory Council" and a political one in the Inter-ministry Committee, in which the political ministries of the sectors involved deliberated on the final characteristics and components of the program and promoted its execution. Having an Advisory Council allowed the engagement of the main spaces for citizen participation and interest groups in this instance, which helped one to organize in a more structured fashion the policy design process of ChCC. After this, the most concrete and final decision-making happened at the level of the ministers, who had more freedom to decide given the preliminary process that provided legitimacy before and secured the acceptance of the interest groups. In the deliberation process, the unanimous approval of the Parliament must be highlighted, given that it mainly had a role of ratification, when ChCC had already been in implementation for two years.

Another relevant point has to do with the social communication strategy, which in the early years had a great relevance to effectively promote ChCC, and specially to inform the public, particularly the parents. However, in time, this has been declining, which affects not only the public but also the teams that implement the policy. On this subject, various implementation issues have been identified, which have grown deeper in recent years.

In addition, it must be noted that ChCC has undergone the transition from a Coalition for Democracy government (center-left) to an alliance for Chile government (center-right), which has shifted the priority of the program, as we saw in terms of budget, the coordination efforts in the field, and the evaluation initiatives.

V. Lessons learned

The lessons learned in this public policy process for the social protection of childhood include the following:
- The political commitment, in this case from the president of the Republic, was a core component in the success at the start and during the deliberation and development of the policy.
- The existence of an Advisory Council, transversal in political terms, and highly qualified in technical terms, which channeled both scientific evidence and the participation of regular citizens and of organized civil society.
- The participation of the public in the formulation process.
- The existence of a single information system at the national level, a key to monitor the policy and supervise its progress.
- Setting the policies in motion is an aspect that must be addressed in a closer relationship with local teams from the start, and it must be maintained over time. Special attention must be given to the training of the human resources and the work modality of model that exists in practice. If there is no biopsychosocial vision installed, it must be worked on with specific measures.
- The evaluation must be defined from the start and with the participation and agreement of the decision-makers at the highest level, so that it will take place effectively and according to the plan.

Chile still has pending challenges related to childhood issues and related to guaranteeing the rights of every children. Clearly, one of them is the lack of a Law for the Social Protection of Children and Teenagers that will articulate all childhood policies. This is a commitment that must be urgently met by our country. The lack of a Law for the Social Protection of Children and Teenagers has an impact on the operation of the ChCC, considering that one of the main criticisms of the subsystem is the lack of articulation between the benefits and the institutions involved in their implementation. This Law for the Social Protection of Children and Teenagers is part of the commitments assumed by Chile in the Convention on the Rights of children, and it is still pending. A Law for the Protection of Rights establishes the rights and benefits to guarantee the rights that children are entitled to, some of which must be delivered by ChCC. Also the need emerges that Law 20.379, which creates the subsystem for the Integral Protection of Childhood, has rules that allow the materialization of its provisions, to effectively guarantee the rights of the Convention on the Rights of the Child.

There are other challenges for the ChCC, including the need to make progress on gender equality, in co-responsibility in child care, and in improving certain aspects of the development of the children, such as language, where the greatest backwardness is observed. There is also a need of making progress in the development of parental capacities, by training the staff that delivers the benefits.

Last, the need has been discussed to expand the subsystem to 8-year-olds, or to generate a new protection childhood subsystem for children and teenagers. Extending it to 6-year-olds is a challenge that has been assumed by President Bachelet in her second presidential term.

In the current situation, the main challenge for the ChCC program is recovering its integral and intersectoral focus, gaining new impulse to better reach the teams and the families, and evaluating its progress and results in a more methodical and deeper manner.

VI. Bibliography

Bedregal, Paula, 2010, "Chile Crece Contigo: El desafio de la protección social a la infancia," in Larrañaga, Osvaldo and Contreras, Dante (eds.), *Las nuevas politicas de protección social en Chile*, Santiago, Chile.

Behrman, Jere *et al.*, 2010, *Encuesta longitudinal de la primera infancia: aspectos metodológicos y primeros resultados*, Departmentso de Economía, Universidad de Chile.

Bronfenbrenner, Urie, 1979, *The Ecology of Human Development*, Cambridge, MA, Harvard University Press.

Buse, Kent *et al.*, 2005, *Making Health Policy*, Nueva York, Open University Press.

Centro de Estudios de Desarrollo and Estimulación Psicosocial (CEDEP), 2013, "Estudio cualitativo sobre la implementación del Taller Grupal de Competencias

Parentales Nadie es Perfecto,"*http://www.crececontigo.gob.cl/wp-content/uploa ds/2013/07/21-Informe-final-Estudio-cualitativo-implementacion-Nadie-es-perf ecto.pdf.*

Consejo Asesor Presidencial para la Reforma de Políticas de Infancia, 2006, *El futuro de los niños es siempre hoy*.

Duarte,Claudio and Torres, Osvaldo, 2010, "Niñez y políticas públicas," in *Revista Mad*, No. 3.

EKOS Consultores, 2013, "Evaluación del uso e identificación de nudos críticos y mejoras al Sistema de Registro, Derivación y Monitoreo del Susbsitema de Protección a la Infancia Chile Crece Contigo," Chile, EKOS Consultores, *http://www.crececontigo.gob.cl/wp-content/uploads/2013/07/19-Informe-Final-Eva luación-del-uso-e-identificación-de-nudos-críticos-y-mejoras-al-SDRM.pdf.*

Galerna Consultores, 2012, "Seguimiento de casos de usuarias del Sistema Chile Crece Contigo," Galerna Consultores, *http://www.crececontigo.gob.cl/wp-content/upl oads/2013/07/10-Informe-final-Estudio-de-seguimiento-de-casos-usuarias-Siste ma-Chile-Crece-Contigo.pdf.*

Gobierno de Chile, *Chile Crece Contigo*, website.

Junta Nacional de Jardines Infantiles (JUNJI), United Nations Children's Fund (UNICEF) and United Nations Organization for Education, Science and Culture (UNESCO), 2010, "Encuesta Nacional de la Primera Infancia," *Preliminary Results*.

Kingdon, John W., 1995, *Agendas, Alternatives, and Public Policies, Policy*, vol. 2, 2nd ed.

Leichter, Howard, 1979, *A Comparative Approach to Policy Analysis: Health Care Policy in Four Nations*, Cambridge, Cambridge University Press.

Ministerio de Desarrollo Social, Gobierno de Chile, 2011, *Encuesta de Caracterización Socioeconómica, CASEN*, 2011.

Molina, Helia *et al.*, 2008, "De la sobrevida al desarrollo integral de la infancia: Pasos en el desarrollo del sistema de protección integral a la infancia,"*Revista chilena de pediatría*, vol. 79, No. 1.

Fundación GESTA – Corporación MOVILIZA, 2009, "Análisis Cualitativo Programa de Apoyo al Desarrollo Biopsicosocial,"*http://www.crececontigo.gob.cl/wp-content/uplo ads/2013/07/1-Informe-final-Analisis-cualitativo-programa-de-apoyo-al-desarr ollo-biopsicosocial.pdf.*

Observatorio Social. Ministerio de Desarrollo Social, 2012a, *Infancia y adolescencia*, CASEN 2011.

Observatorio Social. Ministerio de Desarrollo Social, 2012b, *Mujeres, pobreza y trabajo*.

PNUD, 2011, "Informe sobre Desarrollo Humano 2011. Sostenibilidad y equidad: un mejor futuro para todos," en *http://www.undp.org/content/undp/es/home/librarypa ge/hdr/human_developmentreport2011/.*

Silva Villalobos and Molina Helia, 2010, *Cuatro años creciendo juntos. Memoria de la instalación del Sistema de Protección Integral a la Infancia Chile Crece Contigo 2006–2010* (p. 99), Santiago, Chile.

Vallebuona, Clelia, 2011, *Primera encuesta nacional de empleo, trabajo, salud y calidad de vida de los trabajadores y trabajadoras en Chile. Informe interinstitucional, ENETS 2009-2010.* (p. 160), Ministerio de Salud (MINSAL)-Dirección del Trabajo (DT)-Instituto de Seguridad Laboral (ISL).

Walt, Gill and Gilson, Lucy, 1994, "Reforming the Health Sector in the Developing Countries: The Central Role of the Policy Analysis," *Health Policy Plan*, No. 9.

VII. Annexes

1. Breakdown of ChCC benefits by target population and type of program

Target population	Benefits program name	Benefits
All Children	Universal	"Creciendo Juntos" (Growing up Together) Weekly Radio Program
		Crece Contigo TV
		Fono Infancia (Hotline)
		Website
		Social networks
		Educational stamps collection
		Music collection as support for early children development
		Children stories collection in support to language and reading in early childhood
Children of the public health system (81.6%*)	Biopsychosocial development support Program (PADB)	Strengthening of prenatal development: (1) Standardized protocol for admission to prenatal control. (2) Delivery of the Pregnancy and Childbirth Guide. (3) Delivery of the Purita Mamá dairy beverage 6. (4) Primary care sessions and 1 or 2 sessions in the maternity ward, among other benefits
		Personalized attention for the childbirth process: (1) Integral and personalized attention for pregnant women and their companion in the different moments of the childbirth process (pre-partum and childbirth). (2) Generating adequate conditions to provide care to the women and favoring the first physical contact with the child. (3) Delivery of integral care that favors the development of the mother, father and child link. (4) Promotion of breastfeeding. Timely coordination with the primary health care team
		Delivery of four packages of devices for the newly born at the maternity wards of the public health system
		Integral care for children at the hospital, with a focus on development-oriented care
		Personalized care for children at the Neonatology and Pediatrics Services

		Strengthening of the integral development of the child
		First health control for the mother, father, care provider-child, upon entering primary care
		Admission to the Health Control of the child: (1) Application of the neurosensorial protocol. (2) Identification of risk factors. (3) Active participation of the father in caring for the child. (4) Delivery of educational materials
		Health Control with evaluation and monitoring of the integral development of the child.
		Group or individual psychoeducational intervention focused on the development of parental competencies: (1) Nobody is Perfect workshop. (2) Delivery of educational materials
Children in risk of becoming vulnerable (74%*)	Biopsychosocial development support Program	Formulation of a plan personalized health competencies for each pregnant woman and her family. Incorporation to the Integral Home Visit program. Activation of the Chile Crece Contigo communal network.
	Newborn support program	Integral house visit for the biopsychosocial development of the child: (1) Integral house visit program based on the priorities defined. (2) Implementation of an intervention continuity plan
		Health care for children with integral development deficits
		Stimulation hall at the health center
Vulnerable children (60%*)	Differentiated benefits based on the particular characteristics of GENERAL children	Access to technical assistance for children with disabilities
		Free access to daycare or equivalent modalities (children whose mother, father or care provider are working, studying or looking for a job)
		Free access to extended shift kindergarten or equivalent modalities (children whose mother, father, or care provider are working, studying, or looking for a job)
		Access to partial shift kindergarten for children whose mother, father, or care provider do not work outside their home
		Guaranteed access to Chile Solidario for families of children during pregnancy, if they meet the eligibility criteria for Chile Solidario.

		Guaranteed Family Subsidy (SUF) starting on the fifth month of pregnancy until the child is 18 years old, provided that they meet the requirements established in the law for the benefit
Extremely vulnerable children (40%*)	Differentiated benefits based on the particular characteristics of PREFERENTIAL ACCESS children	Preferential access to a variety of public services based on the development support needs of the children, in programs such as: Remedial education Job integration Improvement of the home and its habitability conditions Mental health care Family dynamics Judicial assistance Prevention and attention of intra-familial violence and children maltreatment

* Percentages correspond to the children with that status that are covered by the benefits.
Source: Prepared internally with information from http://www.crececontigo.gob.cl/.

2. ChCC Budget distribution between 2008 and 2012 (in Chilean pesos)

ITEM	2008	2009	2010	2011	2012
Biopsychosocial development support program	11,121,205.5	25,874,740	26,262,861.8	27,129,536.4	27,889,163.6
Newborn support program	0	14,076,327.3	22,484,465.5	23,909,125.5	24,578,581.8
Municipal strengthening fund	980,427.273	1,041,214.55	1,056,832.73	1,910,363.64	2,805,692.73
Child development support interventions fund	1,894,545.45	2,012,007.27	2,042,187.27	3,048,670.91	3,134,034.55
Grant fund for childhood initiatives	588,256.364	624,729.09	1,556,827.27	669,110.91	687,845,46
Educational program	0	1,207,203.64	2,976,165.45	3,074,378.18	3,160,460
Preschool vulnerability diagnosis program	94,727.27	135,163.64	137,190.909	141,718.18	145,685.46
Fono infancia (Hotline)	132,618.18	140,840	142,952.727	147,670.91	151,805.46
Pre-basic education-JUNJI	0	0	5370,443.64	7,343,210.91	7,548,820
Total investment MDS-CHCC (CLP)	14,811,780	45,112,225.5	62,029,927.3	67,373,785.5	70,102,089.1
Annual variation %		67.20%	27.30%	7.90%	3.90%

Source: Budget Office, Ministry of Finance, Government of Chile.

Part III
Inequalities and Care Policies

THE "WOMAN/MOTHER" AS THE ONLY RESPONSIBLE PARTY FOR CHILD POVERTY? CRITICAL ETHNOGRAPHY OF SOME HEALTH PROGRAMS AGAINST CHILD MALNOURISHMENT (LATIN AMERICAN EXAMPLES)

Charles-Édouard DE SUREMAIN[1]

> I. Introduction: Women, mother, and children—A mutually reinforcing triad? II. Confinement, devaluation, and stigmatization. III. Empowerment reinforces exclusion and poverty? IV. Conclusions: Teachings from critical ethnography? V. Bibliography.

I. Introduction: Women, mother, and children—A mutually reinforcing triad?

Ever since a couple of decades ago, women have been the focus of attention of a large part of the media and also of political attention. This category of stakeholders has a particularly central and privileged position in antipoverty and pro-development programs. Therefore, the systematic association of the terms "women" and "mothers" is older, and it is closely related to the reproductive and domestic roles that have been assigned to women for centuries. This is true to the extent that it was not until the great wars of the twentieth century that the representations based on motherhood were transformed and that the fundamental political and economic roles of women in the global society became appreciated.

There is another equally problematic category of stakeholders that is now linked to that association: that of "children." Today, it is impossible to think separately about the categories of "women," "mothers," and "children" in health- and family-planning projects. It would be inconceivable to act upon one group without affecting the other: anything that benefits women must have a positive impact on mothers and children; conversely, anything that benefits children must improve the life of mothers and women. Regardless of the category of stakeholders the program is aimed at, the result must be "transitive relationship"—that is to say, a relationship between two

---

[1] Anthropology researcher. UMR 208 "Patrimonios Locales & Gobernabilidad." Email: *suremain@ird.fr*.

categories of stakeholders that always involves a relationship with a third category.

This "axiom of development" is based on the idea that all the categories of stakeholders involved have a common feature—"vulnerability"—and that they share economic, cultural, psychological, and scientific assumptions. In antipoverty programs, vulnerability refers to an immutable condition or a condition that potentially will hardly evolve. Used as a noun, "vulnerability" contributes to point out the essence of the stakeholders in a certain role, fixating dynamic phenomena in stable and permanent situations.

My hypothesis is that the wife/mother/child triad and vulnerability are mutually reinforcing concepts. The contradiction is such that it has at least two contradicting consequences: the sterilization of the debate on the responsibility for health and the identical repetition of interventions that are based on the same assumptions. These contradictions may explain several examples of reluctance and rejection *vis-à-vis* health interventions. Using examples from anthropology and nutrition, I ask in this paper how antipoverty programs may overcome the underlying economic, cultural, psychological, and scientific assumptions. Ultimately, how critical ethnography makes it possible to consider other actions to improve antipoverty programs?

II. Confinement, devaluation, and stigmatization

In the sphere of development, and in the scientific world, it seems evident that the fight against child malnutrition has to be associated with the fight against poverty. Is not malnutrition one of the "diseases of poverty," just as HIV/AIDS, malaria, or tuberculosis? This label continues to have consequences over the nature of the interventions carried out. It actually guides the identification of some agents responsible for malnutrition, favoring the construction of the limited target groups on which health programs against malnutrition focus.

1. "Nutrition environment" and malnutrition

In the fight against malnutrition, women/mothers are the main agents in charge of the status of the child. Due to a seemingly exclusive investment in nourishment, they are noted and labeled as "responsible for negligence."[2] In the interviews I made on the subject of the alleged maternal negligence, it is clear that, for the promoters of the health programs, women assume child nutrition and health with a serious lack of knowledge on the subject. In other words, women/mothers are simultaneously incompetent and alone when getting involved not only in feeding their child but intaking care oftheir overall health.

That prejudice, with respect to maternal negligence, is linked to a cartoonish interpretation of the distribution of feeding roles in society. Although women/mothers supposedly have a privileged and almost exclusive relationship with the child, ethnographic studies show that mother–child relationships are much more complex and evolving.

Between one and a half years and two and a half years,[3] that is to say, before the weaning process is complete, the protagonists of the child may be male or female; adults or children; relatives, neighbors, or friends; and so on.[4] With different foods, at varying paces, on many and various occasions, each protagonist participates in the feeding of the child. This is the reason why I proposed the concept of "nutrition environment" to describe the extension and intensity of social relationships in which the eating child is at the center.

In my investigations in Bolivia and Peru, I had the chance to prove that child malnutrition is not systematically linked to poverty and to the lack of education of the mother (Sureinam et al, 2003). A child may be malnourished, and his mother may be educated and relatively well-off; on the contrary, a child may be healthy, and his mother may be poor and without education; and so on. The status of the child continues to be conditioned by the breadth and quality of the network of social relationships he or she enjoys—or not—through investments (in time, money, affection, etc.) from his or her main protagonists, hence the importance of studying the family form to which the child belongs. This family may be extended or reduced; the child may have a special relationship with the patrilineal side, the matrilineal side, or both sides of his family, or a selective relationship; and so on. It would be counterproductive to limit the analysis to the biological family of the child.

---

2   In Peru, an open reference is made to the word "guilty."
3   That is to say, when "malnutrition peaks" associated with foodchanges and digestive characteristics of the children are the most important.
4   See also the studies by Lallemand (1997), Gruénais (1990), Jaffré (1996), Bonnet (1996), Dettwyler (1989), Scheper-Hughes (1992), and Pelto (2001) on the subject.

In the Andes, as in Mesoamerica, "ritual family ties" (the joint responsibility of *compadres*) is an institution with the main function of providing a social security network for the children. It is clear that ritual parents act to a large extent during the feeding of the child, not only in the event of a famine.

In Bolivia, I remember the example of a malnourished child whose mother lived with her mother in relative ease. Our ethnographic research showed that the mother and the child were voluntarily supported by her mother-in-law in a constant status of social isolation. In fact, the mother-in-law showed her disapproval of her own child—the father of the malnourished child—who had failed to follow the steps of matrimonial processes. In other words, her son had not formalized the "trial marriage" period (*sirvinakuy* in Quechua) that forces all men to perform a series of actions *vis-à-vis* his family and his future family, due to the fact that there is a long relationship with a woman foreseen. Being completely isolated, the mother of his child, and therefore his own child, were the victims of direct retaliation for his socially undesirable behavior. In this context, the feeding and the health of the child were altered to the point that he suffered malnutrition.

2. Health card, child malnutrition, and stigmatization of the responsible agents

But the questioning of women/mothers is not restricted to malnutrition. Health professionals also hold them as guilty when considering, in a broader fashion, the issue of the health of their children, particularly their growth and development.

During the visits to the pediatricians at the health centers in the poor rural and urban areas of Bolivia and Peru, I have been able to observe the strong stigma that women/mothers who use the health card of the child suffer. The visits very often were limited to a very short auscultation of the child. At the end of the visit, physicians would quickly inspect the health card to stop at the weight and height charts of the child. This way, they pointed out their limited growth as compared to their age and international standards—knowing they are questionable. Invariably, physicians would conduct their talks on what the mother "did" or "did not do" to meet those standards. More or less abruptly, they would emphasize the responsibility of the mother in the limited growth and development of the child.

Numerous visits would end with the return of the health card, to which a red or green sticker was stuck depending on the severity of the status of the child. In returning it, the physician would sanction the more or less "good behavior" of the mother, in fact, her ability to be a "good mother" or otherwise (Fassin, 1986).[5] But, for the women/mothers, the devolution of the card not only devalues them but also condemns them in the eyes of society.

To the extent that it is considered that they are mainly responsible for the health of the child, it is their entire ability as a mother and wife that is being questioned: With any other recognition apart from that of their social role as child-raisers and their function of protecting, women/mothers feel strongly stigmatized if they fail to fulfill that role. They felt that they were only recognizable through the "careless mother" label, which literally and figuratively is adhered to their skin. On the other hand, the stigma additionally reinforces male domination: Without being mentioned or questioned, men are completely "powerless." They relied on the diagnosis of the doctors to blame their wives.

The stigmatization of the women/mothers has many noxious effects on the operation of health systems. It leads many of them to abandon health structures for a while, despite the sanctions applied to them. In Bolivia, not going to the compulsory children's health control involves losing the right to the reimbursement of the health expenses of the child; in Peru, missing care causes a fine, and, for repeat offenders, the deprivation of citizenship through the cancellation of the electoral card, and so on.

Ultimately, it would seem that poverty and bad health that are imposed on children are the result of the attitude of the women/mothers, at least partially. At that time, the punctual abandonment of the health services is interpreted by health workers as a more or less active reaction of rejection or resistance from the women/mothers to biomedicine, and therefore, to "progress" and "modernity." In this conceptual framework, women/mothers would clearly show their lack of capacity and their negligence in taking care of the children—given that they are supposed to be the main agents in charge of health. The vicious circle in which the system itself is managed is barely questioned.

---

5   Expressions in quotation marks belong to the actors that work in health programs. The interviews were conducted during different anthropological researches in Africa and Latin America.

III. Empowerment reinforces exclusion and poverty?

What could be the possible origin of the devaluation and stigmatization of the target group of the women/mothers? We have seen that the political and ideological premises underlying antipoverty programs are important, but not determinant. Possibly, the careless use of the concept of empowerment, very much in vogue these days, may be against its own objectives. The question now is, in the field of health, is empowerment compatible with the designation of a single responsible agent, in this case the woman/mother?

1. Empowerment and community

The concept of empowerment is simultaneously a theory, an action plan, a process, and a result; it acts at the individual and the collective level; it posits the importance of "community" as an intermediate level between the individual and public policy. The entire focus is based on the "strengthening of community" and in increasing the analytical capacity of its members. Supposedly, it helps one to better identify the problems that individuals will be able to solve, encouraging them to increase their participation in the intervention and providing the means to better sustain "their" development and fight against poverty.

The principles that inspire the concept of community development refer to values such as sharing, consensus, solidarity, redistribution, equality, or exchange. To the extent that the application of these values allows unwinding the divisions and centrifugal forces that destroy general cohesion, anything that promotes community will be functional, leading to social peace and, therefore, to development.

The problem is that the empowerment process is based on a highly idealist and consensual vision of the community that does not correspond to social reality. In fact, it is quite the contrary: Ethnographic studies show that the community is very often governed by divisions, conflict, and inequalities maintained by a social group at the expense of other social groups.[6]

In the developed world, the community is a big political, economic, and cultural challenge, both for developers and for locals. Although the developers have every incentive to identify the collective organization forms they can rely on more easily to implement their subprograms, the locals

---

[6] See the "perspective by the actors." *Cfr.* Long and Long (1992), Olivier de Sardan (1997), Berche (1998), or D'Hont (2005).

mobilize the community to increase their power or to improve their status inside it.

2. Empowerment and target groups

We may also ask how the inclusive social, political, and cultural vision sustained by the empowerment may fit into the exclusive vision that guides the forming of the target groups. One may ask, how is it possible to "build a community" while the interventions are targeted to a single group, in this case, women/mothers, which involves excluding more than half of the population (men, boys, elderly men, etc.)?[7]

The excessive focusing of target groups may explain the alleged "cultural resistance" invoked by developers when trying to understand the deviation or reluctant behavior of women/mothers. In fact, it seems that these conducts reveal more the lack of conformance of the actors to the interventions that any type of cultural resistance, which in itself does not explain anything about the real problem.

I remember a discussion group on the promotion of health with mothers of children under 5 years in Peru. The discussion was interrupted when one of the mothers read the letter of protest that her husband asked her to read in public. In this letter, he explained that he did not understand "why he was not invited to the discussion" to discuss an issue "that also involves him!" He wrote that "even though women take care of the children," he was concerned about "not being considered by the activities of the program"; he explained that he felt a "thoughtlessness" from the doctors; and also asked to "be invited to be heard." The father, in other words, did not want doctors to consider him as "powerless" but as a "real" agent of the health of the family.

Beyond the articulation of the notions of empowerment and target group, the problem of inclusion and exclusion of categories of actors in antipoverty programs is being posited. By stating that women/mothers are the main agents in charge of child malnourishment, it would seem that developers isolate and objectify women/mothers: They consider them as scapegoats. By doing so, they may be creating a huge gap between women/mothers and their children, on the one hand, and the rest of the

---

7   On the exclusion of entire sectors of the population in a program against malnutrition in Congo, *cfr*. Suremain (2007).

actors of the community, on the other—in addition to reinforcing the discrimination mechanisms that were already against them locally.

Examples of this abound. The exclusion derived from an excessively exclusive construction of target groups is clearly a challenge faced by many health programs and, in general, by many antipoverty programs when they use the concepts of empowerment, community, and target group without a critical approach. Could the "un-targeting" of the interventions assist to conceive things differently?

IV. Conclusions: Teachings from critical ethnography?

As for development programs in the field of health, everything happens as if a woman necessarily were a mother or a "potential mother." As a result of a prolonged naturalization process, this statement is questionable and leads to a tautology: Women, mothers, and children are "vulnerable" precisely because they are women, mothers, and children, and vice versa. In their vulnerability, the wife/mother/child triad is presented as the main source of welfare for the child. Logically, this idea states that if the child is not feeling well, it is "natural" to seek the causes and responsibilities for his or her status from the woman/mother.

In this context, what are the spaces to improve anti-malnutrition programs that critical ethnography highlights? As we have seen, critical ethnography allows the examination of the methodological, theoretical, and ethical premises that are the foundation of development programs.[8]

First, it is necessary to advance in the debate on the causative agents of malnutrition. In this regard, the debates have not seen significant changes in decades. They are mainly centered on the wife/mother/child triad, despite the lessons learned from the evaluations and the exams conducted by ethnographic studies on the issue of the responsibility for the child. Without a doubt, one must also stop considering that women/mothers "do not know very well what malnutrition is," that "they do not have good practices with respect to feeding and caring for the child," or that "they do not have a clear perspective of the growth and development of the child," and so on. These premises confine, devaluate, and stigmatize women/mothers. In time, they lead to the resistance and rejection of the women/mothers, not so much *vis-à-vis* the content of the programs, but rather *vis-à-vis* the discriminating

---

8   It is derived from what I call "engaged anthropology" (Suremain, 2013).

focus with which they are applied. More or less explicitly, depending on the circumstances of each case, the questioning of the upbringing and the educational skills of the women/mothers is often accompanied by a significant real and symbolic violence. The women/mothers perceived as "negligent" feel guilty. This accusation is particularly unfair because the nutrition role is solely assigned to them and they are constantly reminded of that by society.

Inthese conditions, health programs should consider instead the family structures and gender relations in the local environment. Not knowing how the societies operate, if the interventions are conducted in haste, it will lead to erroneous interpretations of the alleged "acts of resistance" and the rejection of the actors. Often, actors have very good reasons to oppose a program that will supposedly improve their daily lives. The program has better chances of success if it is consistent with the values and operational customs of the society and if it is based on the concerns of the actors.

Last, the challenge of an overly simplistic causation established between malnutrition and poverty reminds us that child poverty cannot be reduced to quantifiable, economic, or educational variables, although they are important dimensions. Critical ethnography shows that the situation of poverty imposed on the child is a result of the breadth and quality of the network of social relationships he or she enjoys—or not—through his or her main protagonists. These considerations lead us to reconsider the construction and implementation of antipoverty public policies, by way of the core issue of the social isolation of the child.

V. Bibliography

Berche, Thierry, 1998, *Anthropologie et santé publique en pays dogon*, París, Karthala.

Bonnet, Doris, 1996, "Présentation. La notion de négligence sociale à propos de la malnutrition de l'enfant,"*Sciences sociales et santé*, vol. 14.

Dettwyler, Katherine A., 1989, "Styles of Infant Feeding: Parental/Caretaker Control of Food Consumption in Young Children," *American Anthropologist*, vol. 91.

D'Hont, Olivier, 2005, *Techniques et savoirs des communautés rurales. Approche ethnographique du développement*, París, Karthala.

Fassin, Didier, 1986, "'La bonne mère'. Pratiques rurales et urbaines de la rougeole chez les femmes haalpulaaren du Sénégal,"*Social Science & Medicine*, vol. 23.

Gruénais, Marc-Éric, 1990, "Le malade et sa famille. Une étude de cas à Brazzaville," in Fassin, Didier *et al.* (eds.), *Sociétés, développement et santé*, París, Ellipses-Aupelf.

Jaffré, Yannick, 1996, "Dissonances entre les représentations sociales et médicales de la malnutrition dans un service de pédiatrie au Niger," *Sciences Sociales & Santé*, vol. 14.

Long, Norman and Ann, Long (eds.), 1992, *Battlefields of Knowledge. The Interlocking of Theory and Practice in Social Research and Development*, London, Routledge & Kegan Paul.

Lallemand, Suzanne, 1997, "Enfances d'ailleurs, approche anthropologique," in Guidetti, M. (ed.), *Enfances d'ailleurs, d'hier et d'aujourd'hui*, París, Armand Colin.

Olivier de Sardan, Jean-Pierre, 1997, *Anthropologie et développement. Essai en socio-anthropologie du changement social*, París, APAD-Karthala.

Pelto, Gretel H., 2001, "Continuities and Challenges in Applied Nutritional Anthropology," *Nutritional Anthropology*, vol. 22.

Scheper-Hughes, Nancy, 1992, *Death Without Weeping. The Violence of Everyday Life in Brazil*, Berkeley, University of California Press.

Suremain, Charles-Édouard de et al. (eds.), 2003, *Miradas cruzadas en el niño. Un enfoque interdisciplinario sobre la salud, el crecimiento y el desarrollo del niño en Bolivia y Peru*, La Paz, Plural-Institut de Recherche pour le Développement-Éditions de l'Institut Français d'Études Andines.

Suremain, Charles-Édouard de, 2007, "L'entourage nourricier de l'enfant. À partir d'exemples en Bolivie et au Congo," *L'Autre. Cliniques, Cultures et Sociétés*, vol. 8.

Suremain, Charles-Édouard de, 2013, "L'implication Constructive. Anthropologie, Recherche, Développement", *Habilitation à diriger des recherches*, Université Paris Ouest Nanterre La Défense.

COMPARATIVE STUDY OF THE DAYCARE PROGRAMS IN MEXICO (2007-12)

Juan Antonio VEGA BÁEZ[1]

I. Inequality in childcare policies. II. Agenda for democratic care: Body, time, and citizenship. III. Bibliography.

I. Inequality in childcare policies

The morning of June 5, 2009, was an ordinary day on which millions of mothers, extended families, and exceptionally some care-providing fathers performactivities related to the care and upbringing of their children under 4 years of age in Mexico.

Hundreds of thousands of female workers in the country, both in the formal and the informal sectors of the economy, used one of the three systems of child care: care facilities or development devices or establishments in early childhood.[2]

But that morning in Hermosillo, Sonora, the risk protection mechanisms in a childcare center, labeled as a "nursery," failed to detect a fire, precisely in an establishment granted under concession to private

---

[1] Doctoral student of Latin American studies from UNAM. He is the author of articles and publications on childhood, human rights, humanitarian issues and violence policy: *consultoriadh.3@gmail.com*. I want to acknowledge the initial contribution of Dr. Pablo Yanes Rizo (CEPAL) and the attendants of the "Child Poverty, Public Policy and Democracy" Seminar, organized by Equidad para la Infancia, CROP, FLACSO, IIJ-UNAM, and IFE in February 2014, in Mexico City.

[2] We must recall the criterion proposed by the Committee on the Rights of the Child to define "early childhood," in their General Comment No. 7 (2005) *Implementing child rights in early childhood*: "In its consideration of rights in early childhood, the Committee wishes to include all young children: at birth and throughout infancy; during the preschool years; as well as during the transition to school. Accordingly, the Committee proposes as an appropriate working definition of early childhood the period below the age of 8 years." For Mexico, an operational definition of early childhood would be 0-5 years, with the completion of the preschool stage, because primary education starts precisely at 6 years (compulsory age). However, in this paper we want to focus on the day-care services for children in the infant (45 days to 18 months) and maternal groups (19-35 months), a period we can label as the initial early childhood; no analysis is made of the preschool group (3-5 years), whose schooling is compulsory at the age of 4 and 5 years.

operators by government social security. The result was 49 lifeless children's bodies and 76 children with serious burns, respiratory, and other damages.

The fire in the "Guardería ABC" was a tragic event that forced the Mexican public opinion to analyze the childcare and custody systems for children under 4 years. There was a special focus on the failures of the supervision and civil protection standards (disaster risk prevention), but many structural issues were overlooked, such as the inequality of the coverage and of the allocation of resources or the quality of the services.

The above-mentionedtragedy involved a paradox, because until that time, "Social Security" nurseries enjoyed considerable prestige with the public, and in fact, it was one of the daycare systems that had the greatest demand among parents with formal jobs. The public question in the air was, "If this happened with children's bodies that were properly cared for, what might happen with the rest of the children in lower quality facilities, or who are looked after by neighbors or acquaintances or, in the worst-case scenario, locked up in their homes alone or left to be looked after by their older siblings?"

1. The contribution of the Daycare Facilities Program

The case of "Guardería ABC," in 2009, occurred in the context of a government that had launched an ambitious project to increase care and attention coverage for early childhood. This was an initiative to establish collective daycare spaces with the social participation of the mothers and fathers, known as Daycare Program for Working Mothers (PEI), which in its first two years doubled the coverage of the traditional system of daycare facilities and nurseries (IMSS–ISSSTE, see 1.2), which was over three decades old, with a network of a little over 9,000 active establishments.

The PEI started being implemented in 2007 by the Social Development Ministry (Sedesol) in coordination with the National DIF (National System for Integral Family Development), as the training entity and certifier of the staff, by the government of Felipe Calderón (2006–12). Its purpose was "To contribute to eliminate backwardness in the access and/or permanence at work of single mothers and fathers who work, seek employment or study and who have children between 1 and 3 years 11 months, increasing the range of child care and attention services offered."

It was considered as the axis of the social policy for early childhood care, with the delivery of economic support to working mothers and to the establishments affiliated to the "Quality Daycare Facilities Network."[3]

According to the premise argued by Sedesol, based on data from the 2004 National Employment Survey, only 35% of the employed female population had access to social security schemes, including daycare services. In addition, parallely, it pointed out a "backwardness" in the "offer of nurseries for female workers who did not enjoy social security benefits and that, while there were options in nurseries and Daycare Facilities operated by private citizens, they were not always affordable" (Sedesol, s.f.: 2). That is to say, the program argued the need to attack the problem of the low availability of resources to face the costs of child care and attention and, simultaneously, of supporting working mothers who did not have social security, especially those who were in conditions of poverty, in the informal sector, but also in the formal sector of the economy, but without benefits.

According to the 2011 impact assessment by the National Public Health Institute, at the request of Coneval (2011), the main finding at the programmatic level was that "78% of the former beneficiaries agree with the phrase 'While the child was at the daycare facility, I was able to find a job.'" On the other hand, 34% of the active beneficiaries answered that if their support were to be cut, "they would immediately leave their jobs, to take care of their children."

Soon, PEI became a pertinent and timely program, with social or community participation, to provide access to institutional care services for the children of mothers who worked in the informal sector of the economy and to multiply the availability of care establishments for mothers who had formal jobs, but in areas with no or limited availability of "nurseries" from the two formal social security systems created by the postwar social-welfare state: the IMSS and the ISSSTE (Institute for Social Security and Services for State Workers), for persons who were employed in private or social companies and for persons in the state bureaucracy, respectively.

---

3 A standard of living at the national level is established in the "Official Mexican Standard for the provision of social assistance services for minors and senior citizens," from 1997.

2. The irruption of private business *versus* state-provided care

The so-called IMSS "nurseries" were based on a childcare model with a state health orientation, that is to say, with high sanitary standards based on an operation by professional and technical staff hired by the state institution, but with low social participation and accountability, within a management style subordinated to a short-term bureaucratic-political logic that prevented its financial sustainability and its expansion as an universal benefit, given its orientation as a low-coverage system with relatively high costs.

This social benefit was incorporated in 1973 to the Social Security Law (currently, articles 201–207), and its operation was based on the payment of fees by the workers and the companies, that is to say, based on a three-party social solidarity agreement between employers, employees, and government. The right to institutional daycare was offered exclusively to working women-mothers who were affiliated to the IMSS, excluding working fathers, either single or with a couple, with an underlying family-oriented and *machista* focus that assigns that task to women-mothers, which also relaxed employer obligations for groups such as agricultural workers,[4] who generally were members of indigenous nations or of rural communities without land.

With respect to the workers of the state, it was a decade later, in 1983, when it was established as a mandatory benefit by the ISSSTE through "daycare facilities," absorbing, in 1984, the daycare establishments of the entire federal public administration, in a state-health-family-oriented model.

However, institutional and bureaucratic corruption thwarted the growth of both systems, in an adverse context such as the debt crisis of the 1980s. The limited growth of the coverage of IMSS-managed nurseries was due to the "transfer of resources" between the different fields of security: Money was taken from nursery funds and used in the disease and maternity funds, "which has considerably limited its capacity of growth" (Martínez Monroy, 2007: 20).[5]

---

[4] In 2008, there were only 10 indirect benefit IMSS nurseries in the countryside (REDIM, 2008: 40).

[5] These decisions, which blurred the higher interest of childhood in public investments in social security, are a clear example of the weakness of the state protection of the rights of the child *vis-à-vis* the rights of adults, the bureaucracies, the employer sector, and the financial capital.

In the 1990s, starting with the Mexican financial crisis of 1994, the social solidarity system, with universal coverage for formal workers, was changed for a personalized access system. In that context, a new management model was promoted, one with public–private participation, with the creation of the "subrogated nurseries" (IMSS) model or the "hired daycare facilities" (ISSSTE) model, that is to say, allowing the participation of private capital in the construction and operation of nurseries, with the obligation of complying with the law, in exchange for a fee paid to the IMSS for each child served.

Soon, the provision of care through the system subrogated to private actors exceeded in numbers the provision of care through establishments directly operated by the said institutes, as it happened with the IMSS, where the ratio came to be 10 to 1 (1,420 subrogated against 135 directlymanaged establishments, in 2009).

However, as previously mentioned, with the fire in "Guardería ABC" the effectiveness of the supervision and control mechanisms in the enforcement of the regulations for health care under concession to the private sector was questioned; and additionally, it revealed the existence of family ties between the political and economic elites that benefited from the "direct award" (without a public tender process) of establishments and the administration of sizable public funds for child care. With the tragedy that occurred in Hermosillo in 2009, it became public that the owners of "ABC" included families of the local and federal political environment, including relatives of the first lady, the wife of President Felipe Calderón.

Only this trade of influence explains that the nursery was installed in an inadequate building, next to a warehouse of the local government that was filled with paper, allegedly "dead archives," without emergency exits or functioning fire alarms, and without staff training on civil protection. Even though the Supreme Court admitted the investigation and established institutional responsibilities, in practice, there was no independent justice that was able to establish individual criminal responsibilities, and the negligent owners of an unsafe establishment, along went officials and managers who were directly or indirectly responsible for the fire, and those responsible for the supervision went unpunished.

3. Unequal access and service stratification

Mexico has been presented to other countries of the region as a model in terms of investment in early childhood (Quintanilla, 2012: 60), under the argument that it allocates 0.8% of its GDP to this population group, a percentage that is greater than the one allocated by the United States.

However, in the concrete provision of institutional care for initial early childhood, it is possible to notice a trend toward the stratification of the supply and the quality of the services, in detriment of the families that are in the informal economy and in places with less than 5,000 inhabitants, factors that favor inequality and child poverty.[6]

A. Social determinants of unequal access

Mexico is one of the economies in Latin America with a greatest percentage of informal employment, and that is one of the main determinants that condition and limit access to institutional care. According to the National Occupation and Employment Survey (ENOE), the employment informality rate has maintained more or less constant values in the past decade. In the first quarter of 2005, it presented values of 59.3%, whereas in the third quarter of 2012, it had 60.1%. This is a factor that exerts influence in the fact that the coverage of institutional child care is so low, because only 10.3% of children under 4 years had access to IMSS/subrogated nurseries, ISSSTE/hired nurseries, PEI, or private establishments.[7]

---

[6] In this paper we cannot address the problems of other parallel systems with a more pedagogic focus, such as that of the Initial Indigenous Education and Conafe, whose goals only partially cover the goals of childcare; this paper also does not address some local assistance or community attention systems, such as the CADIS of the DIF, or the CENDIS of some universities. The early childhood education system, which dates from before the boom of the Day Care Facilities Program, was reviewed in detail in "*La primera infancia y sus derechos*" (Early Childhood and Its Rights) published by REDIM (2008: 36–54). This paper shall also not address the status of preschool education, whose gross coverage went from 50.5% in 2001 to 84.6 in 2012, an increase resulting from the legal and administrative process that incorporated it as part of basic and, therefore, compulsory, education.

[7] Before 2007, Mexico had informed at the international level that its day-care services coverage reached 20% of the early childhood population. But that figure had been formed by including all the children enrolled in the first year of preschool education, which sought to disguise the very low coverage of institutional day-care services for infants and maternal children (Salvador, 2007, *vid. infra*). The figure of 10.3% of coverage is given by Tuma (2010: 19).

B. Stratification of the attention

By 2009, it was estimated that daycare facilities affiliated to the PEI of Sedesol represented 84% of the early care establishments, serving 56% of the child population that benefits from these services in establishments with public funds. In turn, establishments directly managed by the IMSS and the ISSSTE represented 2%, serving 8% of the population, whereas the nurseries subrogated to the private sector represented 14% of the total establishments of the kind, with a participation of 36% of the population served. The above information means that the PEI program saw an explosive growth at the start of its operations, effectively doubling attention through small and midsize units that, in total, increased the number of establishments fivefold, achieving a greater territorial reach and a proximity to population centers where there had never been a daycare center for working parents (chart 1).

Chart 1. Comparison of population served, number of nurseries or daycare facilities (in percentages)

	IMSS and ISSSTE	IMSS-ISSSTE Subrogated	PEI
Child population served	8	36	56
Nurseries per sector	2	14	84

Source: Prepared internally with information from Gerhard Tuma (2010).

C. Budget allocation inequality

An IMSS nursery received in 2009, on average, 950,000 pesos a month, whereas a PEI daycare facility received an average of 34,680 pesos a month (including the economic contribution from the parents), even though the differences in quota may be significant. However, if we measure per capita budget allocations, the differences are abysmal: in the PEI daycare facilities, a monthly average of 665 pesos was destined to each child (51 USD), whereas in IMSS nurseries the average amount was 4,570 pesos (351 USD), that is to say, almost a sevenfold difference.

Gerhard Tuma (2010: 55) verified the global budget inequality because through the PEI, 23% of the resources were invested on 56% of the children enrolled at care institutions, whereas in the IMSS and ISSSTE, 78% of the resources of the sector were invested on 44% of the beneficiary population.

In consequence, 8% of the child population with access to institutional care was served with very high professional and health standards, 36% with high or medium standards, whereas the remaining 56% was served by staff with cultural-popular knowledge related to care, without professional training (care providers are required to have a minimum high school degree), generally with empirical interest and experience, that is to say, the profile of a volunteer, a situation that is verified with the low or medium wages they earn.

As a result of the above-mentioned data, it can be said that the social policy on early childhood care in Mexico has reproduced social inequalities due to the absence of a universal care policy and of the promotion of institutional services with a different quality and with largely unequal budgets.

4. Child poverty: Caring for care

Recently, the National Council for the Evaluation of Social Development Policy (Coneval and UNICEF, 2013: 9), in a multidimensional measurement of poverty with a social rights perspective in Mexico between 2008 and 2010, detected that poverty and extreme poverty levels among children and teenagers "were higher, compared to the rest of the Mexican population." Although in the general population, 46.2% was in poverty, the percentage for people under 18 years was 53.8% (21.4 million). With respect to extreme poverty, 12.8% of the children and teenagers were in extreme poverty (5.1 million), compared to 10.4% of the Mexican population.

The measurement showed that the segments of children with the highest levels of poverty were those between 0 and 5 years, at 55.5%. This fact is not irrelevant; given a measurement from a decade before, in the year 2000, it was found that the childhood group with the highest incidence of poverty was that between 6 and 11 years, in terms of food poverty, skills poverty, and poverty of patrimony (Sedesol *et al.*, 2002: 38).

A plausible explanation is related to the increase in access to the new social security program (Seguro Popular) and to the basic education promoted by the Oportunidades Program applied to this age group, but an *ad hoc* descriptive and explanatory study would be required.

However, as the years go by this inequality and historic vulnerability worsen among indigenous children, among whom poverty is greater by a third than in the rest of Mexican children. To this respect, the study indicates that the incidence of poverty in homes that have at least one speaker of an indigenous language is greater than 76%, against 53.3% among the general population (indigenous and nonindigenous). In addition, inequality between the rich and poor municipalities is appalling, as previously described by other studies I have analyzed before (Vega Báez, 2011: 303), as they reach a gap of 10 times as much poverty, because in municipalities with very low marginalization only 5.1% of the children and teenagers are in poverty. In addition, over 90% of indigenous children and teenagers presented one or more social deprivations.

In the country, there are structural and multiple discrimination processes that particularly affect five subgroups of indigenous child population that have not been addressed to date by the social programs that lack a childhood and rights-oriented perspective:

> Indigenous infants under 5 years in towns with less than 5 thousand inhabitants, specially in the laborer, temporary resident or migrant sector. Both urban and rural working indigenous children, particularly those who perform seasonal or cyclic migrant work, and who are under 12 years of age. [The children of] Pregnant and breastfeeding girls and teenagers in towns with less than 5 thousand inhabitants. [And the children of] Indigenous teenage girls who experience voluntary or forced early marriages, favored by inexistent civil or criminal laws. Indigenous children with an evident motor or cerebral disability in isolated towns with one or two migrant parents.

Due to the absence of indicators broken down by ethnic identity, indigenous initial early childhood continues to be invisible for the PEI, the IMSS, and the ISSSTE, the only exception being the monitoring of Conafe services and the Initial Indigenous Education.[8]

But the concern related to the population group of initial childhood in poverty in Mexico grows stronger if we analyze in detail the fields to which

---

8 The IMSS and ISSSTE nursery systems do not have information on the ethnical identity of their users, a matter that is in itself discriminatory. As to the PEI, the same omission exists, although they try to remedy it with the indicator of the nurseries located in municipalities with high or very high marginalization which, as is known, in Mexico, at the national level, over 80% of the municipalities with an indigenous majority fall into that category. Therefore, a fourth of the PEI nurseries are in municipalities with those characteristics, although not necessarily serving indigenous population.

that 0.8% of the GDP assigned to the sector was being destined at the end of the last decade: In practice, less than a fourth of it was being invested in care for the early age subgroup, which in volume represented around 50% of the population, and at least three quarters were being invested in preschool education, an area where a major progress in coverage must be acknowledged.

In addition, the differentiated operation, with major operational differences in relation to the standards of each type of establishment in Mexico, is an evidence that highlights the absence of "a" consistent, planned, integral, and integrated policy and that, quite the contrary, everything has been developed by mixing subsystems with different operational rationales, and the goal of universal coverage has been lost.

Due to the above-mentioned information, if we consider the proposal for a minimum investment in early childhood launched by UNICEF (2008) of using 1% of the GDP, Mexico would have to take new steps in its public policies for childhood, overcoming the inertia of the prevailing residual, stratified, and assistentialist models, toward a truly universal model of child care, with the fiscal participation of the formal and informal economic actors that may benefit from adequate services. Only that way could the country be considered as a "regional model" of non-stratified care, with equal access and long-term sustainability.

II. Agenda for democratic care: Body, time, and citizenship

In Latin America, the absence of the state in terms of social policies for the care of people and the care of the household has been notorious, as it has been difficult in the past two decades and a half to earn the recognition of care as a human right of children and, therefore, as a relevant element in the construction of democracy in the long term.

The historical trend has been to maintain the model that focuses on nuclear and extended families, particularly on women,[9] as providers and responsible for child care, an asset that in some South American cases has been used to structure family, neighbor, or community networks for the provision of care services with a peer-orientation. But the Mexican case

---

9   Fernández (2012: 14) has described the "maternalist" paradigm of social policy: focalized policies are "maternalist" and those centered on salary are "spousealist," because both take for granted the role of the women in the home."

shows an increase in interaction of the state with market and private actors in the region, especially among the countries that continue to follow the agenda of the Washington Consensus.

The contribution of the different economic–social sectors to the development of care-related public policy in the region has been notoriously addressed by studies on the economy of care,[10] in dialogue or debate with CEPAL and UNICEF.

However, it is pertinent to introduce new components to the debate, especially from the standpoint of other disciplines and perspectives such as the ethics of care and reproductive work, time sociology, the rights-based, and citizenship perspective of radical democracy, applied to the Latin American early childhood.

1. Reproductive inequality and the ethics of care

In a study conducted in several Latin American countries (Salvador, 2007), it was concluded that the provisions of public care services for initial early childhood between 0 and 2 years have been highly insufficient, attaining very low coverage rates, or even, with a complete unavailability of public statistics as a result of not being a priority issue: Brazil, 1–9%; Chile, 5–12%; Mexico, 10–20%; Argentina and Uruguay did not submit information.[11] The above data resulted in the detection of a public debt in terms of paid child care, a debt that is greater in marginal urban areas without formal employment centers and that grows exponentially in rural and indigenous areas.[12]

---

10   Enríquez (2005) and Pautassi (2007) have contributed to the current of the "care economy." The so-called "crisis of care" refers to the number of persons who require family care and, simultaneously, to the reduction of the proportion of women (traditionally women) in conditions of exercising that function, mainly due to the integration of women into the job circuits (CEPAL, 2009). Based on the above, it has been said that the prevailing thesis that defines domestic work and care-related work as activities under the exclusive responsibility of the families and, in the said units, a traditional responsibility of the women, disguises forms of family, and especially female, exploitation and overexploitation. The work of the late Hoyos (2010) and of Aguirre (2007) may also be consulted.

11   In turn, school enrollment between 3 and 5 years is mostly served, according to the same study, following a descending order: Uruguay with coverage at 42.6 and 96%, for 3 and 5 years, respectively; Argentina, with 39.1 and 78.8%; Chile, with 27.4 and 77.7%; Brazil, with 21.8 and 62.3%, and Mexico, s/d. Salvador (2007), p. 16.

12   In a descriptive manner, we may indicate that the responsible persons of the homes in Uruguay and Argentina, are women, at 84 and 78%, respectively. Continuing with the case of Argentina, in nuclear families with children under 14 years, 90% of the

> In every country, there is a notorious gap in the paid-unpaid work ratio as performed by men and women .... In general, women devote less time to paid and unpaid work due to the need of aligning their responsibilities inside and outside their home ... the burden of the unpaid work performed by women restricts their integration to the job market and the time they devote to that activity .... If we add up the burden of paid and unpaid work performed by each sex, we conclude that women work more, and that limits their leisure and welfare time.[13]

In terms of unpaid child care, which generally takes place inside the home, very few countries have been able to implement measurement systems based on use of time surveys, and for that reason, it is not possible to make a cross-country comparison that includes all countries.

Social policies that seek to adapt to market laws and to the patriarchal relationship between genders and generations seem to bet on the overexploitation of the reserve of reproductive work.[14] In addition, they denote conservatism with respect to the labor rights-family culture tandem, which can be noticed in the timid steps to attain gender equality in care; they externalize and depreciate reproductive work; they associate institutional care services with maternity; they exclude care work from the incentives; they limit or refuse paternity leave; they do not establish public services to prepare and provide psychosocial monitoring for the exercise of paternity or care.

Ultimately, what is in crisis is the sexual division of reproductive work, as a result of a greater female emancipation (Virreira and Calderón, 2010). This position could be supported with the thoughts of feminists such as

---

women are in charge of care and socialization activities, v. the 50% of the men; but if in the home there are senior citizens or ill persons, only 24% of the male spouses assumes the responsibility, compared with 86% of the women. In Brazil, in turn, 91% of employed women perform domestic care tasks, compared to 51% of employed men. As for unpaid domestic work in Mexico, 95.6% of employed women perform domestic work, compared to 58% of the men, although that male participation increased significantly between 1996 and 2002 in tasks such as cleaning, doing the dishes, and doing laundry. The weight of unpaid work of Mexican women is a condition that limits their access to the formal job market.

13   Salvador (2007: 43-44).
14   This is the segment with the greatest value added, not only in the productive workforce but also in the reproductive one. In a geopolitical dimension, this is often the argument to highlight the "competitive" potential of the Latin American workforce compared to workforces from other regions or nations.

Gilligan (2009), who argues that the ethics of care,[15] grounded in notions such as responsibility and a certain otherness, does not compete with the patriarchal concepts of justice based on individual rights: "more than 'justice', it seeks a redefined justice, in which 'care' is at the center."

2. Chronological equality

The reforms to increase labor flexibility that fail to consider the growth of care debt, as if it were an erasable or negligible external issue, jeopardize the capacity for healthy social reproduction of Latin American societies. Unfortunately, ignoring this situation, conditional resource transfer programs have not prevented the overexploitation of the reproductive work of the women, as it happened with the Oportunidades Program in Mexico, which has given the triple female shift an "official certification": productive, reproductive, and community work.

Faced with phenomena like these, critical social thought with a decolonial orientation[16] has been able to confirm that the nations and cultures of the Global South are governed by a chronological hegemony under the horizon of a compressed, linear, universal–formal temporality forced into them from the liberal–neoliberal vision.

According to Santos (2009), it is possible to identify the conditions to materialize a regime where multiple times coexist. For that purpose, in the first place, it is necessary to be aware of the imposition of a monoculture of linear time that has prevailed in a couple of decades as a result of the hegemonic notion of globalization, which has declared any concept with an asymmetrical or disorderly temporality as "premodern,""backward," or

---

15 In Latin America, we may highlight the debate started by Boff (2012) on the application of the ethics of care to human spaces such as the environment, and its sustainability. Also the Colombian compilation by Gaviria*et al.* (2011) may be referred.

16 According to Walter Mignolo and Aníbal Quijano (Castro-Gómez and Grosfoguel, 2007), decolonial thought, which initially appeared in indigenous, Afro-Caribbean, and Latin thought, seeks to unravel the logic of colonialism, that is to say, the system based on an idea of racial/ethnic classification and culture/epistemic, and which is rooted in the rhetoric of modernity, its projects, and institutions, and we may add to these constructions the invention of the concept of childhood in modern times. We may refer, as relevant works to this section, the gender reflections compiled by Villalba and Álvarez (2011) at Universidad de Granada, and on childhood issues, the essay *"Una noche en el museo del niño; miradas decoloniales a los derechos de la niñez"* (Vega Báez, 2013).

"traditional" in terms of the prevailing productive time. Despite the hegemony of compact-linear-global time, Santos opens the possibility of recovering an "ecology of temporalities."[17] At the point where the ecology of temporalities, the care economy, and the ethics of care meet, we can find new solutions for the debate on reproduction time. The condition of these new constructions will be to dismantle the notion of productive time of the global capital as the only and hegemonic dimension, to submit the possibility of other productivities based on economic concepts that are compatible with care, and which overcome overexploitation, in a dialogue with pre- and post-capitalist notions of time such as those that are the foundation of solidary economy, which integrate other dimensions different to a mere economic productivity: democratic participation, environmental sustainability, social equality, and development of local social fabric.

Contrary to the delocalized and disembodied chronological universalisms, the ethical perspective of care encourages the debate on the appropriation of the human and historical possibilities of the present and the future, thus reinforcing the possibility of building social and civilization alternatives: Having different gender relationships is possible, if other (humanizing, sustainable, and ecological) temporalities are feasible.

3. Democracy of care and early citizenship

With a growing frequency, bodies see the prevailing archetypes of the production–consumption model as unattainable. Caring for the bodies in early childhood from the perspectives of ethics, of inclusive gender, of daily democracy, and of alternative chronologies can become a critical perspective to build "another" regional public agenda for early childhood, based on a

---

17 For Santos (2009: 118), this ecology of temporalities involves reviewing the multiplicity of cultural forms overtime: "The relationship between the past, the present and the future; the form in which concepts such as early and late, short and longterm, the life cycle and urgency are defined; the accepted paces of life, the sequences, synchronies and diachronies. Thus, different cultures create different time communities, some of them control time, others live inside time, some are monochronic, others, polychronic; some are centered on the minimum time required to perform certain activities, others, in the activities required to be delivered on time; some give preference to time-schedule, other, to time-events, thus adhering to different concepts of punctuality...some are included in a linear progression, others in a non-linear progression".

democratizing effort that goes beyond the logic of mercantile consumption and of political consumption.

In that sense, it would be advisable that Latin America revises the paradigm of the maximizing of labor flexibility, given that it disguises the reproductive exploitation of family units and because it encourages the breaking of the family and social fabric, which, in conditions of marked social polarization and state vacuums, can lead us to scenarios like those that are being experienced in Central America, in the Caribbean, and in Mexico, with high levels of criminal violence and social conflicts.

Faced with the risk of barbarity, new forms can be explored to apply the principles of democracy and citizenship, from economic-work to gender-care relationships. It is important to expressly state and try to measure the contribution of childcare policies to the development of early citizenship, in a civic and social sense:

- Early citizenship as a construction and recognition of subjectivity: Based on the progressive development of the sense of identity and belonging as a subject of rights, but also on their subjective construction as a subject of rights and of inalienable, permanent, integral rights that cannot be suspended.[18]
- As an element of the process of intersubjective relationships: Considering the transition from objectual to intersubjective relationships; from dependence to gradual and progressive autonomy in the resolution of needs, in the sense of self-affirmation and otherness; in personal awareness; and in the sense of shared responsibility.
- As a construction of social processes for the recognition of their rights: Both in the formal dimension of the legal recognition, in the procedural dimension of the enforceability and justiciability mechanisms, and in the material conditions of the access to the exercise of rights starting with the parents, guardians, or legal representatives.

---

18 In Mesoamerica this statement is urgent and necessary *vis-à-vis* the increase of violent infanticide, child femicide, child disappearance and abduction, and child trafficking for various purposes, including organ trade, child migration and forced displacement as a result of generalized violence or other violence situations and many other regrettable but preventable and eradicable situations.

- As a construction of democratic-participative surroundings or environments: With the promotion of participative, nonauthoritarian relationship and education models; the assimilation of the citizenship in all the dimensions of life: citizen education, social agency competencies, expression, and participation.

Infants are hardly considered as subjects with rights, and much less seen as citizens, even in terms of the hard issues of the protection of their integrity, personal health, and civil registration. Hence, it is important to invokethe rights-based, equality, and participation perspective, three of the fundamental principles defined by the Convention on the Rights of the Child, which is the starting point, not the goal, of any claiming of rights.

The right of children to child care must be exercised as a universal prerogative, in light of the principle-right to nondiscrimination. For that reason, the installation and operation of initial childhood care institutions should be guaranteed, overcoming any inequality based on the characteristics of the infants or of their parents, such as their race, language, opinions, cultural or social origin, ethnicity or national origin, economic status, disability, or any other kind of characteristic.

III. Bibliography

Aguirre, Rosario, 2007, "Los cuidados familiares como problema público y objeto de políticas," in Arriagada, Irma (ed), *Familias y políticas públicas en América Latina: una historia de desencuentros*, Santiago de Chile, CEPAL, UNFPA.

Boff, Leonardo, 2012, *El cuidado necesario*, Madrid, Trotta.

Castro-Gómez, Santiago and Grosfoguel, Ramón, 2007, *El giro decolonial: reflexiones para una diversidad epistémica más allá del capitalismo global*, Bogotá, Siglo del Hombre Editores, Pontificia Universidad Javeriana.

CEPAL, 2009, *Panorama Social*, CEPAL, Santiago de Chile.

Conevaland UNICEF, 2013, *Pobreza y derechos sociales de niñas, niños y adolescentes en Mexico, 2008-2010,* Mexico, Coneval-UNICEF.

Coneval, 2011, "Programa de Estancias Infantiles para Apoyar a Madres Trabajadoras (PEI)," in *Informe de la Evaluación Específica de Desempeño 2010-2011*, Mexico, Consejo Nacional de Evaluación de las Políticas de Desarrollo Social.

Enríquez, Corina Rodríguez, 2005, "La economía del cuidado: un aporte conceptual para el estudio de políticas públicas,"*Buenos Aires Centro Interdisciplinario para el Estudio de Políticas Públicas. Documentos de trabajo No. 44.*

Fernández, Patricia Provoste, 2012, *Protección social y redistribución del cuidado en América Latina y el Caribe: el ancho de las políticas*, Santiago de Chile, Comisión Económica para Latin America (CEPAL), Serie Mujer y Desarrollo, no. 120.

Gaviria, Arango, Luz, Gabriela and Molinier, Pascale (comps.), 2011, *El trabajo y la ética del cuidado*, Medellín, La Carreta Editores, Universidad Nacional de Colombia.

Gilligan, Carol, 2009, "Le care, éthique féminine ou éthique féministe?, "*Multitudes*, vol. 37-38, No. 2.

Hoyos, Marina Chávez, 2010, *Trabajo femenino: las nuevas desigualdades*, Mexico, UNAM, Instituto de Investigaciones Económicas.

INEGI, 2012, "Empleo informal en Mexico,"*Press ReleaseNo. 449/12, December 11, 2012*, Aguascalientes, Instituto Nacional de Estadística y Geografía.

Martínez Monroy, Raquel (ed.), 2007, *Cuaderno de apoyo, Ley del Seguro Social*, Mexico, Chamber of Deputies.

Pautassi, Laura, 2007, *El cuidado como cuestión social desde un enfoque de derechos*, Santiago de Chile, CEPAL, Serie Mujer y Desarrollo, no. 87.

Quintanilla, Maite Onochie, 2012, "Una mirada regional a la situación de la primera infancia," in *Crecer juntos para la primera infancia. Encuentro regional de políticas integrales*, Buenos Aires, Fondo de Naciones Unidas para la Infancia (UNICEF).

REDIM, 2008, *La infancia cuenta en Mexico 2008*, Mexico, Red por los Derechos de la Infancia en Mexico.

Salvador, Soledad, 2007, "Estudio comparativo de la 'economía del cuidado'in Argentina, Brasil, Chile, Colombia, Mexico y Uruguay," Red Internacional de Género y Comercio, *http://www.generoycomercio.org/areas/investigacion/Salvador07.pdf*, retrieved in April 2013.

Santos, Boaventura de Sousa, 2009, *Una epistemología del sur: la reinvención del conocimiento y la emancipación social*, Mexico, Siglo XXI.

Sedesol (s.f.), "Caso de éxito," Mexico, Secretaría de Desarrollo Social, *http://tramitefacil.gob.mx/ index.php/alcance/cases_ex?siglas=SEDESOL* (retrieved in December 2013).

Sedesol, SEP, and Salud, 2002, *Un Mexico apropiado para la infancia y la adolescencia. Programa de acción 2002-2010*, Mexico, Secretaría de Desarrollo Social, Secretaría de Educación Pública, Secretaría de Salud.

Gerhard Tuma, Roberto Gerardo, 2010, "Un diálogo sobre los servicios de cuidado infantil en Mexico," in *Una mirada hacia la infancia y la adolescencia en Mexico. 2009 Seeond UNICEF Prize*, Mexico, Random House Mondadori.

UNICEF, 2008, "The Child Care Transition," in *Innocenti Report Card No. 8*, Florence, United Nations Children's Fund.

Vega Báez, Juan Antonio, 2011, "La discriminación hacia las niñas y niños indígenas," in González Contró, Mónica (coord.) (ed.), *Los derechos de niñas, niños y adolescentes en Mexico, a 20 años de la Convención*, Mexico, Save the Children-Porrúa-UNAM, Instituto de Investigaciones Jurídicas.

Vega Báez, Juan Antonio, 2013, "Una noche en el museo del niño. Miradas decoloniales a los derechos de la niñez," in *Rayuela, Revista Iberoamericana sobre Niñez y Juventud en lucha por sus Derechos*. No. 9.

Villalba, Cristina and Álvarez, Nacho (coords.), 2011, *Cuerpos políticos y agencia. Reflexiones feministas sobre cuerpo, trabajo y colonialidad*, Granada, Universidad de Granada.

Virreira, Sonia Montaño and Calderón, Coral Magaña, 2010, *El cuidado en acción. Entre el derecho y el trabajo*, Santiago de Chile, CEPAL, UNIFEM, AECID.

DO EARLY CHILDHOOD POLICIES PERPETUATE THE HISTORICAL INEQUALITIES BETWEEN COLOMBIAN GIRLS AND BOYS?

Ma. Cristina Torrado[1]
Ernesto Durán
Tatiana Casanova

> I. Introduction. II. Colombian early childhood: Poverty and inequality. III. Early childhood and the Colombian armed conflict. IV. National early childhood policy. V. Policies aimed at reducing poverty. VI. To not conclude. VII. References.

I. Introduction

Today, early childhood has a prominent position in the Colombian social policy agenda, as it happens in most of the countries of the region. Overcoming a certain neglect of the subject that lasted for a few decades, during this quadrennium there were plans to invest around 6 billion in integral attention early childhood (Office of the President of the Republic, 2013) to expand and qualify the services aimed at providing "integral attention" to the youngest children, with a special focus on those living in poverty and in remote rural locations.

In addition, as part of its antipoverty strategy, since 2002 the national government set in motion a conditional subsidies program, known as Families in Action, which today has a presence in the 1,103 municipalities of the country, benefiting 3,000,000 families; its goals include impacting early childhood through nutritional subsidies and with the promotion of the attendance to growth and development programs. The evaluations of the program show limited effects on the health and nutrition of early childhood.

In the past four years, the Red Unidos National Strategy to overcome extreme poverty has been reinforced. It is aimed at "promoting the

---

[1] Master in Psychology; coordinator of the Observatory of Children of Universidad Nacional de Colombia. mcristina.torrado@gmail.com.
PHD Candidate in Social Science; coordinator of the Observatory of Children of Universidad Nacional de Colombia. *ejdurans@unal.edu.co*.
Psychologist; research assistant at the Observatory of Children of Universidad Nacional de Colombia. *tccasanovam@unal.edu.co*.

integration of the poorest and most vulnerable to social services, providing integral attention to that segment of the population, and to provide monitoring and tools that will allow the poorest families to generate income in a sustainable fashion and definitely overcome poverty" (Departmento Nacional de Planeación, 2011: 19). According to data from the National Agency for Overcoming Extreme Poverty, in the first eight months of 2013, 53,374 families have overcome extreme poverty in Colombia, mainly in urban areas, and 588,731 families in rural areas are in the process of achieving the same goal (El tiempo Newspaper, 2013). President Santos claims that 1,300,000 persons had overcome extreme poverty, and 2,500,000 had overcome poverty during his government (RCN News, 2013).

On the other hand, in the past decade, some local governments, such as the Bogota and Medellin governments, have implemented social policies aimed at the reduction of poverty and inequality with good results in some indicators. Those policies have been aimed at improving urban and social services infrastructure and facilitating the access of the public to them.

Despite these efforts, the country still holds a debt with respect to the effective assurance of the rights of children under 5 years, especially those who live in regions and demographic groups that have been historically excluded from the benefits of national development.

Based on the information available, the article proposes a critical analysis of the role and effect of the policies aimed at providing integral attention to early childhood, which, according to the state, are based on a rights-oriented perspective. The core question is, to what extent do these policies, which manage to guarantee the access of children to basic care, generating a minimum "social capital," become or not a factor of reproduction of poverty and inequality in a country where these phenomena have deep historical roots and highly complex determinants.

II. Colombian early childhood: Poverty and inequality

According to the 2005 Census, children under 5 years represent 10.9% of the population of the country (Dane, 2005); this percentage shows a declining trend in recent decades because of the impact of the so-called demographic transition—"characterized by a reduction of fertility, with an annual population increase of 1.6%, lower birth rates, reduction of child mortality and a higher life expectancy at birth" (Ministerio para la Protección Social y Profamilia, 2005: 44).

However, national trends show major variations from one region and demographic group to the other; therefore, the ratio of children under 5 years varies depending on the case. As can be seen in graph 1, an example of the said variations can be seen by comparing the national population pyramid with that of the indigenous groups.

Graph 1. Structure of the population by sex and age, 2005

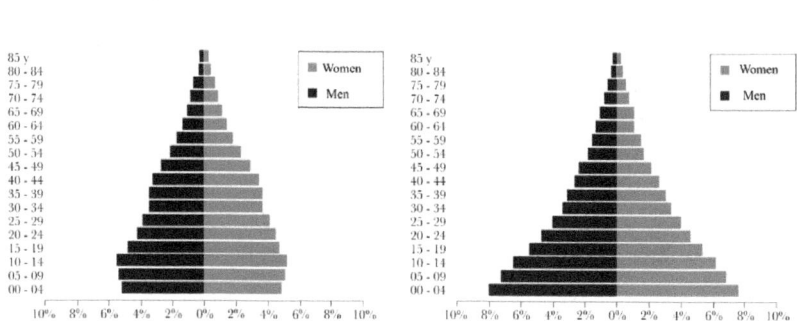

Source: Dane (2007). Colombia: a multicultural nation. Its ethnic diversity.

The population of children under 5 years is estimated to be 5,150,797 in 2013. Of them, 75.9% lives in urban areas and 24.1% in rural areas (Republic of Colombia—From Zero to Forever Strategy, 2013).

It is important to consider that various demographic groups coexist in Colombia, among which child population is particularly numerous. Thus, 14.4% of the population between 0 and 5 years belongs to an ethnic group that is different to the majority, a percentage above the national average estimated by Dane for 2005 at 3.2% of the total population.

Children under 5 years who belong to ethnic groups have the following distribution: Afro-descendant 9.8% (507,272 persons), comprising 3,679 Raizales, 663 Palenqueros, and 502,930 black and Afro-Colombian. About 4.6% belong to an indigenous group, and the Rom population is estimated at 0.0082% of the total (Republic of Colombia—From Zero to Forever Strategy, 2013). Graph 2 shows a summary of this distribution.

Graph 2. Distribution of the Colombian population under 5 years

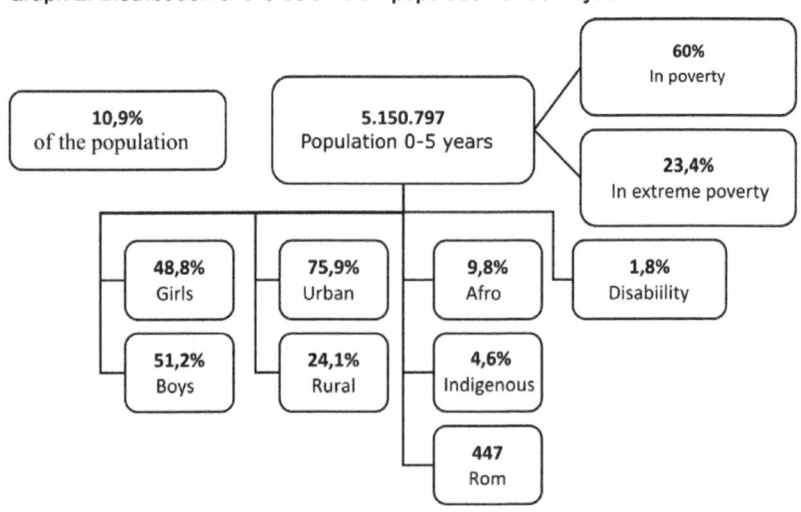

Source: Republic of Colombia—From Zero to Forever Strategy (2013).

However, the proportion of children in the early childhood segment with respect to the total population is not the same in every region of the country; the highest is in departments (states) with an indigenous majority, such as Vichada (20.69%), Guajira (19.59%), Vaupes (19.53%), Amazonas (17.65%), and Guaviare (15.88%), and in departments with an Afro-Colombian majority, such as Chocó (17.61%) (Dane, 2005).

It is precisely in these regions and demographic groups where the highest indicators of poverty and the most unequal living conditions are found. In that sense, Colombia, despite major achievements in economic growth and, more recently, in the reduction of poverty, maintains huge welfare inequalities among its population. Currently, two methodologies are used in Colombia to measure poverty: poverty line by income and multidimensional poverty index (IPM), which take the household as the analysis unit. The IPM includes some variables related to children, and there is only one indicator related to early childhood: access to early childhood care services, obtained through the National Quality of Life Survey (Dane, 2012).

Between 2002 and 2012, the incidence of economic poverty at the national level went from 49.7 to 32.7%. Between 2011 and 2012, the national economic poverty fell 1.34 percentage points, from 34.1% in 2011 to 32.7% in 2012, with 428,000 persons overcoming absolute poverty (Office for Social Development, 2013).

With the IPM, it is estimated that poverty fell 1.4% at the national level between 2011 and 2012. However, this reduction is not reflected in the data of rural areas, where in 2011 there was a poverty percentage of 46.1%, and in 2012 it grew to 46.8%; similarly, the extreme poverty percentage grew from 22.1% in 2011 to 22.8% in 2012. In turn, urban areas report a reduction from 30.3% in 2011 to 28.4% in 2012 (*Pobreza en Colombia se ubicó el año pasado* en 32.7%, 2013).

With respect to poverty data by country department, the Mission for the Assembly of Employment, Poverty and Inequality Statistics (2012) reports that the departments with the highest levels of poverty in 2010, according to income-based poverty, are Cauca (64%), Cordoba (64%), Chocó (65%), La Guajira (64%), and Sucre (64%) (Alcaldía Mayor de Bogotá, 2012). These departments concentrate a significant share of indigenous and Afro-descendant population, where the ratio of children in early childhood is higher than the national average.

The Mission assessed the variation of the Gini coefficient, which accounts for income inequality, with 0.57 in 2002, 0.56 in 2005, 0.57 in 2008, 0.56 in 2010, and 0.539 in 2012 (*Pobreza en Colombia se ubicó el año pasado* en 32.7%, 2013; World Bank, 2013; Mission for the Assembly of Employment Statistics, 2012). As can be seen, there is a very small variation in that decade.

Based on the 2010 Great Integrated Household Survey, the Dane identified that 23.36% of the early childhood population lives in extreme economic poverty, and 60.03% lives in poverty (Republic of Colombia— From Zero to Forever Strategy, 2013). As can be seen, while among the general population three out of every 10 Colombians are considered poor, among the youngest children it is six out of every 10 children under 5 years who are poor.

On a different note, the "Measuring inequality of opportunities in Latin America and the Caribbean" study (Barros *et al.*, 2008, quoted in Vélez *et al.*, 2010) was conducted in 2008, which measured five basic opportunities for the Colombian population in 1997 and 2003 through the Human Opportunities Index (IOH). This index combines two elements in a composite indicator:

i) How many opportunities are available, that is to say, the rate of coverage of a basic service; and ii) how equal is the distribution of these opportunities, that is to say, whether the distribution of said coverage is associated to exogenous circumstances, understanding basic opportunities as a subgroup of goods and services that are useful for children, such as access to education, drinking water and vaccines. (World Bank, 2008: 17)

The opportunities considered were as follows: the timely completion of sixth grade and the school attendance of children between 10 and 14 years, access to drinking water, sanitation, and electricity for children between 0 and 16 years. This investigation concluded that, despite having a relatively high income inequality, the opportunities index in Colombia for 2008 was relatively high, as it was in the category of countries with the potential for "transition," along with Brazil and Chile (Vélez et al., 2010).

The report of the investigation recommended expanding the IOH to five additional aspects: early childhood, the results of the investment in basic schooling, access to communications, the legal identity of the teenagers, and protection of teenagers. The following indicators were proposed for early childhood: opportunities associated with minimum nutrition and food security conditions, immunization, institutional birth, legal identity, and the quality of the upbringing (*id*).

Subsequently, Vélez *et al.* (2010) made a study to calculate the human opportunities index for children and teenagers in Colombia. Nineteen new indicators were considered in addition to the five of the regional exercise performed by the World Bank, grouped in the sectors of early childhood, education, housing services, information and communication technologies, nutrition, food security, security, legal identity, and immunization and vaccination, covering three stages of the life cycle between birth and the age of 17: infancy (0 to 5 years), childhood (5 to 11 years), and youth (12 to 17 years).

For early childhood, with data from the 2005 National Demography and Health Survey and the 2008 Quality of Life Survey, the study by Vélez *et al.* found vaccination scheme (94%), prenatal (88%), institutional birth (54%), civil registry (85%), nutrition weight size 0-4 (79%), health insurance (79%), no overcrowding (78%), development control (75%), parental interaction (73%), and preschool attendance between 4 and 5 years (59%) (*id*).

As could be expected, the investigation indicates that there are significant regional differences; therefore, it considers the living site of the child as an important factor with respect to the opportunities available to the children. This way, for the food insecurity indicator by regions, it is possible to notice that the Atlantic and the Pacific regions show significant differences with respect to Bogota, as seen in graph 3 (*id*).

Graph 3. Food insecurity by regions. Colombia (2008)

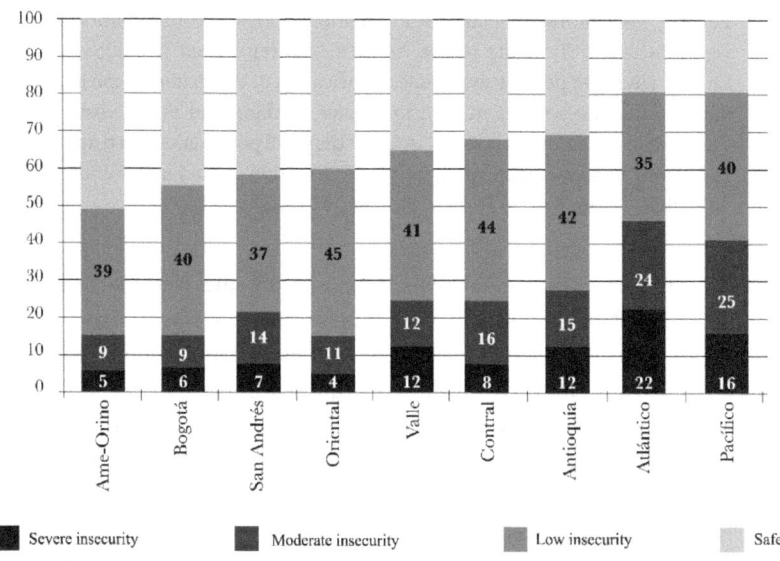

Source: DANE (2008). Estimations by the authors.

To conclude, Vélez *et al.* (2010) identify four circumstances with a determinant role in opportunity inequality among children. These circumstances are education of the parents, urban–rural location, location by region, and the presence of children, the elderly, and disabled persons at home. There are two additional circumstances that need to be considered: the presence of the parents and per capita income.

In consequence, the authors point out the importance of recognizing the significant inequality associated with urban–rural location, and to the region of the country where the children and teenagers live at the moment of designing public policies, giving special attention to the moderate and severe food insecurity status (which in some regions exceeds 40% of the children) (Vélez et al., 2010: 88).

Last, there is an investigation conducted by García*et al.* (2013a,b) that develops the Multidimensional Child and Adolescent Poverty Index (IPM-N), based on the analysis of different variables to recognize the deprivations of the children and teenagers. Its formulation was based on the concept of child poverty provided by UNICEF:

> Poverty, for children, constitutes a situation of risk and of violation of rights in itself. The State of the World's Children stated in 2005 that Children living in poverty experience deprivation of the material, spiritual and emotional resources needed to survive, develop and thrive, leaving them unable to enjoy their rights, achieve their full potential or participate as full and equal members of society. (UNICEF, 2005 quoted in Republic of Colombia—From Zero to Forever Strategy, 2013: 27)

It also considered the dimensions proposed by the National Planning Department (DNP) to measure multidimensional poverty (Angulo *et al.*, 2011, quoted in García *et al.*, 2013a,b) and by CEPAL-UNICEF (2010) to measure child poverty in Latin America (quoted in García *et al.*, 2013a,b). Variables were added to the above, which were the product of an investigation conducted through the voices of participants from different regions of the country; for that purpose the decision was made to include deprivations that would prevent the development of the present and future capacities of the children and teenagers. The new dimensions considered to measure child poverty are security, geographical integration, affection and use of time, care, and leisure (*id.*).

The IPM-N emphasizes deprivations in which the child is the center, not the household, as it used to happen with traditional poverty measurements. The reason for this decision is the characterization of particular needs of the children that can be responded to with the programs they require, being substantially different from those of the adults, both in terms of degree and type (*id.*).

Results indicate that over a third of the children and teenagers lived in poverty in 2011, according to the multidimensional approach. The children and teenagers that live in poverty according to the IPM-N are those with one deprivation in 30% of the variables that make up the index. According to this criterion, 28.6% of the group of children between 0 and 2 years are poor; and the group of children between 3 and 5 years is identified with the most critical levels (37%). The above information is supported in that only 8.4% of the children in this group do not have any deprivation (*id.*).

In a more specific manner, it indicates that the group between 0 and 2 years has very high levels of deprivation due to critical overcrowding and lack of access to green areas, drinking water, and to excreta disposal systems. Over one-third of this group has chronic malnutrition and does not have a complete vaccination scheme. With respect to the group between 3 and 5 years, the most critical dimension is that of initial education, since almost 80% does not have this indicator (the attendance to the ICBF Community Home was considered as a deprivation). Overall, 40% of the group does not have access to drinking water, 45% have no access to basic sanitation, and over 30% have chronic malnutrition (*id.*).

According to this indicator, the most critical departments are Chocó, Cordoba, Guajira, and San Andrés, in which poverty levels exceed 50%. The results in these departments are explained by water and basic sanitation deprivations (*id.*).

To complement the analysis of the poverty and inequality in which the youngest Colombians live, we present below the behavior of some welfare indicators among the population under 5 years.

With respect to low birth weight, it is estimated that by 2013 there were 37,498 cases of children with less than 2,500 g, out of the 406,775 children who were born that year, which corresponds to 9.2% of the total. This percentage increased to 10.5% for the department of Chocó and to 10.3% for La Guajira. Paradoxically, Bogota has 10.9% in this indicator (Dane).

Malnutrition in the early years persists as worryingly high: for 2010 the percentage of children under 5 years with small size for their age (chronic malnutrition) was 13.2%, and it was higher in the rural area (17.0) and even higher (19.4%) in lower income families. The most affected departments were, again, those with an indigenous majority: Vaupes, Amazonas and La Guajira, with twice the national prevalence (Profamilia, 2011).

In the country, child mortality, defined as the probability of dying during the first year of life, was 12.76 per each thousand children born alive in 2010, and the highest was in the Orinoquía–Amazonía region, with an indigenous majority (19.72 per thousand), and the Pacific region, with an Afro-Colombian majority (15.0 per thousand). By department, the highest child mortality occurred in Guainia, Vichada, Chocó, Amazonas, and San Andrés, where there are 20 deaths of minors in a year per each 1,000 children born alive (Ministerio de Salud y Protección Social, 2013).

Another important indicator to show the inequality among the Colombian population under 5 years refers to intra-urban inequality. In the case of Bogota, the Residential Segregation Index (ISR) was established, which considers the location as a spatial dimension and income as a reference variable; it was found that this index increased from 13.1 in 2007 to 17.6 in 2011, showing that segregation has increased in the city. This finding shows the gap that exists between the rich and the poor, as well as the differences in access to education opportunities, in the exposure to risk factors, in the quality of the food, the institutional health and culture services, among others (Alcaldía Mayor de Bogotá, 2012).

Measurements, as the above one, allow making progress in positioning an issue that only recently appeared in literature: the impact of intra-urban inequality on the quality of life of the children and teenagers, and particularly on the early childhood segment. Although there are no studies on the subject yet, it is known that in large cities such as Bogota, Medellin, and Cali, there are children living in very precarious situations.

The conclusion is quite evident: the early childhood segment is one of the demographic groups that are most affected by the poverty and inequality of the country. The situation of many small children makes it evident that Colombian society is characterized by

> A deep social exclusion or, in other words, for maintaining large layers of its population in a perverse and discriminatory way, preventing them from strengthening and exploiting their skills for the enrichment of their lives, the extension of liberties, solidarity, the sense of belonging, cooperation, collaborative construction through democratic institutions and practices, development, economic and social well-being. (Garay, 2002: 13)

III. Early childhood and the Colombian armed conflict

It is not possible to analyze the situation of early childhood in Colombia without referring to the long internal armed conflict, which involves several armed groups that keep complex links with drug trafficking and have deployed abominable strategies against civilians.

Despite the abundant literature on the impact of the Colombian armed conflict on the quality of life and the realization of rights of children and teenagers, there are very few works that are directly related to early childhood. *Colombia: huellas del conflicto en la primera infancia* (Colombia: traces of the conflict among the early childhood segment) published in 2009 states:

> We cannot talk about the incidence of the armed conflict on the early childhood segment as if it were a homogeneous group, but rather of *differential impacts* on specific sectors of the child population, because of the significant differences that exist from one geographic region and social sector to the other in terms of rights and opportunities, also in the probability and intensity of the contact between children, armed stakeholders and the violent events inherent to the conflict. (Torrado *et al.*, 2009: 59)

Throughout the book, it is seen that the most affected by the armed conflict are children under 5 years living in areas of the country that have a convergence of a high ratio of children in the early childhood segment, such as the indigenous communities, high ratios of poverty, and a greater presence of armed actors and violent actions, such as the case of the departments of Chocó, Vaupes, Guajira, and Amazonía.

According to Torrado *et al.* (2009) it can be concluded that:

> The impact of the conflict on the children is not homogeneous, because the risks and effects are greater for some demographic groups. In some cases, the conflict worsens a situation of structural inequality that affects the enjoyment of rights for children under six years, revealing the gap between the indigenous and Afro-descendant communities or the inhabitants of certain rural sectors and the rest of the country. (Torrado *et al.*, 2009: 82)

These communities are the most affected by the strategies used by armed actors, such as the confinement or the fumigation of illicit crops, in the access to food, medicines, or timely health care.

The same source identifies the most critical groups as follows: children under 6 years in the indigenous groups who live in regions where the conflict has a high intensity, such as Putumayo, Vichada, or Guaviare; who live in areas that are infested with landmines in the rural areas of Antioquia, Caquetá, and Guaviare; those belonging to the Afro-descendant communities who are victims of forced displacement; and last, those who live in poverty and exclusion in rural areas with a high presence of armed actors, particularly in the departments of Nariño, Putumayo, Meta, and Arauca.

The findings and conclusions of this study agree with the findings of the 2008 state of the children report: "emergency situations such as those generated by armed conflicts produce food insecurity and an increase in child mortality as a result of nutritional deficiencies, epidemics or outbreaks of certain diseases, scarcity of medicine and other difficulties for the provision of healthcare services" (UNICEF, 2007: 18).

The impacts caused by the armed conflict on children not only seem to expand the existing inequalities but they also create new ones: It creates physical and emotional damages in those who, living in "conflict areas," directly experience the pain and horrors of war, whereas others know them as relatively distant events that are narrated on TV.

Belonging to an indigenous or Afro-descendant family and living in certain areas of the country are the main risk factors for a Colombian under 5 years to potentially die or be hurt in a shooting, or to be killed by landmines, to suffer forced displacement, lose their parents, or even to be kidnapped.

IV. National early childhood policy

Colombia, as most of the countries in the region, has been developing early childhood attention strategies for over 30 years, and these policies have been reinforced in the past six years, and today they have a prominent spot in the social and political agenda of the country. These strategies are addressed to early childhood in poverty, with clear criteria to focus on the population that is in the most critical situations.

The Community Welfare Homes (HCB) program, due to its geographic coverage, amount of users, and investment, has been the main state strategy to attend to early childhood in Colombia for over 25 years. Each HCB has a community mother who is in charge of attending to and providing care to 13 children under 5 years in her own home. The evaluations of the program have found significant difficulties to provide quality attention, such as overcrowding and insecurity conditions in the physical spaces, insufficiency of resources, inadequate nurturing, and capacity of the educators to provide enriching experiences to the children.

At the start of the twenty-first century, the country lacked an integral early childhood policy that would articulate the existing programs and, particularly, a clear direction for initial education; there was scant regulation of private offerings and a significant number of the poorest children of the country attended the HCB program.

In 2009, the HCB had a total investment of $729,682,000,000 to operate. A total of 22.16% of the resources invested by the ICBF came from parafiscal funds. The said investment made it possible to cover 78,700 community homes, where 1,206,287 children participate (Unión Temporal Universidad de Los Andes and Profamilia, 2009).

After a period of almost two decades characterized by a lack of discussion on the sense and orientation of early childhood programs in Colombia, between 2000 and 2002, the issue started to reappear in the political agenda of the country, and important mobilization processes started, involving actors from the public and the private sectors and from civil society. One of the most visible and recognized processes was the performance in 2003 of the international seminar "Early Childhood and Development. The Challenge of the Decade."

Then, in 2005 and 2006, under the direction of the ICBF, a program was implemented to support the formulation of the national early childhood policy, which facilitated the mobilization of numerous actors throughout the country, with the organization of a second seminar "Mobilization for Early Childhood," held in 2005. A result of this process, which saw many discussions and the conduction of a few researches, was the preparation of the document Colombia por la primera infancia (2006). This was the basis for the document prepared by the National Economic and Social Policy Council, Conpes.[2]

This document is a milestone in the evolution of the national early childhood policy, as it seeks to integrate, under a single framework, all the actions and programs aimed at this demographic group under the coordination of different sectors of the public institutions; from that moment started a process that has positioned early childhood among the top priorities of the social policy.

The current policy, known as the "From Zero to Forever Strategy," has significantly increased public investment in an intersectoral model that seeks to guarantee the rights of Colombian children under 5 years.

Despite irrefutable progress in terms of coverage, in the improvement of quality, and the social mobilization around the integral attention of early childhood, From Zero to Forever is based on a social policy model that barely

---

2 Conpes is a technical advisory body of the government on the planning of economic policy.

contributes to overcoming inequality of opportunity for the smallest citizens of the country. This model largely maintains its focus on the poorest and does not strengthen state actors.

> A (social policy) model oriented by the application of four closely interrelated principles: 1) the privatization of social services and social security, 2) the focalization of social public spending, 3) the decentralization of social programs and services to regional and non-government entities and 4) compensation, understood as the action of introducing measures aimed at mitigating the social and political costs of the adjustment programs. (García, 2009: 26)

According to *Conversando sobre políticas sociales* (2013: 2) when social investment is focused on the poorest or most vulnerable segments, while leaving to the market the regulation of the services for the richest, "this means that the poor will go, along with other poor, to poor quality establishments, while the rich will go, along with other rich, to quality establishments." Following this path does not lead to reducing inequality; instead, it is deepened in the long term.

As we have pointed out, when the From Zero to Forever Strategy appeared, a large number of children in the early childhood segment attended HCBs. For this reason, the policy promotes other educational alternatives such as the training of the families and the progressive transformation of the HCBs in specialized institutions to provide integral attention to children. However, the country maintains a more formalized, and better quality, initial education for the children who belong to the higher quintiles of income, thus reinforcing a dual policy model with effects on social cohesion, solidarity, and equity that are well known.To increase the coverage and improve the quality of the attention, the strategy has set in motion throughout the country a model under which private operators are contracted to provide initial education services in the family and institutional environment. This model raises many questions, such as the sustainability and quality of the interventions; in addition, this model does not strengthen the technical and management capacity of local authorities.

Instead of making progress toward an inclusive social policy, it continues to promote the segmentation of the services and social segregation, and this way it maintains and deepens inequality. The impact that initial education may have over social inequality is lost due to the stratification of the quality; at the same time, there is no promotion of a full citizenship for all children without discrimination.

Currently, the educational supply for Colombian children under 5 years includes a large range of care and education environments of varying quality, from sophisticated nurseries and preschool classrooms to child development centers and community modalities such as the HCBs, and other more informal options. Only in Bogota, we have identified six initial education modalities.

This diversity would not be a problem if it was not for the way it corresponds to the "map of inequality." This way, although children under 5 years belonging to the families with the highest income have access to rich educational spaces, the poorest attend programs with less financial and technical resources, as seen in table 1.

Table 1. Percentage of children under 5 years by socioeconomic stratum[3] and initial education program 2007

Program/Stratum	0	1	2	3	4	5	6	% of the total
Community welfare home (%)	61.9	53.4	41.7	15.5				41.8
Family welfare nursery or kindergarten	6.8	22.1	25.7	16.8	7.3			21.9
Social kindergarten, neighbo home, kindergarten of the district (Bogota) (%)		2.3	3.6	4.4				3.0
Other official nursery, preschool or kindergarten (%)	22.7	11.9	9.7	13.6	1.2			11.2
Private nursery, preschool or kindergarten (%)	8.6	10.2	19.2	49.7	91.6	100.0	100.0	22.2
Total (%)	100.0	100.0	100.0	100.0	100.0	100.0	100.0	100.0

Source: CEPAL estimates based on the Quality of Life Survey (2007).

---

3   The Colombian socioeconomic stratification is a classification of the homes based on their physical characteristics and environment. It has six groups or strata, one being the lowest. Retrieved from: //www.dnp.gov.co/Programas/Sinergia/Evaluaciones Estrat%C3%A9gicas/EvaluacionesdeImpacto/Estratificaci%C3%B3nSocioEcon%C3 %B3mica.aspx.

Even though since 2010 the national government has promoted the transformation of the HCB into more formal initial education modalities, and it has implemented an ambitious program to provide integral attention to early childhood in the family context, it has not abandoned the criterion of focusing the policy on programs aimed at the poorest segments, where children receive lower quality services, apart from their peers from other social sectors.

How did this situation come about? Without making a detailed historical analysis, we can say that it is the result of educational and social policy decisions made by the Colombian state throughout several decades, which deepened the differences between public and private offerings, and also within each of them, and placed initial education in the field of social welfare as a residual action[4] through which the state only supports the provision of some services for the poorest children.

Instead of guaranteeing access to a unique educational program for all children, education policy is oriented toward actions that focus on the poorest and most vulnerable segments. To this respect, it is worth remembering that this has been a tendency of Latin American social policy, which has "set aside the importance of guaranteeing homogeneous services with quality standards for all, which would facilitate the development of equal, democratic and sustainable societies, and strengthen citizen participation" (Filgueira *et al.*, 2006: 1).

V. Policies aimed at reducing poverty

To reduce poverty, which they recognize as very high, the most recent government plans have proposed two lines of action: an indirect one and a direct one. The former is based on the premise that encouraging economic growth increases the income of the entire population (which has been dubbed the trickle-down of resources to the lower income population) and the latter seeks to act upon the deprivations of those in extreme poverty, promoting their access to basic social services.

The problem is that in the current economic model, economic growth is not equally beneficial to all. The benefits are distributed unequally; therefore, as López and Núñez (2007: 188) propose, economic growth on its

---

4 The residual model is the one that limits the provision of protection or welfare policies to the poor, that is to say, to those who demonstrate a need or incapacity.

own is insufficient, because it reduces poverty and destitution in a residual manner.

On the other hand, the Colombian state has implemented a strategy based on conditional cash transfers, following a trend that has spread throughout the region (Minujin et al., 2007). These programs are characterized by being highly focused on those who are in poverty or in extreme poverty, by mainly having women as the receivers, by agreeing commitments and responsibilities with the beneficiaries, by having significant coverage, and by being highly centralized in terms of design and structure (Serrano, 2005).

In the Colombian case, the transfers are specifically aimed at families with children under 18 years, preferably families with women as heads of family and/or victims of forced displacement; these families are selected through a classification system known as the System for the Identification of Potential Beneficiaries of Social Programs (Sisben) (Flórez et al., 2008). Transfers would be aimed, as per the program, at the improvement of child nutrition and health, and school attendance, with a view to protecting and promoting the development of human capital in that age range. The basis of these initiatives is the program known as "Families in Action," which started its pilot stage in 2001, with the support of the World Bank and the IDB, and it has expanded. This program has been granting cash transfers to female heads of family with children under 18 years in economic vulnerability. The transfer may be a nutrition subsidy for children between 0 and 7 years, subject to the condition that mothers have to take their children to development and growth controls at health centers, and to completing all the vaccination plans offered by the state.

The evaluations of the program, conducted within its own conceptual framework, indicate that it has an effective incidence in the mitigation of the effects of poverty on child nutrition and school attendance, but it simultaneously creates a level of dependence that encourages the permanence in the program for extended periods.

The other major strategy, known as the RedUnidos, works from the results obtained with the application of IPM, which identifies the most critical deprivations, and the geographical location of families in extreme poverty. The program seeks to have a more integral effect on the situation of the families, transferring not only resources but also services from the different state programs. It works with a dual focus: a path to improve the generation of income, raising the educational level and job preparedness, and the improvement of the inhabitability conditions of the families in terms of water, basic sanitation, and the conditions of the home.

Both strategies seek to provide the poorest with minimum conditions to subsist and to be included in society. They are focused on "providing the poorest with instruments that will help them to manage risk to have more opportunities to overcome poverty" (Giraldo, 2007: 144).

With these programs, poverty is assumed not as an economic and social problem, a consequence of an unequal and unfair system, but as a transient situation in which some households are caught, depoliticizing the debate and disguising the core causes of the problem. They generate a dependence of families on state assistance, contributing to forming new political clients.

VI. To not conclude

The analysis conducted seeks to make progress in responding to the question on the relationships between early childhood policy, social justice, and the exercise of the social citizenship of the younger children. As we have indicated, a policy to provide integral attention to early childhood as the one currently being implemented by Colombia will improve the access of the poorest and most excluded children to some social services, but it causes no impact on the enormous gap between groups of the child population, a product of historical inequality.

Without a doubt, in the past eight years the Colombian state has increased public investment and attracted private capital to improve the quality of the programs aimed at early childhood and to integrate the actions implemented from various sectors and public actors (health, education, family welfare, and nutrition), in what has been dubbed as the strategy for "Integral Attention to Early Childhood."

Despite the existence of all this framework of programs aimed at early childhood, and of others that seek the reduction of the extreme poverty of families, the information available shows that inequalities of opportunities and capacities among Colombian children under 5 persist and are reproduced. To a large extent, this is a result of the approach of the policy, which focuses on the poorest demographic segments and in hiring private actors for its implementation.

Although it is necessary to update the numbers to incorporate the achievements of the national early childhood policy in the past five years, no significant changes are expected in the historical trends of inequality and quality of life and the exercise of rights by Colombian children under 5 years. It is not only a matter of improving the coverage of the programs but also a matter of fighting social segregation and of reducing the gap between the demographic groups of children.

The process of discussing and analyzing the Colombian policy on early childhood must continue, as it constitutes a key element in the development of public policy aimed at guaranteeing the enjoyment of social rights from the initial years of life, which is indispensable in the fight against inequality, discrimination, and social exclusion in Colombian society, if we consider their individual and collective effects in the medium and long term.

VII. References

Alcaldía Mayor de Bogotá, 2012, *Plan de desarrollo 2012–16. Plan de desarrollo económico y social y de obras públicas para Bogotá Distrito Capital 2012–16 Bogotá humana*, Bogota, Colombia, Alcaldía Mayor de Bogotá.

Colombia por la primera infancia, 2006, *Política pública por los niños y niñas desde la gestación hasta los seis años*, Bogotá, Colombia por la primera infancia.

Conversando sobre políticas sociales, 2013, "Focalización: un atentado contra la igualdad," *http://voces.latercera.com/2013/08/27/claudia-sanhueza/* (retrieved on September 13, 2013).

Dane, "Nacimientos por peso al nacer, según departmentso y área de residencia de la madre. Año 2013 preliminar."*Chart 6. Statistical Information*, Dane.

Dane, 2005, *Sistema de consulta información censal*, Dane, 2005 basic census.

Dane, 2007, *Colombia: una nación multicultural. Su diversidad étnica*, Bogotá, Dane.

Dane (2008). Quality of Life Survey in Colombia.

Dane, 2012, "Pobreza en Colombia," Dane, Press Release, *http://www.dane.gov.co/files/investigaciones/condiciones_vida/pobreza/cp_pobreza_2011.pdf* (retrieved on September 2013).

Departmento Nacional de Planeación, 2011, "Resumen Plan Nacional de Desarrollo 2010–14 Prosperidad para todos," Departmento Nacional de Planeación, *http://www.dnp.gov.co/LinkClick.aspx?fileticket=4-J9V-FE2pI%3D&tabid=1238* (retrieved on November 30, 2013).

Dirección de Desarrollo Social, 2013, *Pobreza monetaria y desigualdad del ingreso. Análisis de los resultados recientes 2010–12*,Colombia, Dirección de Desarrollo Social.

El Tiempo Newspaper, November, 2013, "53.300 familias han salido este año de la pobreza extrema," 2013, El Tiempo newspaper, *http://www.eltiempo.com/economia/ARTICULO-WEB-NEW_NOTA_INTERIOR-13164049.html*.

Filgueira, Fernando *et al.*, 2006, *Universalismo básico: una alternativa posible y necesaria para mejorar las condiciones de vida*, Washington, DC, Banco Interamericano de Desarrollo-Planeta.

Flórez, Carmen *et al.*, 2008, *Diseño del índice SISBEN en su tercera versión*, Bogotá, DNP.

Garay, Luis Jorge, 2002, *Colombia entre la exclusión y el desarrollo. Propuestas para la transición al Estado social de derecho*, Bogotá, Contraloría General de la República.

García Andrés, 2009, *Los programas de transferencias condicionadas: mecanismos de legitimidad política del orden neoliberal en América Latina. El caso de Familias en Acción*, Bogotá, Universidad Javeriana, Master's Thesis in Social Policy.

García, Sandra *et al.*, 2013a, "Análisis de la situación de la pobreza infantil en Colombia," *Notas de Política*, Bogotá, vol. 14, No. August.

García, Sandra *et al.*, December, 2013b, *Análisis de la pobreza multidimensional en niños, niñas y adolescentes en Colombia: metodología y principales resultados*, Bogotá, Colombia, Preliminary Version.

Giraldo, César, 2007, *¿Protección o desprotección social?*, Bogotá, Desde Abajo, Fundación CESDE, Centro de Estudios Escuela para el Desarrollo, Universidad Nacional.

López, Hugo and Núñez, Jairo, 2007, *Pobreza y desigualdad en Colombia. Diagnóstico y estrategias*, Bogotá, DNP.

Ministerio de Salud y Protección Social, 2013, *Análisis de Situación de Salud según regiones Colombia*, Bogotá, Ministerio de Salud y Protección Social.

Ministerio para la Protección Social y Profamilia, 2005, "Encuesta Nacional de demografía y Salud," http://www.profamilia.org.co/encuestas/02consulta/01capitulos.htm (consultado el 28 de agosto de 2013).

Minujin, Alberto *et al.*, 2007, "El boom de las transferencias de dinero sujetas a condiciones. ¿De qué manera estos programas sociales benefician a los niños y niñas latinoamericanos?," *Salud Colectiva*, Buenos Aires, vol. 3, No. May–August (2).

Misión para el empalme de las series de empleo, 2012, "Mesep estimates based on the Household Surveys by DANE-Encuesta Continua de Hogares 2002–05, assembled by Mesep and Gran Encuesta Integrada de Hogares 2008–10."

Pobreza en Colombia se ubicó el año pasado en 32.7%, 2013, *Revista Portafolio*, Bogotá, No. April, http://www.portafolio.co/economia/cifras-pobreza-y-desigualdad-colombia-2012.

Presidencia de la República, 2013a, "'Hoy podemos decir con satisfacción que cumplimos las metas en materia de reducción de la pobreza': Presidente Santos," http://wsp.presidencia.gov.co/Prensa/2014/EneroPaginas/20140108_07-Hoy-podemos-decir-con-satisfaccion-cumplimos-metas-materia-reduccion-pobreza-Presidente-Santos.aspx (retrieved on January 10, 2014).

Presidencia de la República, 2013b, "Inversión para la primera infancia en el cuatrenio será de $6 billones," http://www.deceroasiempre.gov.co/Prensa/2013/Paginas/1307

02-Inversion-para-la-primera-infancia-en-el-cuatrienio-sera-de-6-billones.aspx (retrieved on January 10 2014).

Profamilia (2011). Encuesta Nacional de Demografía y Salud 2010.

RCN News (2013). "Cumplimos en materia de reducción de la pobreza": Santos. Published in January 2013. *http://www.youtube.com/watch?v=eJBtgv6yOL0*

República de Colombia—Estrategia de Cero a Siempre, 2013, *Fundamentos políticos, técnicos y de gestión de la Estrategia de Atención Integral a la Primera Infancia*, Colombia, Imprenta Nacional.

Serrano, Claudia, 2005, *La política social en la globalización. Programas de protección en América Latina*, Santiago de Chile, CEPAL.

Torrado, María Cristina *et al.*, 2009, *Colombia: huellas del conflicto en la primera infancia*, Bogotá, Save the Children-OEI.

UNICEF, 2007, *State of the World's Children/United Nations Children's Fund—UNICEF. (2007). State of the World's Children 2008*, New York, Child Survival.

Unión Temporal Universidad de Los Andes and Profamilia, 2009, *Evaluación de impacto del Programa Hogares Comunitarios de Bienestar del ICBF*, Bogota, Unión Temporal Universidad de Los Andes and Profamilia.

Vélez, Carlos *et al.*,2010, *Oportunidades para los niños colombianos: cuánto avanzamos en esta década*, World Bank, Colombia-Banco de la República de Colombia-Departmentso Nacional de Planeación.

World Bank, 2008, *Midiendo la desigualdad de oportunidades en América Latina y el Caribe*, Washington DC, World Bank.

World Bank, 2013, "Índice de Gini," *http://datos.bancomundial.org/indicador/SI.POV.GINI* (retrieved in August 2013).

REFLECTIONS ON CHILD POVERTY, QUALITY OF LIFE, AND LOCAL PUBLIC POLICY

Nelson ANTEQUERA D.

I. Introduction. II. Conceptions of development and poverty. III. Child poverty and quality of life. IV. Conclusions. V. Bibliography.

I. Introduction

This article presents a reflection on the conceptions of child poverty, quality of life, and local public policy. Based on this reflection, we may redefine the concept of child poverty from the paradigm of "Living Well." The importance of redefining or extending the concept of child poverty from an alternative paradigm to economic development tradition lies in the fact that this exercise opens the possibility of also redefining public policy for childhood from a different perspective. This perspective is oriented to an interpretation of reality that assumes a conception of poverty in terms of the access to goods and services, but it simultaneously assumes a conception of poverty in terms of "quality of life."

For this purpose, we developed our arguments as follows. In the first section, we present and analyze the conceptions of development that are used to define child poverty as a phenomenon and a problem. We will see how this definition of childhood poverty is the basis for the core programs of the Bolivian State policy on childhood, which are implemented by the different levels of government. This exercise seeks to prove that the definition of child poverty that is restricted to following qualitative poverty indicators results in interventions that are necessary but insufficient.

In the second section, we present a part of the results of the qualitative human development diagnosis performed in the municipality of La Paz. In this section, we present some aspects of childhood-related problems in three areas: early childhood, teenage, and working children. We seek to highlight the aspects that challenge both the conceptions of childhood poverty and the role of the state, the community, and the family around the quality of life of children.

In the third section, we submit our proposal of "Living Well" as an alternative development paradigm that is synthesized in the concept of "community with quality of life." Based on the paradigm, we state the terms in which we propose a redefinition of the concept of "child poverty" from the paradigm of "community with quality of life" and the core implications of this redefinition in terms of the local state intervention.

II. Conceptions of development and poverty

In 1985, the new cycle of economic (neo)liberalism in Bolivia started with a series of radical measures that sought to respond to the aggravation of the structural crisis the country was undergoing. The 1990s was marked by the intensification of the neoliberal model. One of the most significant measures of the period was the passing of the Popular Participation Law (1994), which introduced important modifications to the Bolivian democratic system. A fundamental change produced is the expansion of the concept of municipality, which allows planning and channeling resources to rural and urban towns.

"Human development" arose in this context, as an alternative to economic developmentalism both from economic thought and from international organizations. Human development was assumed by the Bolivian state in the context of municipalization with an approach that primarily focused on meeting basic needs and "reducing poverty."

As a consequence of this approach, we must to highlight two characteristics of the human development policy implemented in the context of municipalization.

The first characteristic is the basic needs approach. The 1999 Municipalities Law establishes, under the "Sustainable Human Development" subheader, a wide range of municipal competencies such as the planning of human development, tourism, production projects, land issues, territorial zoning, health insurance, attention to disabled persons, environmental protection, gender equality, complementary nutrition, and so on. Under the "On infrastructure" title, it stipulates that the municipality is in charge of building, supplying, and maintaining infrastructure in the education, health, culture, sports, micro-irrigation, basic sanitation, urban roads, and gravel roads sectors. Human development is conceived as the construction of educational, sports, or health-related infrastructure to improve the conditions of these services.

The second characteristic of the national and municipal human development policies is their focus on the "vulnerable" segments of the population. This way, both infrastructure works and other meager social programs focused precisely on the reduction of poverty and on serving the marginalized segments of the population. The focalized policy is based on a conception of human development understood as a social response to the perverse effects of the neoliberal model and aimed at the containment of the growing social demand they generate.

Local governments implemented programs aimed at serving the demographic segments identified as "vulnerable groups," which mainly include women, children and teenagers, and senior citizens. This way, social programs only serve those who, in the eyes of the state, are considered as poor, impoverished, marginal, or vulnerable. Social spending is justified not in terms of the rights, but of the needs. To put it differently, rights are conceived as unmet basic needs, and citizens as persons in extreme need, due to their lack of capacity to generate economic resources.

This conception of development in general, and of human development in particular, based on a basic needs and "vulnerable groups" approach, gives rise to a conception of child poverty and to the policies that are derived from it.

The concept of child poverty assumed by the Bolivian state is found in one of the official documents that explicitly deals with the issue: The *ChildPoverty and Disparities in Bolivia report* (Unidad de Analisis de Politica Social y Economica (UDAPE)-UNICEF, 2009: 34).

The *Report* highlights the need to have a precise concept of child poverty, as "this will be the basis for the design of anti-poverty policies" (UDAPE-UNICEF, 2009: 34). In addition, it establishes the need forhaving specific policies to fight child poverty based on the verification that poverty has a particular impact on children, as it compromises their development and future life.

Building on UNICEF's definition, considering the particularities of the case of Bolivia and "based on the available data," the Bolivian state defines child poverty as follows:

> The deprivation or limitation in the access to resources such as health, education, housing, sanitary services, information, a situation that compromises the integral development of capacities and potential, limits the full exercise of rights and restricts social integration as a full member of society.

The definition of child poverty provided by UNICEF contemplates, in addition to deprivation of material resources, the deprivation of "spiritual and emotional" resources needed to survive. This broader definition has four characteristics. The concept of deprivation refers to "lack" as a characteristic of the environment. Deprivations must be analyzed by taking into consideration the mutual relationship of the deprivations and not by viewing them as isolated indicators. Child poverty, from the perspective of the relationship of the deprivations, will be multidimensional. Last, it is established that the economic criterion (income) to define poverty is important, but it is not the only one, or the core one.

However, the definition of the Bolivian state does not contemplate the spiritual and emotional aspects, and it emphasizes basic services. In a footnote, it states that "unfortunately, there is no information that allows us to incorporate the emotional and spiritual aspects of poverty to this study. Collecting this information is a pending task." It is not our purpose to analyze the conceptual or methodological consistency of the document cited. What we mean to show is that this definition of child poverty that "will be the basis for the design of anti-poverty policies" is based on "the information available." We can thus infer that the public policy on child poverty is largely based on the availability of information, and it does not respond to the issue in its real dimension.

Based on this definition and the data availability criterion, basically four fields of analysis are identified: housing basic service (sanitary services and safe water), information, education, and health. In each field, the indicators are determined, once again, based on the data available.

"Deprivation in education" is understood as the school attendance rate—attending or not attending school. It can be seen that 10.6% of the population between 0 and 17 years does not attend school or "had severe deprivations" (UDAPE-UNICEF, 2009: 41). In the area of health, it uses indicators of vaccination coverage (third dose of anti-polio vaccine and triple vaccine for children under 2 years) and of health care in the event of a disease. According to these data, 8% of the child population "faces severe health deprivations." In the area of housing, a house is considered "adequate" if it does not have dirt floor and if the child does not experience overcrowding conditions. It is then concluded that 31.5% of the children live in homes with dirt floors, and 15.3% live in overcrowding conditions. Combining these data, it is concluded that almost 40% of the total of children live in homes with dirt floors and/or overcrowding conditions. In the area of safe water, the only indicator is the "type of access to water," for which it establishes that 14.4% of the child population presents water access deprivations. In the area of the deprivation of sanitary services, it establishes that 29% of the child population lives in homes where there are no bathrooms. The deprivation of information is defined as a lack of access to telephone, radio, television (TV), or newspaper at home. Results show that 13.8% "present information deprivations" at home.

In this approach to the conceptions of the state with respect to development and child poverty, we would like to highlight the following aspects.

First, they reflect the will of the Bolivian state to explicitly work for the reduction of child poverty indexes through the planning of sectoral programs and plans.

However, at least according to the *ChildPoverty and Disparities in Bolivia report* (UDAPE-UNICEF, 2009), they are based on a conception of child poverty that is limited to the data that are available, which are not adequate enough to sustain a policy that seriously accounts for and faces the incidence of child poverty.

Reducing "education deprivation" to an attendance rate issue implies a simplistic response from the state: giving the children a grant that will encourage school attendance and permanence. This may have improved school attendance rates, but the quality of the education, as a fundamental right, has not been improved. Analyzing the health problem in terms of the coverage of sanitary services and the vaccination rates reduces it and distorts it in a cartoonish way, where the health policy is reduced to increasing vaccination coverage and "births" assisted by a medical professional. Also at the extreme of this technical-methodological reductionism of the issue of child poverty is including the "quality of the floor of the home" or the access to a TV as a factor in the measurement of "deprivation." In other words, we do not consider that one of the most serious problems that Bolivian children are experiencing is the quality of the floor of their homes, or the lack of a TV.

The indicators guided by the basic needs approach may account for a part of the child poverty situation, and they may give rise to policies aimed at improving these indicators. However, the analyses and policies guided by the basic needs approach are necessary as a point of departure, but they are insufficient. It will be then necessary to reformulate the orientation of the policies from the underlying conception of development and poverty.

To reformulate the orientation of the policies, it will be necessary to build on the particularity of the incidence of the deprivation among people who are in a situation of dependence and in a certain stage of development. Child poverty compromises the current living conditions of this segment of the population, as well as their development and their future. Despite the lack of quantitative data, the emotional and spiritual aspects that are related to the development of the affection and identity bonds in the family and the community or, alternatively, to the progressive deterioration of social ties must be taken into consideration.

These aspects will be addressed in the following section, based on the data of the human development diagnosis for the municipality of La Paz.

1. Beyond the figures. The relational dimension of child poverty

We present some aspects of childhood-related problems in three areas: infancy and childhood, teenage, and working children. The data are part of the results of the qualitative human development diagnosis performed in the municipality of La Paz. That diagnosis has sought to collect the population's perceptions of and concerns about social problems in general. This way, our analysis and conclusions are based on the testimonies collected aboutthe problems of childhood, teenagers, and working children. The testimonies herein seek to open the discussion to concrete situations that express that child poverty involves aspects that are not limited to the lack of services or to economic indicators. In this section, we seek to highlight the aspects that challenge both the conceptions of childhood poverty and the role of the state, the community, and the family in the quality of life of children.

2. Infancy and childhood problems

Behind "poverty" indexes lie the worries and efforts of provider parents in relation to guaranteeing the subsistence of their children and the ensuing situation of abandonment that children experience, either with respect to the single head of the home (mother or father) or to both: abandonment because the only head and provider of the family must go out to work to satisfy the biological needs of the day: "most of them are with their mothers, and the mother has to go to work, they leave at 5 am, come back at night, and at that time they must prepare the food, the kids arrive, and I do not know if they know, if they will eat or not" (director, UE Ladislao Cabrera, morning shift, 2012E); because "there they do not have enough" and both parents must go to work:

> Now the problem is that parents, due to the current situation...have to devote more hours to work, and therefore children are semi abandoned, because their parents leave at 7 or 8 in the morning and come back at 8, 9, 10 in the night, children are pretty much on their own, because parents cannot provide the attention they require. (Eva Riveros, coordinator, Fundación La Paz, 2012, CUE 11)

In some cases the mother, or both parents, had to migrate to guarantee the basic conditions of subsistence; they had to leave town or the country:"many parents go to work in other countries and their children are here, with their grandparents, uncles and aunts" (director, UE Ladislao Cabrera, morning shift, 2012E), because one or both parents need to work a lot more in order t covernot only more than the basic needs;"if you want to provide comfort for the children, it is even worse, you have to try harder, and spend most of the time looking for a way to provide all the comfort, economic resources, that is the key" (David Patty, president Community Association District 7).

That is to say, in the eyes of the parents of different socioeconomic levels, either from monoparental, biparental, or extended families, the abandonment of the children is an indispensable requirement to satisfy the material conditions of subsistence of the family:

Children are almost not taken into consideration with too much care, because people or the parents mostly are trying to find economic resources, we neglect the issue of the children, the issue of health, we address it a little bit every time they get sick...in this times of economic downturn it is very difficult to be present...the neglect of the children is mainly due to the economic issue, that is the reason, because we parents are more concerned with how to provide food and a roof to our children, that is what concerns us, anything else, affection, their upbringing, which go pretty fast, we out their mouth first, don't we?, their stomach, and then everything else, don't we? (David Patty, President, Community Association District 7) Although the quote refers to mothers and fathers who must guarantee the subsistence of their children, generally through self-employment, without any job security and protection, this effort would only cover some basic physical needs of the children, such as their feeding.

Family fragmentation causes the reconfiguration of the roles and the rupture of primary ties. The sense of protective relationships of the family, regardless of its type, toward the children is more related to satisfying the basic needs, such as their feeding and educationfor the children to become successful persons. However, family ties are generally associated with the exercise of violence, either as a teaching, corrective, or sanctioning method, as can be identified in the following fragment:

> I have a pathetic case. In front of my house. I do not think she is the only one that goes through this, many women must go through it (the neighbor was abandoned by her husband and) she was left with two children. She does not have a professional degree, she can't get a job and she has taken her children to a private school. Can you imagine the pressure she is under, having to raise her children on her own, and paying for their school. So she is going crazy, she looks for jobs, she accepts any job she can get, earn money any she can, but all the pressure, she takes it out on her children, because she gets home and they haven't done their homework, she starts beating them and makes life impossible for the two kids, and I don't think that only happens to her, it is happening in many homes, in many lives, both to men and women. (Yolanda G., Community Association, District 1)

According to an investigation conducted by Fundación La Paz, children internalize the expressions of violence of the adults as educational acts "for their own good,"and even as demonstrations of affection. The reasons argued for the exercise of violence generally include that children disobey their parents, and with respect to infants, the fathers or mothers generally "cannot explain it," although they point out various factors that lead them to lose their temper. Another of the reasons that starts to emerge as a frequent explanation to exercise the different forms of violence against the integrity of the child is that it is a way to get back at their spouses, through their mutual kid, or the kid of the other. The most extreme cases are the murder of minors by the partner of the mother, which are more frequently communicated by sensationalist media; however, this practice of punishing the mother (more frequently), through her children, has become commonplace. These forms of rationalization and naturalization of violence seem to respond more to a need of disguising or denying the dimensions of violence that encompass the entire subjectivity of the person, and which always finds avenues to be expressed or to emerge at that or other times.

On the other hand, sexual violence against children, which according to the records of municipal attorney offices, is scant and generally takes place within the family. This way, the problem is in many cases concealed and shrouded in shame and complicity.

3. Teenagers and youths

Teenage, the same as childhood, is a category that acquires meanings based on the contexts in which it takes place. Although this stage of transition, identified from other disciplines approximately between 11 and 17 years, defines the physiognomy of the sexually defined body, the process does not guarantee the definition of the subjective world of the teenagers. That is to say, teenage is both a biological and a political process with tensions, ruptures, and definitions with respect to the conceptions and practices of the world of the adults, which may lead to the definition of their autonomy of thought. In this framework, the physical, emotional, psychic, and social dimensions of the teenagers acquire a greater capacity and power to transform their individual and social world: "A source of initiatives, full of a transformative energy, able to find creative solutions in dead-end alleys" (Tiba, 2009: 20).

One of the predominant characteristics of the current situation of the teenager person is the condition of abandonment, not only by the other social dimensions but possibly from their own particularity. In this sense, most of the teenagers who study in state units spend their lives alone, either because they come from nearby or remote communities where their father and/or mother and relatives live or because their father and/or mother are immersed in their job activities and their contact is scant, either because of their rebellion, which make them incomprehensible, or because of an overly protective relationship that the father and/or mother have with them, which prevents a relationship of mutual recognition or respect.

Situations of violence against the teenagers are added to the abandonment and lack of affection. One of the recurring situations at the attorney offices with respect to teenagers is that the mothers, sometimes the fathers, appear to request that the institution acts as an intermediary in the incontrollable situation of their children: a situation generally associated with the consumption of alcohol, debauchery, and involvement with youth gangs, among others.

In this framework of absences, with pressure both from the conditions of subsistence of the families and from the expectations of working mothers and/or fathers, not only to satisfy the physiological needs of their children but to enable them to study and "be something," the traditional problems associated with teenagers continue to appear, including premature pregnancies, violence, the formation of gangs, the use of alcohol and drugs, although at a greater pace and more widely, which is additionally associated with the growing insecurity.

Possibly one of the most visible expressions of sexual violence is the issue of unwanted pregnancies and abortions, as one student points out: "Pregnancies and abortions are everyday matters. In my class there are three pregnant girls." In this framework, the new problem appears to be more related to the issue of clandestine abortions. Another of the expressions of sexual violence, mainly against teenage girls, is human trafficking. The problem starts with family violence situations that force the girls to run away from their homes and to become economically independent, and it is intermingled with the increase of organized crime, which puts the youths of any social or economic status in danger.

One of the problems associated with the abandonment, the early start of sexual relations, and violence is the consumption of alcohol and other drugs. This practice is growingly frequent, and it tends to start at increasingly earlier ages, regardless of the social strata and gender. The explanations for this problem, in the opinion of the school authorities interviewed, are family disintegration, the absence of leisure spaces, and the existence of places that sell alcohol near the educational units.

Another problem is the increase of violence and the forming of gangs. From an adult perspective, the issue of violence is considered as one of the expressions of what the teenagers live in their homes: "The violence among the youths is terrible, they come here with a lot of anxiety and pressure, because they are beaten at home," says one of the interviewees. According to the records of the attorney offices, the second stage in which the children are most punished by their parents is the teenage years.

In this framework of identification of some angles of the problems, mainly from the perspective of the adults, the specific demands in the area of care basically refer to the settting up of care centers for teenagers, centers that provide their needs of food, education, and leisure in a social environment:

> A demand that has emerged has been to create school canteens, linked to recreational school support services, and cultural services for children and teenagers, because many times it is not possible to come back at lunchtime because of work, then the children sometimes eat alone, they are alone, the response to that is that there should be school canteens...with the youngest children and teenagers, the youngest children, or many teenagers, also come back from school, they are alone, they have no activities to do, then, in the case of Hampaturi we have proposed to create off school services for children and teenagers, and also in Mallasa, there should be more of these services, they should be created, because they don't exist. (Systematization of the Dialogue "Women: the right to care with joint responsibility" Hampaturi, 2012)

These general guidelines of what is demanded from the adult perspective for the teenagers keep appearing with the different institutions that work with teenagers, with more or less elements:

> Of course, it is about making playrooms, with an arts corner for music, dance, arte, poetry, sports, board games, then the child is better entertained, he will have several options and he will leave here when he actually has to get home, right? to sleep, but all of this without neglecting his school performance, because we have to open a space for them to make their homework, the area does not have a library, only Villa Copacabana, a little boy comes all the way from Pacasa, it's very far for him, and with the current risks, even worse, then well, opening spaces for the articulation of those activities, and that the Municipality has to open the (sports) court, at least twice a week, free court. (Raúl Peláez, CEDIN-Fundación La Paz)

Here it is important to recognize that the daily life activities include a lack of services specifically aimed at teenagers. However, the extension of care services for teenagers may be linked to the restitution of the social, community, and family fabric, the weakening of which is the cause of a more complex problem that becomes manifest in early pregnancies, abortions, violence, alcohol consumption, and others. That is to say, faced with affectional, emotional, social, psychic, and other forms of abandonment that make up the subjectivity of the teenager, and which occur in the framework of material deprivations, but furthermore, of emotional and spiritual deprivations, aspects that are very necessary in a stage when the identity is conformed.

4. Working children and teenagers

From the perspective of the working children and teenagers (NNAT) interviewed, child labor is considered as a way of participating in the activities that contribute to the home, or as a space of learning; because for several class segments, working at certain ages and situations is associated with a condition of "being poor," it is even convenient for the children and teenagers to disguise their job as a circumstantial hobby.

The NNAT perform various economic activities to cover their basic needs in terms of food, clothes, education, and additionally

> If they don't decide to go out and generate income, unfortunately they will stop studying, they don't eat and they can't get dressed. These children are very aware of reality, because they do it consciously...out of need, and in addition, there are children who contribute, who give to their mother, "here mom, this is what I have earned," they distribute it among the siblings, specially the eldest ones, in some cases, they keep something for their own expenses. (Jannet V., head of the NNAT program of the Municipal Government of La Paz, 2012)

That is to say, they are children and teenagers who, faced with the option of "letting themselves die" with their families or going out to the street to sell anything, have chosen to go out and work to survive. In other cases, the role is assumed by the entire family; because the income earned by one or both parents is meager and circumstantial, they must be supported by their children: "They are street vendors, same as the child, then they cannot make ends meet, if the child sells anything, it helps, they will obtain income to buy something else" (*id.*).

In the case of the NNATs, several institutions, including the municipality, perform assistential work through services aimed at meeting their urgent needs in an eventual manner.

III. Child poverty and quality of life

The breadth and complexity of child poverty described in the preceding paragraph shows the insufficiency of a concept of child poverty that only responds to the variables of deprivation in the access to health services, education, protection, or care, and that seeks to reduce the indexes build with the basic needs approach. At the same time, it presents the need of an alternative development paradigm that may result in a state intervention that is consistent with these challenges.

This alternative development paradigm emerges from the redefinition of the Bolivian state with the enactment of a new constitutional text in 2009. This paradigm is defined as "Living Well," as opposed to the liberal development model. There are at least two core characteristics of this concept that we would like to review. First, its pluralist character: From this perspective, there is not a single development model or a single way of "Living Well" that is the goal of the paradigm. The second one is the community character of the paradigm. Although there is an insistence in using indigenous, native, or farmer communities as a model and inspiration of the "community spirit," the concept is much broader and richer in terms of the political proposal that may come out of it.

The concept of community with quality of life refers to this proposal of "Living Well" stated in the new constitution. From this perspective, Living Well must be first construed in the context of the community. Living Well may only be achieved in community. This means that Living Well must encompass all the members of the community. But it also means that "community" is the *sine qua non* condition for human development. Community is the basic space and social unit in which the frameworks of meaning that facilitate the transactions, the relationship with the world, and the representations that make them possible are generated.

Therefore, this ultimate reference of identity, the community, must be construed from three areas for which we make an analytical distinction: the relationship with the world, social organization, and ideological configurations.

The first dimension of the quality of life is the quality with respect to the world, which must be understood in two aspects: the access to resources that facilitate the material reproduction of the individuals and a harmonious relationship with nature. The access to material goods, although not the ultimate goal of development, in this proposal is indeed a necessary condition for quality of life. By material goods we mean basic services, adequate housing, employment, salary, transport, leisure spaces, clothes, and food. Living Well is not a subjective statement of welfare, but the need to enjoy the material conditions that facilitate the realization of a good life. The quality of our relationship with the world, with nature, will be a goal to attain quality of life, but also a condition. Without a propitious natural environment, the quality of the air, of the water, and of the land; the preservation of green spaces and of biodiversity; and food security, quality of life is not possible.

The second dimension is related to the quality of social relationships. We are living in a time when the core concern of society is about the quality of social relationships, especially in the cities. The increase in the levels of intra-familial violence, abandonment, insecurity, and violence in all its forms and areas are symptoms of a decline in that aspect.

The third dimension of the quality of life from the community approach is related to culture in a broad sense. That is to say, it is related to the "framework for understanding" that determines economic transactions and social interactions. Pluralism has a significant value in the context of a society as diverse as ours. It is the starting point to conceive a new development paradigm that questions precisely the linearity of its own evolution. Currently, there is no single concept of development or a single ideal of society, humanity, or culture that is preponderant. The development of the community will be marked by what the community decides to be. The concept of community also refers to the construction of an identity and a sense of belonging, despite, and based on, the differences.

The "quality of life," the expansion of freedoms, not only becomes the ultimate goal of development but is also a change in the relationship between the state and society. The community becomes the main actor in its own development, and the state will be a part of the community, the local government, that in our case is no longer that benevolent and totalitarian "father" that claims the right to outline the fate of the community.

From this perspective, the definition and analysis of child poverty must not be understood as a "deprivation of resources," but also in terms of the "quality of the dad relationships" and as a process of expansion of the freedoms through the development of capacities.

The first dimension, the relationship with the world, refers to the material resources that facilitate children, now and in the future, to live a long and healthy life, have access to education and to a dignified standard of living, and participate in the life of their community and in the decisions that affect their lives, based on their own concept of a good life. From this perspective, health services, drinking water, housing conditions, protection services, or care services, among others, are a necessary condition to overcome child poverty situations.

The second aspect of the relationship with the world is related to the relationship with nature. The quality of life also involves the enjoyment of a healthy natural environment, the direct contact with nature, the access to drinking water, clean air, adequate, and nutritious food.

The quality of life, in addition to the materials and ecologic conditions, fundamentally involves the quality of the relationships. In the diagnosis presented in the preceding section, we saw that child poverty is precisely characterized by the decline of these relations of affection, care, and attention that are fundamental to the development of the human being.

In this respect, it will be necessary to turn our focus on the people to listen to their aspirations and their needs, to question ourselves as to what can we do as a state actor to strengthen family and community cohesion processes, and to reestablish the social ties that are undermined by modern rationality. It will be the agency of the community that will enable to make the decisions that will orient public policy toward the welfare of the children. From this perspective, the state and the local government must leave aside their totalitarian aspiration of claiming the right to outline the fate of the community and of its children. Nothing comes out further from this perspective than to characterize itself as the central protagonist of the social changes that translate into a triumphalist reduction of the numbers of dirt floors or into an increase of the school attendance rates due to the benevolence of the politician that hands out economic grants.

The third aspect of the quality of life is related to a pluralist vision of the idea of development. We have seen that child poverty cannot be exclusively characterized with statistical variables. The diversity of "deprivations" is expressed in a range of problematic situations that are derived to a large extent from material deprivations, but also in the life ideals that lead to the deterioration of family relationships, in the lack of affectional and identity references among children and teenagers, and in the search for better living conditions. In the diagnosis, we have identified that, paradoxically, this effort to satisfy the most urgent needs is giving rise precisely to the condition of abandonment as a central characteristic of child poverty. This way, the participation of the community in the search for development alternatives that make it possible to overcome child poverty involves a change in the relationship between the community and the local government. From the local government, it is expected to focus on an ability to listen, creativity, proactivity, and above all, opening spaces for the community, the family, the children, and teenagers to actually participate in the construction of a good life.

IV. Conclusions

We started by analyzing the conceptions of development, human development, poverty, and child poverty that define poverty in general and child poverty in particular, both as a phenomenon and a problem. These definitions simultaneously guide the intervention of the state through its policies, programs, budget allocation, and so on. It is evident that the definition of child poverty from an approach that focuses on the lack of income has been largely exceeded. An alternative to this definition assumes a multidimensional approach that contemplates "the deprivations in the access to educational, health, information, and other resources" that poor children experience. However, this multidimensional approach is exclusively based on analyzing the information that is available. This way, the "education" indicator is reduced to the "school attendance rate," the health indicator, to "access to vaccines and healthcare," and so on. The greatest difficulty of this proposition is not in its methodological or technical deficiencies, but in the fact that child poverty is characterized using these reductionist criteria, and that defines the type of interventions that the state will implement. These set of interpretations and analyses that are the basis of the policies of the state are based on a concept of poverty that is reduced to the failure to meet the basic needs of the individual (ENB), in this case, the person under 18 years.

The basic needs approach responds to the paradigm of "welfare-poverty." This paradigm says that the less the poverty, the greater the welfare. By poverty it means, with respect to childhood, the deprivation of goods and services. Several poverty measurement exercises, poverty reduction policies, attention to vulnerable groups, and others have been carried out within this scheme. The underlying logic of this conception and the practices derived from it is that welfare is attained with the access to goods and services that are regulated by the market. Therefore, poverty is the inability to plentifully participate in the market due to the lack of income, and therefore, to gain access to these goods and services that would realize the "welfare" of the individual.

Human development as part of state policy, from this perspective, is oriented to two strategies. First is the direct and indirect subsidization of goods and services, making up for the deficiencies of the liberal mercantile system and mitigating its consequences. The second strategy is the increase of income through grants, to increase the possibility of participating in the market of goods and services, thus improving the levels of "welfare."

This approach and the data derived from it address the issue of child poverty in a manner that is so restricted to sectoral indicators that it ultimately distorts it. This way, public policy guides its efforts to improve the numbers derived from these analyses as a path to reduce child poverty.

The empirical evidence presented in the second part of the paper shows that the problem involves a greater complexity. The deprivation of public health, education, or protection services is only a part of the problem. The drama of child poverty is precisely grounded on the fact that the public policy evades due to the "lack of data" or due to a lack of will or capacity to address them. The most evident expressions of poverty are the situation of abandonment of the children and teenagers, the growth of violence toward the youngest ones, the reproduction of peer violence in the schools and neighborhoods, the consumption of alcohol and drugs, teenage pregnancies, and others. The response of the state through the local authorities only cover the most extreme and urgent cases with the implementation of care and protection services that are growingly insufficient with assistentialist programs that somehow mitigate the situation. Their urgent and remedial character causes interventions to be isolated, focalized, and sectoral.

With these data, we propose a framework to facilitate understanding that will overcome the economic approach or the basic needs approach, and that responds to the "relational" character of child poverty, building on the concept of community with quality of life. From this perspective, the idea is to rethink child poverty, the methodologies for data generation, but above all, the orientation of state policy. The efforts to overcome the direst, and most widely spread, expressions of child poverty, such as abandonment and violence, must not be assumed as a lack of services experienced by minors, but as a consequence of the deterioration of the social fabric, and the community and family relations.

The Living Well paradigm aims at quality of life in the community context. We said that "there is no quality of life without community and there is no community without quality of life." From this paradigm, quality of life must be understood not only as the access to or deprivation of goods and services but also from the relational perspective—the relationship with the world, with society, and the symbolic space that facilitates these relationships (shared vision). Therefore, this is a much broader perspective. The mediation to attain a good life is no longer (exclusively) from the market, but is also from the community.

In summary, quality of life partially is the deprivation of access to goods and services. But there is also the relationship with nature, social relationships, life projects, shared values, and others. From this paradigm, development must be understood as "living well" in accordance with the values and projects of the community.

An initial difficulty is the development of "quality of life" indicators. We must build on the indicators of poverty, but also develop other indicators at the individual, family, and community level, and only use the indicators related to individuals as the basis for the design of social policies.

Then, what is the role of the state and, in our case, of the local government? It is not about dismissing the progress made so far in terms of social policy, but about transcending the welfare-poverty paradigm to start walking toward the Living Well, or the "community with quality of life" paradigm. We cannot suddenly go from one paradigm to the other. A process is necessary. However, it is also necessary to consider that the public policy on early childhood must be designed from a different paradigm.

The paradigm of Living Well, or of a community with quality of life, refers to a different reading of reality, which is based on the relational analysis (community) and not only in the access to goods and services. Building on this reading, diagnosis, and interpretation of social issues, we may outline new social and sectoral policies. The role of the local government must emphasize the generation of the conditions to strengthen community authorities with the existing and new programs. The starting point will be to redirect subsidy programs to make the transition toward new programs that seek the improvement of the "quality of life" of the population based on the agency of the community and the central role of the local government.

If the absence or deficiency of quality of life is a consequence of the deterioration of the relationships, and therefore of the community, it will be necessary that policies, programs, activities, benefits, and others are ultimately oriented to the strengthening (or in some cases, to the creation and development) of the community at every level. Then, the alternatives to this situation must be oriented toward the reconstruction of the community and its immediate expression, the family, and other more mediate expressions, such as the educational or neighborhood community. Based on this recovery of the central role of the social actors in the development of the community in general, and in the protection of childhood in particular, we may specify the root causes of child poverty and the alternatives to overcome it. This does not mean that the state should abandon its share of responsibility; rather it means that the state and its local administrators will not limit themselves to responding to the guidelines indicated by international organizations, and to reducing poverty indicators, and that the society will not be limited to waiting for the state to do something else than that.

Any situation of poverty, child poverty in particular, deserves urgent and determined attention, because each day that goes by is another day in which thousands of children and teenagers experience material deprivations, but above all, violence and abandonment, which have irreversible and unimaginable consequences.

V. Bibliography

Antequera, Nelson and Coria, Isidora, 2013, *Comunidad con calidad de vida. El desarrollo humano en el contexto municipal*, La Paz, Gobierno Autónomo Municipal de La Paz.

CEPAL-UNICEF, 2010, *Pobreza infantil en América Latina y el Caribe*, Santiago, CEPAL-UNICEF.

Edo, María, 2002, *Amartya Sen y el desarrollo como libertad. La viabilidad de una alternativa a las estrategias de promoción del desarrollo*, Bachelor's Thesis in International Studies, Universidad Torcuato di Tella.

Ministerio de Planificación, 2006, *Plan nacional de desarrollo*, La Paz, Government of Bolivia.

Pautassi, Laura, 2007, *El cuidado como cuestión social desde un enfoque de derechos*, Santiago, CEPAL.

PNUD-UNICEF, 2008, *Gobernabilidad local y derechos de la niñez y adolescencia: Un análisis de siete experiencias de políticas públicas locales*, Panamá.

PNUD, 2006, *Informe Temático sobre Desarrollo Humano en Bolivia. Niños, niñas y adolescentes en Bolivia. 4 millones de actores del desarrollo*, La Paz-Bolivia

Provoste, Patricia, 2012, *Protección social y redistribución del cuidado en América Latina y el Caribe: el ancho de las políticas*, Santiago, CEPAL.

Sen, Amartya, 2000, *Desarrollo y libertad*, Buenos Aires, Planeta.

Soares, Alice, 2012, *Género e infancia y ética del cuidado*, La Paz, EDOBOL, UNICEF-CIDES.

Tiba, Icami, 2009, *Adolescentes: quien ama educa*, Mexico, Aguilar Fontana.

UDAPE, 2008, *Bolivia. Inversión social en niñez y adolescencia. Un análisis del gasto público social en niveles subnacionales*, La Paz, UDAPE-UNICEF.

UDAPE-UNICEF, 2009, *Reporte nacional Bolivia. Estudio global pobreza y disparidades en la infancia*, La Paz, UDAPE-UNICEF.

Ul HAQ, Mahbub, 1995, "El desarrollo humano sostenible, nuevo enfoque del desarrollo," in PNUD, *Desarrollo humano sostenible*, Seminar organized by the UNDP for senior officials of the national government of Bolivia.

Wanderley, Fernanda, 2011, *El cuidado como derecho social: situaciones y desafíos del bienestar social en Bolivia*, Santiago de Chile, OIT Publicaciones.

ibidem.eu